Rural Fictions, Urban Realities

Rural Fictions, Urban Realities

A Geography of Gilded Age American Literature

Mark Storey

Oxford University Press is a department of the University of Oxford.
It furthers the University's objective of excellence in research, scholarship,
and education by publishing worldwide.

Oxford   New York
Auckland   Cape Town   Dar es Salaam   Hong Kong   Karachi
Kuala Lumpur   Madrid   Melbourne   Mexico City   Nairobi
New Delhi   Shanghai   Taipei   Toronto

With offices in
Argentina   Austria   Brazil   Chile   Czech Republic   France   Greece
Guatemala   Hungary   Italy   Japan   Poland   Portugal   Singapore
South Korea   Switzerland   Thailand   Turkey   Ukraine   Vietnam

Oxford is a registered trademark of Oxford University Press
in the UK and certain other countries.

Published in the United States of America by
Oxford University Press
198 Madison Avenue, New York, NY 10016

© Oxford University Press 2013

First issued as an Oxford University Press paperback, 2016.

All rights reserved. No part of this publication may be reproduced, stored in a
retrieval system, or transmitted, in any form or by any means, without the prior
permission in writing of Oxford University Press, or as expressly permitted by law,
by license, or under terms agreed with the appropriate reproduction rights organization.
Inquiries concerning reproduction outside the scope of the above should be sent to the
Rights Department, Oxford University Press, at the address above.

You must not circulate this work in any other form
and you must impose this same condition on any acquirer.

Library of Congress Cataloging-in-Publication Data
Storey, Mark
Rural fictions, urban realities : a geography of Gilded Age American
literature / Mark Storey.
p. cm.
Includes bibliographical references.
ISBN 978-0-19-989318-8 (hardcover); 978-0-19-027242-5 (paperback)
1. American fiction—19th century—History and criticism.   2. Rural conditions in
literature.   3. City and town life in literature.   4. Farm life in literature.   5. Pastoral
fiction, American—History and criticism.   I. Title.
PS374.R87S76 2013
813'.409—dc23
2012015367

CONTENTS

Acknowledgments *vii*

Introduction: Rural Fictions, Urban Realities   1
1. Lines of Time, Sight, and Capital:
   Train Journeys   25
2. Commerce and Carnival at the Canvas City:
   Traveling Circuses   54
3. The Place of Medical Knowledge:
   Country Doctors   83
4. A Government of Men and Not of Laws:
   Lynch Mobs   116
5. Landscapes of the Future:
   Utopias   148
Conclusion   168

Notes   *173*
Works Cited   *187*
Index   *197*

ACKNOWLEDGMENTS

During the years this book has been with me many people and institutions have been an integral part of the process. I can't possibly hope to mention them all, but I want to make a few specific acknowledgments.

The financial backing of the Arts and Humanities Research Council, the University of Nottingham, and the Eccles Centre at the British Library made it all possible in the first place. The expertise of staff at the University of Nottingham libraries, the British Library, the Library of Congress, the Clifton Waller Barrett Library of American Literature at the University of Virginia, and the Newberry Library in Chicago was essential. I am grateful to them all. This book is also very much a product of the age of digital humanities, and would have been impossible without the archives that online sources have made available – and, of course, the often unacknowledged people who make such sources freely available. I therefore want to mention the Sarah Orne Jewett Text Project compiled by Terry Heller, the Wright American Fiction archive hosted by the Indiana University Digital Library Program, the University of North Carolina's "Documenting the American South" site, Northern Illinois University's dime novel digitization project, and Project Gutenberg Extraordinary resources such as these are transforming the way we do literary studies.

It is the people that I've met along the way, however, that have made it such a rewarding experience. Peter Rawlings first sparked my passion for American literature more than a decade ago, and set me off on a road I'm still on. At Nottingham, Peter Messent deserves a special thank you for his encouragement, judicious guidance, and meticulous attention to detail. Douglas Tallack was instrumental in the early period of writing, while John Fagg offered equally wise counsel a bit later in the game. To all three, for their help and humor, and for agreeing to come with me on this excursion to the countryside, I owe a great debt. Richard King, Jacob Smith, and Robin Vandome kindly commented on portions of the work in its early stages. Peter Stoneley and Graham

Thompson read the whole thing at a crucial stage, offered generous advice, and continue to be sources of support. Ann McQueen deserves thanks for making life a lot easier. Sharon Monteith has been fighting in my corner for a long time now, and for all her support, academic and otherwise, I am deeply grateful. At OUP I have been fortunate to have Brendan O'Neill as my editor: his capacity for patience far exceeds mine, and his guiding hand and faith in the project has been invaluable. Thanks to the anonymous readers for making this a better book, and to Mary Jo Rhodes and Ginny Faber who knocked the whole thing into shape in the final stages.

From the beginning I have been blessed with friendships that have rarely been anything but detrimental to my efficiency – and I mean that in the warmest way. Warren Dockter, Colin Gallagher, Keith Nottle, Bill Smith, Nick Witham and Jenny Woodley all offered a rare and welcome combination of scholarly debate and unscholarly conviviality. Ceri Gorton has put up with it more than most, and kept me afloat even when I started sinking; she knows, I hope, how important she's been. Adrian and Richard manage to keep their little brother's feet on the ground even from the other side of the world; I'm pretty sure this isn't the sort of book they normally read, but I hope they'll find room for it on their shelves. It is really John Storey, my father, who takes any credit that might be due: the example he sets, and his support along the way, have made all the difference. Who'd have thought those visits to Huntingdon Library on Saturday mornings would end up here.

And a final thank you. During the course of writing this book, my mother, Carol Storey, passed away. It never occurred to me when I started that she wouldn't see me finish, and even though she was, I know, vaguely bewildered by the whole enterprise of spending your life poking around in old books, the love and encouragement she offered never stinted. In ways far beyond the academic, this book is a product of her life – and of the things she's left behind.

**

Parts of some chapters have previously appeared, in different form, as "Country Matters: Rural Fiction, Urban Modernity, and the Problem of American Regionalism" in *Nineteenth-Century Literature* (65:2, 2010), as "A Geography of Medical Knowledge: Country Doctors in Elizabeth Stuart Phelps and Sarah Orne Jewett" in the *Journal of American Studies* (44:4, 2010), and as "Huck and Hank Go to the Circus: Mark Twain Under Barnum's Big Top" in the *European Journal of American Culture* (29:3, 2011).

INTRODUCTION

Rural Fictions, Urban Realities

With its dewy-eyed title and cloyingly sentimental plot, James Lane Allen's early novel *Summer in Arcady: A Tale of Nature* (1896) appears to confirm why its place in American literary history is usually limited to margins and footnotes. At odds with its romantically nostalgic tone, however, are occasional moments that signal something quite different—buried but still-glowing embers of the clamorous and transformative world in which it was written. Take, for instance, this description of a horse ploughing a field:

> The old horse kept his gait up and down the rows as evenly as though urged along by the pressure of steam; it would have been as likely for an alarm whistle to have blown off through one of his ears as for him to have stepped by mistake on a hill of corn. (9)

It is a passing and seemingly inconsequential moment, but one that suddenly evokes the previously absent notion of mechanization. Pausing over the metaphor, we see not only an old animal tilling the soil but also the way in which a world out of sight—rational, efficient, driven by the new technologies of an urban-centered capitalist economy—exerts and reveals itself even when it does not form the object of the text's diegetic address. For all its apparent insignificance, the line quietly registers the ongoing replacement of traditional agricultural technologies, and the subsequent obsolescence of animals from (as well as the minimization of human input in) the farming process—an aspect of modernity that the plot of the novel studiedly avoids.

While I do not claim that all the writers addressed in this book are only capable of registering the processes of modernity in this oblique or evasive way, it is on many similar moments, across a wide range of texts, that my argument ultimately hinges. This book seeks to treat the urban and the general markers of modernity itself as "absent presences" in rural fiction, reading the novels and short stories that seem to have only a tenuous connection with the urban-industrial realities of Gilded Age America[1] firmly back into that context. In doing so, I argue, a new understanding of the relationship between literature and modernity can be gained through a kind of geographical estrangement—by approaching notions of the urban and the modern from places and positions that appear most distant from them. In this way, literary representations of rural life and rural space can offer an original method of addressing, understanding, and unveiling the transregional transformations of urban-industrial capitalism. As such, my approach is underpinned by a belief that literature can act as a unique form of historical record; as Bill Brown articulates it, "literature has the capacity to preserve (however marginally) residues of phenomena that remain in some sense unrecognizable…in our existing historiographic registers. Within literature the detritus of history lingers, lying in wait" (4). It is my hope that by tracing specific ways in which rural fiction enables us to recover and map the disparate phenomena of modernity, this book will contribute to a broader field of archaeological-literary study.

Although each chapter that follows therefore takes a distinctive line of inquiry, they are fundamentally underpinned by a single question: how are the intimately connected processes of urbanization and modernization reflected, refracted, embedded, and encoded in the thematic concerns and generic makeup of Gilded Age rural fiction? By focusing on how these texts both consciously and unconsciously record the constellation of influences and conditions in which they were written, I will argue that rural fiction is a unique record of modernity's impact on socio-cultural life and literature, and that it allows us to approach the connections between modernity and fiction in a way that is distinct from more conspicuously engaged urban fiction. I further suggest that, in privileging the latter, literary criticism has tended to marginalize the not-urban in its understanding and conception of modernity.

A project like this requires (indeed, is motivated by) an approach to the cultural context of the period that resists a literary-historical tendency to prioritize urban representation. If the key geographical marker of Gilded Age modernization has been understood to be what Arthur M. Schlesinger once called "the rise of the city," then urban representation has naturally enough become the privileged site for critical accounts of the period's cultural history. The problem is that such prioritization effectively identifies a particular historical period—the maturation of capitalism and its accompanying urban-industrial systems in the late nineteenth century—with those works of fiction, usually considered through the lens of realist or naturalist aesthetics,[2] that we call "urban" or "city" fiction. The equally large (if not larger) number of works of fiction from the period that represent other types of space or that are less generically stable have subsequently been siphoned off from modernist literary histories and either considered quaintly obsolete or, more recently, granted their own politicized subcategories. Allen's metaphor points to the way this book seeks to undo such critical characterizations. By reading rural fiction against the geographical, institutional, and epistemological shifts of the Gilded Age, and foregrounding the increasing similarities between geographically distinct areas of rural life, we can better understand the standardizing and flattening processes of modernity.

On one level, then, my argument revisits a classic theme of literary criticism: the relationship between the country and the city. Far from reiterating this relationship in romantically oppositional or static terms, however, it explores how the categories "urban" and "rural" both break down and constantly reassert themselves in the pages of rural fiction, how they remain legitimate geographical classifications and yet become increasingly fictitious concepts. The representations of rural life found in these works of fiction act as archives for the mapping of the very real fluctuations and deterritorializations in the national geography of Gilded Age America. Such considerations partly follow the path already suggested by historian William Cronon in *Nature's Metropolis* (1991): "More and more, I wondered whether it made sense," he writes, "to treat city and country as isolated places.... Would these Wisconsin farms be here without the city in which to sell their crops? Could the city survive if those crops failed to appear? The answer to both questions was surely no, but then did it make sense...to draw a boundary between it [rural nature] and the urban world next door?" (8). David Stradling has developed similar ideas in his discussion of the relationship between New York City and the Catskill Mountains, pointing out that although "our culture holds city and country as polar opposites, they have in fact created each other" (10). My argument relies on a certain transference of that same thinking to the understanding of literary representation.

Likewise, it relies on an engagement with the heterogeneous scales of space that Hsuan Hsu has recently argued operate within nineteenth-century American literature: the "home, region, city, nation, and globe" (10) that he traces all shape the idea of the rural as it is articulated here, and all ultimately play a part in constructing a geography of Gilded Age fiction that refuses to be circumscribed by narrowly sociological or demographic definitions of rurality. This book begins from an assertion that there is a continuing boundary between urban and rural representation that exists in literary scholarship, evidenced by the critical noise around urban representation and the critical silence around rural representation, and that this distorts and disguises the intimate connection between the two. *Rural Fictions, Urban Realities* goes some way toward redressing the balance by bringing *rural* fiction to the center of the relationship between literature and modernity.

Furthermore, the relative absence of any notion of rural fiction in American literary history tends to retain a historiographical problem that those works of fiction offered us a chance to overcome. The unique perspective on modernization that we find in representations of rural space, as well as the generic instabilities of the representations themselves, suggest an approach to the analysis of narrative that builds on Fredric Jameson's suggestive comments:

> [B]oth the interpretation of historical change and the analysis of narrative structure require us to come to grips with what in structural terminology is known as the "diachronic"; the problem arises, however, from the apparent necessity of the mind to grasp diachrony in what are essentially "synchronic," or static and systematic, terms. Thus, it would seem that to "understand" history involves a translation of flux or change into some relatively fixed relationship between the two states or moments—the "before" and "after" of the historical transformation. ("The Vanishing Mediator" 17)

Reading the rural fictions of Gilded Age America as I do here provides a handle on the processes of historical and geographical transformation that resists synchronic characterization. Rather than suggesting any neatly teleological progression from a rural "before" to an urban "after" of post–Civil War society, these texts insist on the ongoing mediation between the two. Allen's throwaway metaphor of a working horse, read in this light, is useful because it exposes the historical conditions necessary to make the metaphor work in the first place: the coming into being of mechanized agriculture and, simultaneously, the persistence of traditional horse-drawn farming Such details not only locate it within a specific historical period but also capture what Raymond Williams would call the "residual" and "emergent" periods it lies between (*Marxism* 121). In other words, it unconsciously foregrounds the diachronic historical conditions that determine its parameters of reference.

Alongside the more sociological concerns that Allen's metaphor evokes, this book also addresses, as already mentioned, the relationship of rural fiction to the various generic currents usually attributed to this period of American fiction. In keeping with the resistance to linear narratives of change that the quote from Jameson begins to develop, a closer examination of the aesthetics of rural fiction illuminates the often contradictory and fluctuating life of literary genre in the Gilded Age. A novel that stands as a key work of nineteenth-century rural fiction, Edward Eggleston's *The Hoosier School-Master* (1871), might be adduced here as a particularly useful illustration. Hugely popular in its time, the novel has become something of a curiosity in histories of Gilded Age literature: cited as an important early instance of local dialect fiction, it sits uneasily between the sentimentality of popular fiction and the emerging self-consciousness of literary realism. It is precisely this position, however, that marks it out as an important document of literary historiography, foregrounding as it does the historical simultaneity of those seemingly antithetical generic modes.

At one point in the novel, as we follow the hero Ralph on a walk with his future lover Hannah Thomson, the narrative breaks to make an oddly self-reflexive address to the reader:

> You expect me to describe that walk.... You wish me to tell you now of this true-hearted girl and her lover; of how the silvery moonbeams came down in a shower—to use Whittier's favorite metaphor—through the maple boughs.... But I shall do no such thing. For the moon was not shining.... Novelists always make lovers walk in the moonlight.... Moonlight is never so little needed or heeded, never so much of an impertinence, as in a love-scene. (56)

Eggleston stresses his rejection of moonlight as a narrative motif, claiming to deny us this hackneyed device in favor of a fidelity to something more realistic, when what actually happens, of course, is that the posture of realism is adopted to evoke the sentimental tropes it professes to withhold. In a similar moment later in the novel, even the melodramatic-sounding title of the chapter itself ("A Struggle in the Dark") is undercut by a narrator coaxing his sensation-seeking reader into a place beyond the mere thrills of mass-market fiction: "And you... who have blunted your palate by swallowing the Cayenne pepper of the penny-dreadfuls...you wish me to make this night exciting by a hand-to-hand contest between Ralph and a robber" (77). A whole series of social and generic postures are being struck here, the reader being positioned as a consumer of penny-dreadfuls at the same time as the narrator seems to refute the connotations of the chapter title and prepare us for something more attuned to sober realism.

Daniel Borus recognizes the difficult line Eggleston's writing treads, pointing out that although the novel does not "entirely forgo formulaic plots, stereotypic characterization, and authorial editorializing" (15), it nevertheless seems to gesture toward a way of writing that is seeking to leave romanticism and sentimentalism behind—it is, for Borus, "proto-realist." Bev Hogue similarly identifies Eggleston's prose as "an uneven mélange of realistic incident, comical dialect, and sentimental description" (233), while Gavin Jones recognizes that "[h]ere was a writer who...professed 'provincial realism' yet fell back on the humorous stereotype and romanticism he eschewed" (53). Eggleston's novel is not only enmeshed in the various competing and yet available generic conventions of its moment, but speaks of the multiplicity of literary genres spread through the nineteenth century, an unstable form that evokes, for example, both Washington Irving[3] and Mark Twain. Somewhere in those moments of self-reflexivity in *The Hoosier School-Master* is the place where the various generic modes operating across Gilded Age literature reside simultaneously and antagonistically. It is this generic instability that forces us, in other words, to grasp literary history diachronically.

I briefly draw on Eggleston's novel because it offers a usefully condensed example of one of the central arguments of this book. Lloyd Pratt, following Fredric Jameson and Wai Chee Dimock in his less strictly classificatory approach to genre, has recently suggested that genre theory is most productively deployed when it "focuses more on the internal incoherencies of genres than on clearly divisible categories" (13). If anything as circumscribed as a genre of rural fiction does emerge in this book, it is to illustrate that it serves as an exemplary site for the dismantling of genres themselves. Operating restlessly within the literary currents of its time, its subject matter and metaphorical range frequently call upon the romantic, sentimental, melodramatic, pastoral, and gothic traditions that late nineteenth-century fiction emerges out of and remains partly embedded within. Nevertheless, the turn to realist and naturalist modes among a literary elite in the same period exerts a formal pressure that many of these writers chose, or felt compelled, to participate in. Such characterizations of Gilded Age fiction are nothing new—Eric Sundquist memorably referred to the period's resistance to "convenient generic classification" as "the country as the blue" ("Country" 5), while the realist/romantic impulses bound up in literary naturalism have been well discussed. Part of my argument here, however, is to point out that rural fiction serves as an especially useful site for defining and understanding American literary history in this period exactly because it refuses to adhere to whatever linear narratives or taxonomic categories we might be tempted to ascribe. It asks us to think not only about how any given period privileges certain modes or genres, but about how our very conception of periods and genres breaks down when we turn to those texts that have traditionally been sidelined as artistically incoherent or historically irrelevant. This is not an attempt to reclaim the writers I discuss as supreme stylists or preternaturally attuned social commentators; Edward Eggleston is no Henry James. It is because rural fiction operates in this anxious aesthetic place, however, because a range of genres speak simultaneously within it, that it allows us to reconstitute the complex and sometimes erratic experience of the extratextual world it emerges from.

While the foregoing provides an introductory outline of the concerns of this book, it is important to expand on and develop in more detail two particular areas: firstly, "rural fictions"—the ways in which representations of rural space have been dealt with in previous American literary scholarship—and secondly, "urban realities," the specific historical context of urbanization and modernization that I ultimately seek to illuminate.

* * *

The first task is to stake out a clearer sense of what is meant by the term "rural fiction." A good starting point is Nancy Glazener's comment that, because American regional literature focuses "more or less on rural life," it can be "productively considered as part of a larger enterprise of writing the rural": "Writing the rural involves distinguishing the rural from the urban, assessing the practical and symbolic value of the rural to the nation as a whole, and representing rural life—representing it specifically *as rural*" (191–92, emphasis in original). While such comments evoke the rural as a useful critical category, Glazener's insistence that it must be distinguished from the urban and then have its "practical and symbolic value" assessed does tend to reiterate a potentially limiting binary logic. Maria Farland has more recently suggested an understanding of the rural that is closer to my own use throughout this study, arguing for the need to "better understand the complexity of the category of the rural" (913) and focusing on early twentieth-century modernist poetry as a site where the diversity and dynamism of such a category can "transcend regional and even national borders" (930).

It is worthy of note that while the relatively unproblematic category of "urban fiction" has been the subject of continued and sustained interest in literary criticism for many years,[4] the notion of rural fiction has either been narrowly conceived or absent altogether. Caroline Sherman, as far back as 1938, was insisting in her essay "The Development of American Rural Fiction" that rural fiction must be a closely focused depiction of agricultural farming, opening her argument with the questionable claim that "[t]he development of American rural fiction has taken place within the twentieth century. Only three novels published before 1900 are now considered to be genuine studies of rural life" (67).[5] The few other studies of rural fiction that have followed tend to employ the same quite specific approach to the rural and the same twentieth-century focus. Roy W. Meyer's *The Middle Western Farm Novel in the Twentieth Century* (1965) exemplifies a strain in writing about rural fiction that can feel somewhat parochial, and he maintains an oddly deterministic and sociological stance towards the relationship between literature and rural life. More recently, William Conlogue's *Working the Garden: American Writers and the Industrialization of Agriculture* (2001), updates the conversation by pointing out that "scholars have long read American fiction through a pastoral prism" (6), a perspective he seeks to unsettle by offering a more historically grounded study of agricultural life through a range of twentieth-century writers. While Conlogue's work begins the important task of placing rural life into discussions of modernization and literature, like Sherman and Meyer before him he focuses only on twentieth-century texts and defines the rural as something specifically oriented around farming. George Henderson's *California and the Fictions of Capital* (1999) reads selected novels from the late nineteenth and early twentieth century against a detailed analysis of agricultural economics, and offers some illuminating insights into the uneven distribution of capital in turn-of-the-century California. Most recently, there have been some isolated efforts to place the farm novel and rurality more generally into the discussion of American literature.[6] These studies, while more focused on economic or regional concerns than my range of texts and themes, do at least take the notion of the rural seriously as a legitimate category of literary study and have begun to establish such a notion in the vocabulary of American literary history. More often, especially in synoptic histories of American literature, the idea of rural fiction is simply absent.[7] As Farland points out, although the last thirty or so years have seen a glut of city-and-literature studies, "what these approaches share is a substantive erasure of the rural as an analytic category" (912).[8]

This book situates itself in this significant gap in American literary studies, and does so by expanding the very idea of what rural fiction might actually be. In identifying what we define as a piece of rural fiction (a categorical anxiety of a kind that urban fiction studies rarely entertains), it serves us well to employ a more expansive definition than simply those texts that represent farm life. Some texts are obviously set predominantly in cities, but others—those representing farm life, of course, but also those representing ranch life, or life in communities centered around rural economies such as fishing, mining, and forestry—can legitimately be labeled rural partly because they think of themselves as rural, and partly because they represent what would commonly be thought of by others as a rural way of life.[9] This is not to say that regional identity or pastoral idealism is not also consciously part of their representative strategies, just that among the many ways of discussing and analyzing these works of fiction there is a category, relatively undeveloped in American literary criticism, that is both shared and transregional.

Shifting the perspective away from the usual ways in which rural representation has been approached in American literary criticism—the pastoral and the regional in particular—begets some interesting questions. What would the category of the rural in American literary historiography offer to an understanding of particular historical contexts—in this case, the maturation of urban-industrial capitalism in the late nineteenth century—that the pastoral has tended to dehistoricize and that regionalism simply misses? To put it another way, what would this change in emphasis bring to our understanding of both the literary and the wider cultural history of the period?

The pastoral is in many ways the most entrenched of these existing categories, and it certainly has a long and complex history within literary criticism that it is not my intention here to either rehearse or wholly disperse. It is important to my argument, however, because its political and emotional connotations have tended to obscure the kind of historicized notion of the rural I am pursuing. Raymond Williams notes precisely this tendency within an English literary context at the beginning of *The Country and the City* (1975); in each age, Williams points out, there has always been a sense that an essential, organic, more "natural" life is passing away, that the notion of a society living its days in a morally pure pastoral idyll is "just back...over the last hill" (18). Even though Williams explicitly connects his exploration of the pastoral with the legacy of feudalism and enclosure in English history, it is a pertinent point to begin a discussion of the pastoral in American literature because it emphasizes the dehistoricized and mythological resonance of the pastoral ideal. It is this resonance that made the notion of the pastoral so important to an earlier era of American literary criticism and obscured a more contextualized understanding of rural life under a symbolic and mythic-critical vocabulary.

Departing from the more specific meanings of "pastoral"—the classical shepherd poetry of Theocritus and Virgil—the term in its American context came to loosely mean an idealization of and nostalgia toward rural life, a sensibility given a distinctively nationalistic twist by what Sarah Burns calls "the spectacles of Crèvecoeur and Jefferson" (6): the insistence on virtuous agrarian values in early republican rhetoric. The transmission of this pastoral idealism has subsequently concerned many landmark studies of American literature and culture; traces can be found in D.H. Lawrence's *Studies in Classic American Literature* (1923), and the notion certainly comes to the fore in Henry Nash Smith's *Virgin Land: The American West as Symbol and Myth* (1950) and Morton and Lucia White's *The Intellectual Versus the City* (1962). The pastoral's organizing concept—the alignment of cultural and moral values with fairly circumscribed definitions of country and city—continue to play an important role in many areas of American literary criticism, from Toni Morrison's essay "City Limits, Village Values: Concepts of the Neighborhood in Black Fiction" (1981) to William Barillas's *The Midwestern Pastoral: Place and Landscape in the Literature of the American Heartland* (2006).

Despite this long history, the ur-text of American pastoralism remains Leo Marx's *The Machine in the Garden* (1964). Marx's succinct summary of what the pastoral means in this context—"the ordering of meaning and value around the contrast between two styles of life, one identified with a rural and the other with an urban setting" (94)—forms the framework of his readings of several canonical American writers. He makes much, for instance, of a short sketch written by Hawthorne in 1844 that describes an idle afternoon at Sleepy Hollow suddenly disturbed by the whistle of a steam train—a symbolic moment that carries the full weight of Marx's thesis: "The...appearance of the machine in the garden is an arresting, endlessly evocative image. It causes the instantaneous clash of opposed states of mind: a strong urge to believe in the rural myth along with an awareness of industrialization as the counterforce to the myth" (229). The key phrase, perhaps, is that such an episode sees the "clash of opposed states of mind": it is a contest of ethics, an assumption that notions of agrarian virtue occupy an antithetical position to that of industrial modernity. The conciliation of this opposition is the middle landscape of complex pastoralism that Marx sees in the best American literature, but compromise is what it remains—two ideological spheres, embodied in the geographical organizations of the city or the countryside, that are assumed to be mutually exclusive and that exist outside of historical time (indeed, the terms Marx uses—"myth" and its "counterforce"—suggest a timeless battle). We need look no further than that guiding metaphor of the "machine in the garden" to understand Marx's use of the pastoral ideal: the timeless world of country life is penetrated and disrupted by the presence of a new, alien body.

While I do not wish to caricature Marx's argument here,[10] such was the influence of *The Machine in the Garden* that the pastoral ideal as applied to American literature became a historically uprooted and ideologically immutable template for a great many subsequent works on urban-rural relations. A certain enthrallment to the explanatory power of the Marxian "pastoral ideal," for instance, is found twenty years later in James Machor's assessment of eighteenth- and nineteenth-century intellectual history. What he calls "the urban-pastoral vision" was "an alternate 'middle' realm" apparently dreamed up by those concerned with the rise of urban life, whereby the city "contains within its boundaries urbanity, complexity, and sophistication combined with the physical or social attributes of simple rusticity." In this way, Machor claims, "the ideography of urban pastoralism...substitutes for the rural-urban dichotomy an opposition between the overcivilized city, cut off from nature, and the organic city that maintains contact with pastoral values" (14). Marx's legacy is much in evidence here: presumably "pastoral values," along with "simple rusticity," can be located in the same mythic agrarian republic that Marx claimed had such an influence on American writers.

While the pastoral has served as one dominating lens through which rural representation in American literature has been viewed, a more recent field of critical inquiry has addressed it from a somewhat different perspective. Regionalism (or "local color" writing; critics use both terms, sometimes interchangeably, sometimes quite pointedly, but usually to designate a similar grouping of late nineteenth-century texts) has become a vibrant and active subfield of literary study in the last couple of decades, and is relevant here because it encompasses many of the writers and texts that are central to this study.[11] According to Judith Fetterley and Marjorie Pryse, two of the most prominent critics to address regionalism in recent years, regional fiction is a genre in its own right located somewhere "alongside realism and naturalism as a parallel tradition" (4). This sense of it being a distinct genre or body of texts is something that virtually all studies of regionalism share. I should state straight away that this book does not seek to offer a wholesale re-reading or theorization of regionalism; neither is it out to undo critical regionalism as a broader scholarly project.[12] I do want to spend a few moments, however, questioning the tendency in regionalist discussions of Gilded Age literature to section off these texts as a distinct literary form and assign them a particular political role. Some of this criticism has run the risk of turning late nineteenth-century rural texts into a repository for certain scholarly agendas and fashions and of ignoring a nonregional concept of the rural altogether.

The old consensus, solidified in works such as Warner Berthoff's *The Ferment of Realism* (1965) and Jay Martin's *Harvests of Change* (1967), viewed regional writing very much as a "minor" stream in American literary history (Henry James's famous assessment of Sarah Orne Jewett's work as a "beautiful little quantum of achievement" nicely captures the mixture of admiration and condescension that was typical). In Richard Brodhead's words, the huge body of "regional" stories and novels that appeared in the period—usually in influential periodicals such as the *Atlantic, Arena,* or *Century*[13]—presented a literary elegy that performed the task of "memorializing a cultural order passing from life at that moment and of fabricating, in the literary realm, a mentally possessable version of a loved thing lost in reality" (*Cultures* 120). This assessment has been rejected or tacitly embraced in varying degrees by many of regionalism's new standard-bearers, but most agree that nineteenth-century regional writing has something more nuanced to say about the place of regions and regional people—especially as it emerges in an era when the idea of region and nation was so politically fraught.

In two influential accounts, Amy Kaplan and Richard Brodhead each argue that the genre's cultural work was to act, as Brodhead puts it, as a "literary supplement to a more general production of inhabitable backwardness" (*Cultures* 133). In other words, regional fiction provided urban consumer-readers with an imaginatively knowable rural "other" against which they could favorably compare their own sophistication. Kaplan states the case most succinctly: "regionalist writers...were published by a highly centralized industry located in Boston and New York that appealed to an urban middle-class readership; this readership was solidified as an imagined community by consuming images of rural 'others' as both a nostalgic point of origin and a measure of cosmopolitan development" (251).[14] Regionalism ultimately reflects, in its ossification of rural life, the worldview of an urban middle class recently initiated to the pleasures of tourism: "Its operation is to produce a world marked as foreign; but also to make that foreignness fully graspable; and so to confirm the superior inclusiveness of the culture in which the reader is positioned" (Brodhead, "Literary Field" 55).

Other critics have moved away from this market-oriented account toward one that imbues the genre with a more autonomous and politicized narrative agenda, concerned with the often-cited "minor" canonical status of regionalism.[15] In the introduction to Stephanie Foote's *Regional Fictions* (2001) she states that regional writers' "nostalgic tone shows them to have been profoundly shaped by an awareness of the globalizing and standardizing tendencies of urbanization and industrialization" (3), resulting in a fidelity to "local customs" and an assertion of the "value of ordinary rural lives" (6). Read in this way, regional fiction "works to preserve local customs, local accents, and local communities" (4) against, presumably, the eroding influence of all that is not local. In a similar fashion, Donna Campbell has argued that "by representing itself as the site of exclusion from and, implicitly, opposition to the dominant national culture, the region as it is constructed in local color fiction paradoxically resisted integration into mainstream American life even as it represented itself as uniquely and purely American" (95).

This approach to regionalism is perhaps most fully exemplified by Fetterley and Pryse's highly influential *Writing Out of Place: Regionalism, Women and American Literary Culture* (2003). Here, regionalism is redefined as a politically charged genre of women's writing that radically questions its status (and the status of women more generally) in relation to the dominant male-, urban- and white-centric mainstream. This redefinition allows them to claim that "region becomes mobilized as a tool for critique of hierarchies based on gender as well as race, class, age, and economic resources" (6). Fetterley and Pryse essentially end up conflating regionalism with feminism, melding the two into a union of disaffection that means "'woman' and 'region' share similar locations within dominant discourses" (37). The same implicit ethical binary is at work once again, regional fiction becoming the site of resistance against the oppressive operations of a hegemonic national culture. Fetterley and Pryse have no doubt that "regionalism is in effect a women's literary tradition" (13).

Present in all these accounts is an idea that regional literature's motivation and/or value lay in its ability to present a counternarrative to nationalist and urban culture. Tom Lutz has identified the same currents in regionalist scholarship, persuasively arguing that many studies of the genre are intent on reading it as either "hegemonic" or "counterhegemonic," as either guilty of marginalizing the provinces or engaged in a cultural battle against that marginalization (27). Following my comments earlier about the desire to think of genres as untidy and unruly entities, I avoid entering too deeply into discussions about the parameters of regionalism partly out of a reluctance to grant it too much stability as a genre in the first place. The problem with circumscribing a varied group of texts as regional is not only that it potentially narrows critical understanding to something June Howard has called "interpretation by classification" ("Unraveling Regions" 365)—that is, classifying texts beforehand as regional preordains that they are read "regionally"— but also that it threatens to replicate, however indirectly, pastoral and romantic logical structures vested in an ethical binary. That binary was once city versus country (or even more fundamentally, civilization versus nature), but has now been recast as center versus region. The effort to resituate regional writing in its political and social context is vital work, and has recovered many of the previously neglected writers that this book also discusses. At work in some of those studies, however, has been an assumption that the texts in question represent points of either resistance or admission to processes intent on the hostile takeover of a purer, more humane local identity. Those points can sometimes be read as denial, fictional elegies of an agrarian world that seal out signifiers of modernity, but more often are read as politically active, demonstrating the value of identities (female, provincial, marginal) that antagonize an urban-defined norm. The regional writing of the late nineteenth century is rediscovered as a kind of victim's testimony to the insidious inequalities of mature-capitalist America, so that it can be read against the excluding ideologies it supposedly resists.[16] This viewpoint can seem unable to move beyond a region/center binary that carries some immanent moral charge, and a critical project geared toward the exposure of an ideological structure (exemplified by a rising urban modernity) that is always already unequal.

The emphasis in *Rural Fictions, Urban Realities* is very different. Rather than theorizing the construction of regional or local identity in the context of nationalism and globalization, or thinking of "regional" texts in relation to reader-response theory and print culture, it redeploys a range of texts not usually considered together and argues that their representations of rural life can provide a more geographically intricate understanding of nineteenth-century modernity. While I do retain a sense of the argument about the distribution of rural fiction—that it served a generally middle-class and generally white audience through urban-based periodicals and publishers, and that its narrative methods therefore often imply a particular, urban-based reader—the primary focus is on the relationship between cultural materiality and literary aesthetics, rather than on distribution and reception networks. I want to emphasize how the rationalizing and standardizing nature of Gilded Age modernity actually militates against regional recalcitrance, a process that necessarily dissolves regions of rural life into one another as much as it dissolves rural life itself into larger urban networks. Anthony Giddens suggests that a defining characteristic of modernity is the "disembedding" of "social relations from local contexts" (21), so that "the 'visible form' of the locale conceals the distanciated relations which determine its nature" (19). Similarly, J. Nicholas Entrikin sees modernity as a "decline in the areal variation of ways of life" (28), while Marshall Berman simply claims that modernity "cut[s] across all boundaries of geography" (15). The point here is to turn the attention to how the aesthetic rendering of rural life in literature *reveals* the social reach and cultural penetration of modernity's geographical dimensions.

The notion of the rural does not necessarily insist that regional or pastoral considerations should be abandoned, just that being aware of the rural as a historically grounded, transregional category has the potential to open up new avenues of socio-literary investigation.

* * *

More explanation is needed of what is meant in my title by "urban realities," and one way to begin such explanations is to go back to Raymond Williams. A preoccupation of *The Country and the City* is tracing what Williams calls the "Romantic structure of feeling—the assertion of nature against industry and of poetry against trade" (100), a viewpoint that grows out of an anti-urban sensibility and leads to the idealizing of a rural way of life that supposedly maintains a fundamental, organic connection to the natural world. Such aesthetic idealization, Williams goes on to argue, can in turn lead to a simplified political alignment:

> Defence of a "vanishing countryside"—"the open air," "the life of the fields"—can become deeply confused with that defence of the old rural order.... Thus in a strange relation to an active delight in trees and flowers and birds there is a virtually unconscious extension to the values and attachments of an unjust and arbitrary society. (237–38)

There can be an acknowledgement of and a preference for the obvious environmental differences between cities and the countryside, but this does not mean that their epistemological worlds have to be similarly divided. One does not have to absurdly claim that there is no difference between the streets of New York City and the fields of New York State, but that difference does not have to be extrapolated into an ethical and intellectual binary. "Clearly the contrast of country and city is one of the major forms in which we become conscious of a central part of our experience," Williams states, "but when this is so, the temptation is to...abstract even these most evidently social forms and to give them a primarily psychological or metaphysical status" (347). It is the "historical variety" of the "social forms" that are urban and rural life that I consider here.

Urban modernity has proved a notoriously slippery concept for theorists and critics, and simply summarizing theories here would be a mammoth and futile project.[17] The point needs some careful attention, however, as what is at stake within the parameters of this book is not simply an account of how the United States came to be a more fundamentally urban society in the years after the Civil War, but of the changes—intellectual, institutional, ideological and aesthetic—that the establishment of this urbanized society brought about. While statistics give us some sense of the population shifts that were taking place in the Gilded Age,[18] they do not provide a wholly satisfactory way of understanding urbanism and its establishment as the organizing structure of society. As is well documented, the late nineteenth century saw the consolidation of a society connected in ever-more intimate ways to cities, underpinned by an economic system that necessarily found the focal point of all exchanges, markets, and political life in urban centers. This is hardly a new idea, as Louis Wirth explains in his influential essay of 1938, "Urbanism as a Way of Life":

> The degree to which the contemporary world may be said to be "urban" is not fully or accurately measured by the proportion of the total population living in cities. The influences which cities exert upon the social life of man are greater than the ratio of the urban population would indicate, for the city is not only in ever larger degrees the dwelling-place and the workshop of modern man, but it is the initiating and controlling center of economic, political, and cultural life that has drawn the most remote parts of the world into its orbit and woven diverse areas, peoples, and activities into a cosmos. (2)

When Wirth later argues that identifying urbanism with "the physical entity of the city" so that it becomes "rigidly delimited in space" results in an inadequate conceptual model (4), it is clear that urbanization is being constructed not only as a statistical or material phenomenon but also as an ideological and epistemological one.

In Henri Lefebvre's *The Urban Revolution* (2003) we find an extension of these ideas. Although it originates in a later twentieth-century and European context, Lefebvre's argument is that in order to truly understand the place of cities in a modern society we need to lose sight of "the city" as a clearly defined, scientific object, and instead view "the urban" as a system of social, economic and political relations. "These relations are both legible and illegible, visible and invisible," Lefebvre goes on to argue, relations that are "projected onto the landscape in various places: the marketplace, stock and commodity exchanges, labor exchanges, et cetera.... Once they are grasped at this level, the urban reality assumes a different appearance. It becomes the sum, the home of various markets" (46–47). As Lefebvre points out, while there are "visible" examples of the city's encroachment into the countryside, there is an equally fundamental "invisible" world of relations, ideologies, and markets. The city may still act as a spatially recognizable accumulating point for "knowledge, technologies, things, people, wealth, money, and capital" (24), but the centrality of urban life to modern societies means that these accumulated systems reach beyond the built environment of the city.

"Rural life" may remain distinct in obvious topographical ways—the fields and the farmhouses—but its systems of organization and sustainability become part of an urbanized network. Richard Ohmann discusses the Gilded Age in similar terms when he argues that America was essentially "an urban society by the end of the [nineteenth] century. The city was the main locus of production and power; it figured centrally in people's understanding of what their new world had become" (119). That sense of cultural and social urban-centrism is crucial here, a point echoed in more specifically economic terms when Alan Trachtenberg points out that "the countryside found a place fashioned for it within the urban system: it became...a market colony, a cheap source of food, labor and certain raw materials" (115). It is the concept of urbanism that allows us to move beyond a city-country binary to an understanding of modern society that allows room for the rural to be considered as part of a distinctly modern experience. As Williams says, "the city is not only...a form of modern life; it is the physical embodiment of a decisive modern consciousness" (*Country and City* 287). The arrival at this modern consciousness comes with the structural realignment of social and cultural life around a fundamentally urban-oriented society, one that includes physically different types of space within a newly configured system.

Yet "modernity" itself is hardly a straightforward concept. Conceived variously as an epoch, a process, and a sensibility, located anywhere from the European Renaissance to the twentieth century, and described as something people "have been going through for close to five hundred years" (Berman 15–16), modernity is a notoriously nebulous term. Indicative of the colossal critical work it is often called upon to perform is Jürgen Habermas's list of modernity's "bundle of processes," each of them "cumulative and mutually reinforcing":

> [T]he formation of capital and the mobilization of resources;...the development of the forces of production and the increase in the productivity of labor;...the establishment of centralized political power and the formation of national identities;...the proliferation of rights of political participation, of urban forms of life, and of formal schooling;...the secularization of values and norms; and so on. (2)

The breathless "and so on" points to the even broader field that this comprehensive list does not already mention, and to the endless complexity of "modernity" itself. In effect, and with no apologies, I am selecting just one of the many historically located "modernities" to anchor my argument in: the late-nineteenth century acceleration of urbanization and industrialization. Crucially, and as Habermas states, it is impossible to isolate elements of modernity in this way without considering other, "mutually reinforcing" factors; as such, this study uses urbanization as a lens through which to also take account of issues such as the flow of capital, rationalization, the rise of professionalization, and technological industrialism. In short, the explicitly geographical framework of this book ends up being a means of probing into more abstract and distanciated fields.

Modernization theory has a certain explanatory attraction because it can "integrate the whole social process of change" (Ohmann 38) into a coherent narrative of causality, and while I borrow heavily from such a narrative here it is also my intention to offer points of resistance to it. One major explanatory term I do retain is "rationalization," the process Max Weber famously located at the heart of modernity. Roughly summarized as the shift from value-oriented societies (essentially irrational) to goal-oriented ones (essentially rational), rationalization, for Weber, was the process by which customs and traditions, and the institutional structures of society arranged around them, were displaced by a commitment to efficiency and calculation. The ultimate economic realization of this drive is, of course, mature capitalism, but it manifests itself in a more tangible sense in any form of social organization or practice in which the rationalization of human actions might occur: "There can...be rationalizations of the economy, technology, scientific work, education, war, the administration of justice, and of other forms of administration" (Weber, "Prefatory remarks" 365–66). The chapters of this book are anchored in those more tangible and traceable forms, but implicit throughout is the sense that they can themselves be partly understood as manifestations of these metahistorical processes.

The problem here, however, is that we might end up doing away with an ahistorical binary of city and country only to replace it with an oversimplified narrative of modernization. Part of my purpose in examining rural fiction in this book is to unsettle this tendency. Cultural historian Jackson Lears offers a way of refining the discussion when he points out that farmers in Gilded Age America "eagerly embraced participation in the international market, invested heavily in mechanization, and sought to master the 'science' of economic forecasting" (108). He neatly summarizes, in fact, a point often made by historians of American agriculture.[19] Rural life in the late nineteenth century did not simply (or one might say romantically) remain preserved in pastoral amber, nor was it always the site of a premodern and technologically stagnant way of life. But, as Lears goes on to say, it is equally misleading to suggest that the imperial reach of modernization is absolute or uniform. Rural space does not automatically become "modern" (whatever that would look like) as a result of its deeper integration into the urbanized and rationalized social network. Financial instability (especially the economic depressions of the 1870s and 1890s) and what Ohmann calls an ongoing "agricultural crisis"—"the rising value of land, high interest rates, erratic prices for farm produce, and the eternal vicissitudes of the weather" (120)—ensured a certain skepticism toward the processes of modernization, a "feeling that the world was not entirely susceptible to rational management" (Lears 108–09). Rural life and its representation becomes a site of critical interest exactly because it most transparently exposes the historical contradictions and uncertainties of its time, a space where the inchoate *process* of change, rather than simply the *result*, is most readable.

While I am seeking to construct a working understanding of urban modernity, I am not suggesting that life throughout Gilded Age America simply switched from traditional to modern forms. Using the Civil War as a convenient fulcrum in the historical narrative of the nineteenth century, there is a temptation to parcel up the social and cultural history of the time into a "before and after" periodization: the traditional agrarian society bought over from the earlier nineteenth century that gave rise to romantic modes, and the modern urban society of the late nineteenth century that gave rise to realistic modes. The point of using rural fiction as the lens through which to view this period is that it seems to present a counterfactual alternative to this characterization—to locate modernity in environments that do not seem modern, and to understand the history of literary genre through fiction which is generically inconsistent. Modernity and the markers I am using to identify it, are, as the quotes from Giddens and Berman earlier on suggested, highly indiscrete notions, refusing to be bound by prescriptive geographical terms. Although this does not mean that all experiences of space and place become homogenized, it does mean that all experiences of space and place bear some impression, however faint, of modernity's impact. In other words, although the city feels and looks like the pre-eminent expression of modernity and the exemplary geo-social site for elucidating what modernity constitutes, the spaces that wear those changes less overtly are not only still relevant but might actually provide a distinct, de-centered perspective on the very same conditions.

* * *

The rest of this book proceeds with such considerations very much at its heart. The simplest way to outline the approach the book takes, in fact, is to cite Bill Brown again. I share his understanding of the "archaeological task" of literary criticism as "developing a chain of associations that seem, retrospectively, to have converged already in the literary work," a task charged with "representing that convergence as an image that freshly elucidates the signifying structures and material changes of everyday life—the task, in other words, of producing the history that lingers within neglected images, institutions, and objects" (4–5). Producing the history that lingers within the neglected body of Gilded Age rural fiction is the task of this book. While that history is not always produced (or reproduced) through fragments or passing moments—there are, importantly, more traditional readings of rural texts that I engage in—there are also occasions where that history is transmitted through moments that seem quite incidental to larger structural or narrative considerations. Roland Barthes saw these "superfluous" details as integral to the "reality effect" of literary realism (11), while Brown himself sees the incidental material references embedded in literature as moments able to "materialize...an absent presence" (16)—a sign of a "material unconscious." This book does not seek to develop a rigorous notion of an "urban unconscious," but such a notion is suggestive of what my purpose is: less a cartography of Gilded Age print culture, and more an intimately historicized reconstruction of the period's geographical imagination. By piecing together the way in which an urban fabric became part of the material of rural representation, I demonstrate just how casually, and therefore powerfully, the modern world became part of the way people thought.

While I have so far offered a generalized outline of how modernity is understood throughout this study, I want to focus briefly on the way the following chapters will take a more specific approach to the material—and, importantly, why that approach underpins the broader arguments being staked out. Arranged not around particular regions or authors, but instead around key discourses or themes of modernization—namely transport, entertainment, medicine, and law—each chapter addresses these themes through a close analysis of what I will call a "synecdochal counterpart": respectively, train journeys, traveling circuses, country doctors, and lynch mobs. While this is not in any way meant to represent an exhaustive list—other themes might well have provided equally illuminating paths to follow—these particular examples operate as signposts for the relationship of rural fiction to urban modernity because they stand out as narrative preoccupations, frequently appearing in novels and stories set across all regions of rural life and being employed as conspicuous narrative occasions, incidents, or characters so often that they take on a paradigmatic quality. In organizing the chapters around them, the idea is that a chain of synecdochal logic can be implicated by moving, for instance, from a detailed exploration of how train journeys are frequently employed as narrative occasions in rural fiction to a better understanding of something altogether more abstract and harder to grasp: how the modernization of transport networks altered the period's geographical imagination. Implicit throughout is the important point that these themes are also deeply interconnected: from the simple fact that traveling circuses relied on trains to reach rural communities, or that medical sideshows were often part of circus day, to the more abstract drive toward codification shared by medical and legal modernization and the concern among the medical profession that train travel was adversely affecting the health of passengers.[20] While each chapter necessarily approaches its topic as a relatively discrete entity in itself, the mutual imbrications between them should not be forgotten.

One obvious risk is that this explicitly thematic approach may seem to oversimplify these contested issues into something blandly unified or typological, or to turn works of fiction into data sets for a kind of questionable sociological analysis. As will become clear in the detail of each chapter, however, the aim is to understand how the literary multiplicity of rural fiction—its various generic stances, its transposition of material referents into metaphor and simile, its stylistic and syntactical patterning—allows us to recuperate these histories in a way that resists straightforward or hegemonic narratives of modernization. Individual agency, gender relations, racial and ethnic identity, class stratifications, and ideological biases have a crucial bearing on the way in which those cultural and institutional histories are told, and as such I pay them due attention throughout this study. The defamiliarizing lens that rural fiction provides on the period works to cast the intricate interplay of geography and identity in these diverse experiences of everyday life in a new, often startling light.

With this rationale in mind, chapter 1 deals with the issue of transport through a reading of the train journey as it appears in rural fiction. I start here partly because the train has been widely discussed as a potent symbol of modernity in its own right, something Wolfgang Schivelbusch describes as the most "vivid and dramatic...sign of modernization" in the nineteenth century (xiii), and others have called a "constituent part" of a wider "machine ensemble" (Beaumont and Freeman 13). As such, it offers a particularly tangible and immediate entry point into the central concerns of the book. The chapter explores how descriptions of train journeys reveal the altered relationship between a perceiving subject and the landscape that subject is traversing, and how this in turn encodes much about the relationship between individuals, rural space, and urban-industrial capitalism. Chapter 2 asks similar questions of popular entertainment, this time using the traveling circus as its focal point. It argues that as a paradoxical site of both carnivalesque excesses and industrial efficiency, exotic escapism and commercial manipulation, the circus destabilizes realist representation in a way that remaps the antagonistic fusion of capitalist modernity with rural life.

From these examples grounded in the material experiences of modernization, the remaining chapters move into more abstract territory. Chapter 3 looks at how the rise of scientific medicine contrasted with the more traditional (and increasingly discredited) forms of medical knowledge found in rural communities, and how the figure of the country doctor—a contested and geographically indeterminate identity in its own right—serves as a deeply unstable mediation between a range of competing forms of medical knowledge. Chapter 4 takes the most provocative form of justice in the late nineteenth century, the lynching, and examines how its literary representations reveal not only the changing status of law but the geographical dimensions of law's jurisdictional reach. Integral to these chapters are not just considerations of how certain groups of people inflect and inform these wider histories (the place of female doctors in rural practice, or the racial dimension of lynching as an extralegal practice, for instance), but the various ways in which rural fiction represents these events aesthetically—mixing sentimental, romantic, realist, naturalist, even modernist, generic practices. To bring these four chapters together, and to explore their underlying themes in a more overt way, the final chapter then turns to a particular late nineteenth-century genre—the utopian novel—and considers how its imagined geographies of the future unveil the social and literary anxieties around the changing nature of urban and rural space in its own time. Focusing on the hugely popular and prolific body of utopian novels that sprang up in the last two decades of the nineteenth century, it explores how they explicitly discuss, and often struggle to reconcile, the transformed relationship between urban and rural life. As should be clear, this book seeks to draw a range of diverse and significant themes together into a comprehensive analysis of the relationship between rural fiction and "urban reality." Despite the chapters' markedly different topics, the recurring argument in them remains the same: that the processes of modernity also happen in rural space, and that in representing that space, sometimes counter to their intentions, works of rural fiction uniquely record the social experience and cultural impact of modernity's transformations.

There should be a final note on the writers and texts that this book addresses. The sheer quantity of works of fiction from the period that present us with depictions of rural life means that this is inevitably a selective overview, and I discuss a somewhat idiosyncratic collection of names, many of which may be unfamiliar. This is both necessary in terms of articulating the relevancy of these texts to a fuller understanding of the literature of the period, and desirable in terms of performing that aforementioned task of reconstructing the history that lingers in neglected places. Bringing together unknown or forgotten texts with those that are more familiar is part of a resistance to the critical tendency to sift out texts that fall foul of particular value judgements. Philip Joseph admits in his study of regionalism, for instance, that he discusses only those writers "most capable of making a lasting modern contribution"—which means, in effect, not those regionalist works that "feed the fantasy of a hermetic community, sealed off against the corrosive effects of modernity" but instead "those that might enter actively into a more progressive public dialogue" (3). A similar selection policy underpins Fetterley and Pryse's key discrepancy between "local color" (nostalgic, touristic or nativist) and "regionalism" (politically engaged and resistant to the machinations of centralized power). This effort to stake out the boundaries of genres is important, of course, not least because it determines which works of fiction we do and do not teach, but the historicizing drive in this study insists that even texts that do fail artistic or political criteria are still valuable exactly because their narrative employment of certain tropes, figures, and themes unavoidably (and sometimes inadvertently) breaches that hermetic seal and connects them to the flux of their contemporary moment.

Two of the better known figures discussed extensively here are Sarah Orne Jewett and Hamlin Garland; their critical value for me lies partly in the fact that, because they have been the focus of so much regionalist scholarship, they offer especially provocative points for pushing back against some of regionalism's assumptions, but mainly because their work frequently presents moments where rural space and modernity come conspicuously into contact. Some of the other names will be familiar to readers of nineteenth-century literature, while some may not: works by Edward Eggleston, Maurice Thompson, Mary Noailles Murfree, Elizabeth Stuart Phelps, Constance Fenimore Woolson, Bret Harte, Booth Tarkington, Owen Wister, Charles Chesnutt, Joseph Kirkland, Alice Brown, Edward Bellamy, and Paul Laurence Dunbar are all discussed, not so those writers can be recast into anything like a genre of "rural fiction" but because those works present important and illuminating instances of rural representation. The only substantial foray into what might be called the traditional canon is my discussion of William Dean Howells, Stephen Crane, and Mark Twain, but as is the case with all these writers, my interest is not in canonizing them as "rural" but in focusing on how they present us with examples of rural representation that help us to map, in all its complications, the geographical imagination of Gilded Age America. Indeed, it is in an effort to avoid any project of generic taxonomy or categorization that the many critical lenses through which these diverse range of writers have been examined—through notions of realism, naturalism, regionalism, the western, romanticism, dialect fiction, African American literature, feminist literature, sentimentalism, and so on—all have a crucial part to play here.

It is through a selection of relevant works by these writers and a handful of others that this book argues for the value of a rural category of literary inquiry. American rural fiction in the Gilded Age is frequently aesthetically and generically inconsistent, and undoubtedly engaged in the construction of a rural image that is sometimes romanticized and sometimes politically progressive. It is this multiplicity and indeterminacy, however, that means the texts examined here refuse to provide easy evidence for grand historical and literary narratives, asking us to look again at the generalizations we make about the literary and cultural history of the late nineteenth century. Through the arguments, readings, and analysis in the chapters that follow, the representation of rural life in American fiction emerges as a rich field of investigation in coming to grips with the intricacies and entanglements of modernity.

CHAPTER 1

Lines of Time, Sight, and Capital: Train Journeys

"Up the Coolly," one of the best-known stories from Hamlin Garland's *Main-Travelled Roads* (1891), opens on a scene that serves as both an introduction to and a condensation of the themes of this chapter. As Howard McClane travels by train back to his family home in the midwestern farmlands from his life in New York, he sits back and gazes out of the window:

> The ride from Milwaukee to the Mississippi is a fine ride at any time, superb in summer. To lean back in a reclining-chair and whirl away in a breezy July day, past lakes, groves of oak, past fields of barley being reaped, past hayfields, where the heavy grass is toppling before the swift sickle, is a panorama of delight, a road full of delicious surprises, where down a sudden vista lakes open, or a distant wooded hill looms darkly blue, or swift streams, foaming deep down the solid rock, send whiffs of cool breezes in at the window. (42)

So many of the issues important to this chapter appear in this passage that I will to return to it as I progress, but one point worth making now is that it serves as a representative example of a narrative device common in rural fiction. A train journey from a specific urban departure point to a generalized destination in a rural region (here, from Milwaukee to the La Crosse valley in Wisconsin) is a classic opening for rural narratives, just as the reverse came to be something of a cliché for the period's urban realism—Carrie Meeber's journey from "the familiar green environs" of her village to the "great city" of Chicago (1) had an almost archetypal quality about it by the time Dreiser wrote *Sister Carrie* (1900).

This chapter considers the significance of such a ubiquitous device. Departing from the usual ways in which the railway has been discussed in this context—most notably, again, Leo Marx's focus on George Inness's painting *The Lackawanna Valley* (1855)—it considers less the mythic-symbolic resonance of the train-in-the-landscape and more the intimate connection between historicized forms of subjective experience and the train journey itself. Anchoring the discussion in a close consideration of how rural landscapes are created, read, and projected from the narrative point of view of a rail traveler, the chapter is underpinned by particular guiding questions: what are the implications of the "annihilation of time and space"—an often-cited effect of the new railroad technology—for literary representations of rural space? More specifically, in what ways does the train alter and mediate the subjective experience of rural space and, by effect, alter and mediate the literary representation of a rural landscape that it so conspicuously traverses, reveals, and frames?

Other issues tied up in the experience of the train journey are important here. Garland's opening paragraph also makes a passing reference to the reclining chair, which not only locates the story historically (reclining chairs did not become commonplace in train carriages in America until the 1870s) but also, perhaps more importantly, classifies the narrator: only the middle classes and above could afford to travel in the first-class carriages equipped with reclining chairs, and they were, of course, invariably white. The way in which train carriages implicated the social status of their passengers—ranging from the draftiness of economy cars to the luxury of Pullman carriages, first manufactured in 1864—is important because it is here that many of the stratifications and divisions of nineteenth-century life became especially visible. Julia Lee, for instance, has written about the "persistent association between the railroad and racial conflict" (346) at the turn of the century, fired by the central role that trains played in the *Plessy v. Ferguson* case of 1896, and how this reinforced the sense that train carriages were a conspicuous arena for the manifestation of America's fraught racial politics: "rather than having a democratizing effect, the reorganization of spaces served to underscore the categorical differences between groups of people" (351).

Paul Laurence Dunbar, writing just two years after the Plessy defendants had lost their Supreme Court appeal, opens his story "The Ordeal at Mt. Hope" (1898) with a black character aboard a train. The Rev. Howard Dokesbury, an erudite African American preacher, is newly arrived in the somewhat desolate Southern village of Mt. Hope, where he alights from his carriage:

> [H]e descended, bag in hand, from the smoky, dingy coach, or part of a coach, which was assigned to his people, and stepped upon the rotten planks of the station platform. The car he had just left was not a palace... [b]ut he watched the choky little engine with its three little black cars wind out of sight with a look as regretful as if he were witnessing the departure of his dearest friend. (11–12)

Dokesbury is portrayed as a civilized, educated figure throughout the story—certainly in contrast to some of the villagers he encounters—but on the train any social standing or authority he may have is nullified by his racial categorization. The "dingy coach" is "not a palace," pointing out the fact that the "separate but equal" justification behind Jim Crow legislation was rarely borne out in practice. Nevertheless, the train does represent opportunity, both literally and metaphorically. As it pulls away it seems like a last chance to escape the "gloom and desolation" of the town (12), but by the end of the story the Reverend has proven to be an elevating presence, and Mt. Hope is "rising above the degradation in which Howard Dokesbury had found her" (24). Dunbar recognizes the very different connotations the train holds—racially, of course, but also in terms of linking poor rural areas into more prosperous networks—and uses it to signpost the story's ambivalent attitude to contemporary America. The train is an especially prominent site for the perpetuation (even initiation) of racial discrimination, but it is also a herald of a modernity that carries at least the potential for social progress and mobility.

More often than it highlights racial concerns, however, the train functions in rural fiction to imply particular class positions. While the economic status and social position of the passengers are not necessarily traceable in Garland's opening scene, for instance, they are subtly present in their personal experience of train travel, even down to the view they have from the window. An edition of the *Railroad Gazette* from 1893 explains that expensive carriages, along with plenty of leg room and luggage storage, are "glazed with double windows, so that passengers can see out in frosty weather"; the cheap cars, in contrast, are cramped and badly lit, and the "single glass in the windows... prevents an outlook by the condensation on the glass" (qtd. in Gordon 178). While I treat certain aspects of train journeys quite separately here—the experience of train time as distinct from the view from the window, for example—they are ultimately connected by the way in which they can reveal some of the embedded and often invisible social conditions of everyday life.

Such connections point to why the train is a fitting subject for the first chapter of this study, serving as it does as one of the prime symbols (or, in my usage, synecdoches) of urban modernity. The railroad system, as well as trains themselves, typified the larger processes of modernization and acted as a focal point of those changes; in the 1870s, Walt Whitman famously described the train as a "Type of the modern" and an "emblem of motion and power" (359) in "To a Locomotive in Winter," while modern critics often cite the railway journey as a place where "nineteenth-century people encountered...themselves as moderns, as dwellers within new structures of regulation and need" (Schivelbusch, xv). In more explicitly geographical terms, Carl Condit suggests that trains mirrored the urban world in which they were constructed, becoming "a special kind of microcity moving over the ground" (x). At stake, therefore, is an understanding of how the train transformed and regulated the relationship between rural subjects, the landscape they inhabit, and the incursions of urban-industrial modernity. How did the ubiquity of the train increasingly make itself known—both consciously and unconsciously, in direct representation as well as on more allusive, metaphorical, linguistic levels—in rural fiction?

These questions are dealt with in greater depth as the chapter progresses, and I use them to frame my readings of the literary texts. First, I offer an extended reading of Maurice Thompson's short story "Hoiden" to expand on how the railroad acted as a manifestation of urban-industrial capitalism in the rural landscape, making tangible the often hidden flows of urbanism. I then discuss two distinct ways in which the train altered the personal and communal relationship to the rural landscape and rural life: the temporal and the visual. Focusing on a number of indicative moments in texts by Sarah Orne Jewett, Joseph Kirkland, and Garland, I explore how the standardization of train time in 1883 played a crucial role in installing a time consciousness that was at odds with the more traditional, cyclical temporal patterns of rural life. Again using Garland and Jewett, as well as William Dean Howells's *Their Wedding Journey* (1871), I then turn to the issue of vision, and specifically to the ways in which traveling on a train mediated the visual perception of the rural landscapes through which the passengers moved. The final section draws these strands together by illustrating their mutually defining nature: through readings of particular scenes from Stephen Crane's "The Bride Comes to Yellow Sky" (1898), Booth Tarkington's *The Gentleman from Indiana* (1899), and Owen Wister's *The Virginian* (1902), I argue that the more subjective and representable notions of train travel are themselves encoded with the economic and social patterns of urban modernity.

***

Such a vital and revolutionary new technology as the train did, unsurprisingly, establish a firm place in the wider cultural imagination. Dime novels such as Edward Sylvester Ellis's enormously popular *The Huge Hunter, or The Steam Man of the Prairies* (1868)[1] utilized a growing cultural preoccupation with trains—the First Transcontinental Railroad, started in 1863, was just a year away from completion when it was published. Telling the story of a young inventor who constructs a ten-foot-tall automaton (complete with waistcoat and top hat) driven entirely by steam power, the story opens with two crudely drawn stereotypes—the Yankee and the Irishman—gazing out in wonder across the prairie as a peculiar sight draws ever closer to them: "a gigantic man could be seen approaching... a black volume of smoke issued either from its mouth or the top of its head, while it was drawing behind it a sort of carriage" (108). Ellis's fantastical "steam man" is not actually a train, but is described in the very same terms; it is coming at the two men at "railroad speed," and when it stops to blow its nose it throws out "a jet of steam with the sharp screech of the locomotive whistle" (108). The description of the "steam man" that ends the chapter leaves no doubt about the analogy Ellis is drawing, with its iron face, boiler chest, and a knapsack of steam-driven valves. Popular fiction like Ellis's exploited the connotations of such an instantly recognizable technology, its ability to capture something of modernity's uncertainties and excitements—especially when contrasted with the more traditional technologies of the prairies—and in doing so captures the extent to which the train became a shared imaginative reference point.

There were, of course, more sustained and direct representations of the train in rural landscapes. Maurice Thompson, virtually forgotten even by contemporary critics intent on resurrecting such figures,[2] was a popular writer of stories set in the farmsteads and small towns of Indiana, and his first collection, *Hoosier Mosaics* (1875), includes a story in which many of these issues come together. "Hoiden" tells the tale of Luke Plunkett, a middle-aged farmer whose huge tract of land, "some two thousand acres of rich prairie" (128), is under threat from railway developers who want to run a line through it. Luke is bitterly opposed to such a development, soon raising a series of telling objections:

> He did not want to see his farm cut in two, his fields dis-arranged and his fences moved, nor did he wish to see his livestock killed by locomotives. The truth is he was bitterly opposed to railroads, any how. They were innovations. They were enemies to liberty. They brought fashion, and spendthrift ways, and speculation, and all that along with them. (132)

Luke's objections are a neat distillation of the general complaints made against railroad development in the nineteenth century. There is something of the luddite spirit coupling "They were innovations" with "They were enemies to liberty" in much of the antirailroad rhetoric of the time, while underpinning the same coupling is a kind of crude Jeffersonian viewpoint that envisions industrialization and liberty as mutually exclusive. In this story, Luke articulates his objections to the railroad in the personal terms of the effect on his farm, and then broadens to a more general complaint that railroads bring to the countryside the ways of modernity—and, by implication, the city.

But such complaints are soon muted by the sudden appearance of—what else?—a beautiful young woman. Watching a horse-drawn carriage go by, Luke spots a "rosy, roguish girl's face within. The beauty of that countenance struck the great rough fellow like a blow" (132). In a somewhat hackneyed coincidence, the woman turns out to be Hoiden Pearl, daughter of Elliot Pearl—the railroad prospector who wants to run a line across Luke's land. Beneath these contrivances, however, a series of interesting gendered expectations are being played with: Hoiden is in some senses the embodiment of the train's threat to Luke's land, yet as a beautiful woman she represents the antithesis to what the railroad had come to be associated with in the period. Amy Richter has written extensively about the cultural representations of women both in train carriages and in the wider railroad industry, and points out that popular cartoons, for instance, often played on the apparent contrasts between delicate femininity and the muscular, dirty life of the railroad: "Women, such jokes implied, were out of place among the powerful machines that propelled so much of America's industrial and commercial life" (32). Hoiden's narrative role as the feminine love interest is inextricably bound up in an otherwise "masculine" story of the modern transport business. Her appearance heralds the train's threat to bucolic peace, yet it also induces in Luke an overwrought and romanticized appreciation of the rural landscape around him: "The landscape at Rackenshack, as if by a turn of the great prisms of nature, suddenly took on rainbow hues...[T]he woods, a wall of dusky emerald, were wrapped in a roseate mist, stirred into a dreamy motion by the breeze" (134). The coming of the railroad, an apparent example of masculine mechanization that stands as an anathema to quiet rural life, is in fact heralded by a woman who provokes a slippage from the story's usual realist register into something far more romantically pastoral.[3] The train crosses boundaries of literary genre and gendered expectations in a way that undermines a simple connotative binary between modernity and rural life.

But this peculiar mixture of industrialization and romanticized rural landscapes was not such an incompatible juxtaposition. It returns us partly to Leo Marx's "complex pastoralism" but is more directly connected with William Cronon's argument regarding the way the railroad was grasped metaphorically and linguistically in the period of its greatest expansion. Cronon points out that the boosterism that surrounded railroad development in some quarters after the Civil War employed a descriptive language dominated by metaphors of nature or naturalness, so that people effectively "assimilated the railroad to the doctrine of natural advantages, merging first and second nature so that the two became almost indistinguishable. The railroad's presence was no less inevitable, no less 'natural,' than the lakes and rivers with which it competed" (72). The train was understood, in other words, through the existing semantic framework of the picturesque natural landscape, "as an inanimate object that had somehow sprung to life, the mechanical herald of a new age" (73). In the face of perhaps the most striking form of rationalized modernity, the impulse was to subsume the alienating effect of the train into a worldview still anchored in nature, tradition, and enchantment.

Yet the curious shift that Luke Plunkett undergoes, the move in tone from criticism of railroads to enraptured description of the rural landscape, does not involve any dialectical synthesis of the two. The train remains a discrete rational entity, threatening agrarian life, but it also brings with it the potential for romantic love—it is this that romanticizes Luke's view of his surroundings. He does in fact allow the railroad to be built across his land in the belief that it will allow him to get closer to Hoiden, yet the story ends (somewhat inevitably) on an unhappy note. While Luke is away on business in Cincinnati Hoiden and her father leave for South America, Thompson unable to resist the melodramatic irony that their journey begins at the very railway station that Luke has allowed to be built. Returning home, Luke is distraught to find that the object of his affections has fled—the desertion made all the crueler by the box of things he has brought back for her from the city: "great hoops of gold and starry rings and pins—a gold watch and chain, a beautiful gold pen and pencil case, and trinkets and gew-gaw things almost innumerable" (161). Luke's original objection to the railroad, that it brings "fashion, and spendthrift ways," turns out to be another bitterly ironic twist: it has brought these things, but via him. Hoiden Pearl is the modern outsider who represents a chance for Luke to escape the hard toil of farm life, but the railroad, the manifestation of modern industry, has to be accepted into the rural scene if its attendant opportunities are to be grasped. Once it is installed and the traditional life has surrendered itself to progress, however, the gloss of its promise fades and moves on, leaving behind an altered landscape and emotional ruin. It is a tale that replicates on the level of personal drama the negative social and economic impact of the railroad on nineteenth-century rural life.

Lynne Kirby offers a useful summary of the way the train acted as a conspicuous manifestation of the lines of economic flow and social arrangement when she labels it "a physical extension of an imperialist vision," something that heralds "the hegemonic expansion of an economic and cultural power, a principle of incorporation and arrangement, and of the discipline of heterogeneous territories" (27). The train literalizes the lines of flow that comprise the possibilities and problems of mature capitalism, the corporeal reminder of the ever tightening squeeze that railroad corporations had on agrarian economic autonomy (it was, after all, the overexpansion of railroads that had sparked the financial crisis in 1873). Henri Lefebvre viewed the city itself in these same terms, arguing that each new mode of production gives rise to cities that "express" their historical period "in a way that is immediately visible and legible on the environment, by making the most abstract relationships... tangible" (24). The train, as a vehicle born out of urban-industrial capitalist need, makes legible and tangible in the environment processes of incorporation and rationalization—it writes capitalism across the rural landscape. As Luke Plunkett seeks the hand of Hoiden Pearl, he becomes modern in the sense of becoming what Schivelbusch calls a dweller "within new structures of regulation and need." His economic autonomy succumbs to the incorporation of the railroad just as his emotional autonomy succumbs to the young urban outsider. That Thompson's story dramatizes this structure of industrial exchange, dramatizes it by also playing it out in literary and domestic terms, reveals the structure as not just an abstract economic process but a personal one as well. It writes capitalism across the human landscape.

Thompson's story deals with the transformed relations between urban and rural space that the railroad brought about, but it does not incorporate the subjective experience of train travel itself. As much as it tells us about the literary recognition of rural space's changing relationship with modernity, the train itself is only ever a determining absence in the story, missing from any direct narrative description. The same is true in Edward Eggleston's *The Mystery of Metropolisville* (1873). Following on from the popularity of *The Hoosier School-Master*, Eggleston sets his story back in 1856 in order to describe the decline and abandonment of a once-prosperous country town. Here, once again, the economic impact of the railroad is a crucial factor in the narrative—only this time it is the absence of the train, and the prosperity it would have brought with it, that causes the crisis. Villages and towns could simply wither away if they did not happen to find themselves on a rail line, and rural communities were at the mercy of rail developers. Eggleston's town is no exception: "Metropolisville is only a memory now. The collapse of the land-bubble and the opening of railroads destroyed it. Most of the buildings were removed to a neighboring railway station" (231). Like "Hoiden," Eggleston's novel allows us to read the human story of the railroad's economic hold over the organization of rural America.

* * *

Yet as my opening quotation from "Up the Coolly" suggests, as the postbellum period progressed rural fiction more often dealt with the train journey as a distinct form of modern experience, representing and revealing the altered contours of subjective perception—both the subject's temporal relation to rural space and his or her visual apprehension of it—that themselves reveal, however obliquely, the principles of capitalist rationalization. Between the stories of Ellis, Thompson, and Eggleston and the story I turn to in a moment—Sarah Orne Jewett's tale of an old woman's first (and last) train journey, "Going to Shrewsbury" (1889)—a vitally significant change took place in the daily lives of Americans that partly accounts for this shift in emphasis to the subjective experience of rail travel. The story of the adoption of standard time on November 18, 1883—"the day of two noons" the press called it at the time—is a familiar one,[4] but a crucial context for this discussion. It ushered in a new age of time-consciousness, a system of temporal organization that transformed the relationship of rural areas to the growing incorporation of an urban-defined society. Michael O'Malley cites the *Atlanta Constitution* from the day itself, where an editorial noted that "[f]ormerly the rising and setting of the sun was the standard of time in all localities, and in the country the almanac[5] and the sun together enabled many a farmer to do without his watch or clock" (127). Such statements underline Lloyd Pratt's argument that the new travel technologies of the nineteenth century signal "a process that permanently unhinges the measurement of time from the contingencies of space" (25). The train therefore stands as a significant marker in the broader processes I outlined in the introduction, the distanciation of time and space and the construction of "supralocal social reaffiliation[s]" (Pratt 25). From some often quite brief narrative moments set on board a train, a chain of synecdochal logic can be followed through that illuminates just how deeply literary texts were registering the processes of modernization.

Tied up in ideas about the uniformity of time across geographic space are a host of implications that impacted on the way rural space was conceived and imagined. Kirby explains that with "the rationalization of time came the rationalization of markets coordinated by the railroads—which could now steam through the last remaining local obstacles that impeded the efficient pursuit of profit on a national scale." It meant, in effect, that "the country could be regulated in relation to the city, and all territories could be bound together in the post–Civil War era" (51–52). Where issues of rail journeys and time appear in rural fiction, especially when they figure as new social imperatives, we read, not only the day-to-day changes and eccentricities that this seemingly artificial system caused, but also the buried traces of capitalism's maturation and ubiquity—an often unconscious residue of the transformed conditions of everyday life.

Thomas Allen, for instance, has recently argued that attention to the various ways in which time was organized is fundamental to an understanding of the nascent sense of national identity emerging in nineteenth-century America. "The complex cultural history of temporal experience in America," he writes, "in which time could be, at once, both natural and artificial.... [makes] it possible to imagine nationality as an ongoing negotiation, in narrative, of heterogeneous temporal modes" (4). It is this quality or effect of standardized train time that reintroduces and underlines my larger point about the transregionality of modern experiences. The train not only provides a literal link between rural and urban places, but in a more abstract sense serves to symbolize what Anthony Giddens called the "disembedded" and "distanciated" nature of geo-social relations. Richter puts it in plainer terms when she argues that "for passengers from rural communities a train journey carried them beyond local knowledge and drew them into the orbit of urban life…Within the cars, regional distinction yielded to an imagined connection to the nation" (19). The moments in the fiction to which I am about to turn where train time appears as a determining force carry the weight of these complex series of implications; it is not simply a linear story of natural or seasonal modes of temporal organization giving way to artificial or mechanical ones, but the gradual and uneven shift from a diverse and localized system of timekeeping to a nationalized, incorporative one. The representation of the train serves, ultimately, as a synecdochal counterpart to these broader and less tangible changes.

A case in point is Jewett's "Going to Shrewsbury." Its opening sentence alone highlights many of the points I have been making: "The train stopped at a way station with apparent unwillingness, and there was barely time for one elderly passenger to be hurried on board before a sudden jerk threw her almost off her unsteady old feet and we moved on" (700). The hurriedness of the train is made apparent by the series of impatient signifiers—stopping with "unwillingness," "barely time," the "hurried" and "sudden jerk"—which themselves are already qualified by the scene of the action revealed at the beginning of the sentence: this is an anonymous "way station," not a principal stop and seemingly insignificant (it provides only one elderly passenger) to the economic imperative of the railroad timetable. It is worth pausing to wonder at what point such sentences could have actually been written: its sense of urgency and the narrative tone this sets are determined by the weight of the economic, social, and cultural contexts it both describes and emerges from. Pratt is right to point out that "the penetration of American life by standardized linear clock time did not all at once supplant earlier systems of timekeeping" (41), and Jewett's line enables us to begin to reconstruct this indeterminate moment: it registers not just the arrival of standardized time but the actual transition to it as well, the simultaneous existence of incommensurate forms of temporal organization.

Jewett would occasionally use the train as a narrative device in her short stories—train journeys structure the plots of "A Late Supper" (1878), "A Little Traveler" (1880), and "The Dulham Ladies" (1886)[6]—and it appears, often only in passing references, in some of her novels. In *A Country Doctor*, for instance, Dr. Leslie is on his way to pick up Nan from the railroad station when he instinctively performs a task that, read in this context, leaps off the page: "As he passed a group of small houses he looked at his watch and found that there was more than time for a second visit to a sick child" (225). Jewett is perhaps only emphasizing in a somewhat heavy-handed way Dr. Leslie's compassion and sense of medical duty, but his need to check his watch draws attention to the contrast between the leisurely independence of his mode of transport (he is in a horse-drawn carriage) with the timetabled demands of the train. The time-consciousness that the train instills is one of the aspects Nicholas Daly has argued characterizes the whole genre of sensation fiction that flourished in England in the 1860s (472); the drama of such stories relies to some extent on the introduction of standardized rail times[7] as much of the tension in any up-against-the-clock plot device requires, after all, that everyone agrees what the time actually is. Jewett is certainly a long way from sensation fiction, but the same kind of historically specific conditions exert themselves in the fragments quoted here. In simply describing a mundane activity, the text records the spectrum of historical conditions that operate, simultaneously, both within the text and in the extratextual world it seeks to represent.

It is worth pausing over this notion of temporally determined writing. A moment in Joseph Kirkland's popular novel of rural life in Illinois, *Zury:*

The Meanest Man in Spring County (1887), illustrates the kind of effect that the new temporal imperatives of the train can have on the mode of writing itself. Characterized by a familiar mixture of sentimentalism and realism, Kirkland's novel includes a moment at a railroad station that seems to actively acknowledge the narrative role of the train in determining a particular generic mode. A classic sentimental set piece, the tearful goodbye, is denied by the new technological conditions:

> So the parting came… The train slowed up—stopped—they alighted. Phil was kissing them and saying "Goodbye mother, goodbye Meg; for just a little while," and he was back on his engine and the train was off again! Before they knew that the dreadful time of trial had arrived, it came, was here, was past. (483)

The reluctance of the parting is mirrored in the reluctance of the novel to pass over this loaded moment of emotional farewells, but the train is a higher force than even heartfelt family dramas. The train's need to remain faithful to a timetable means that the protracted histrionics of sentimentalism are necessarily forestalled. A new era of transportation determines the rhythm of scenes like this in a way that the horse-drawn carriage did not, and so demands a certain narrative realism that necessarily cancels out the residues of previous generic modes.

The point is that the time consciousness organized and ordered by the train comes into direct confrontation with a time consciousness that adheres to more organic or traditional patterns, so that rural space becomes the site where the effects of that confrontation might be read and understood. I am suggesting that this temporal confrontation appears in both the casual, passing references of rural fiction, as in the opening line of "Going to Shrewsbury," and in the more pointed, yet still unsettled, representation of train time that Kirkland illustrates. Returning to Hamlin Garland's *Main-Travelled Roads* allows for a more expansive example of these points, especially in the story "The Return of a Private." Here, a freight train is bringing a small group of Northern soldiers back from New Orleans to their homes in Wisconsin after the Civil War. Rather than the urgency of Jewett's opening line, however, it is the slowness of the journey that makes itself felt: "A long journey, slowly, irregularly, yet persistently pushing northward" (108–109). The train's apparent reluctance to get back to La Crosse County only exacerbates the men's misery, a misery that itself is partly created by the train's slow procession home and their awareness of the time:

> The train jogged forward so slowly that it seemed likely to be midnight before they should reach La Crosse. The little squad grumbled and swore, but it was no

use; the train would not hurry, and, as a matter of fact, it was nearly two o'clock when the engine whistled "down brakes." (109)

The men here are at the mercy of the train's own pace, having no connection to those in charge of their transport and no ability to alter its speed, and such frustrations are marked, importantly, by the time. A brief discussion between the men about money for a hotel emphasizes the hard economic situation into which they are arriving, and the sense that the battles of war are being replaced by less dangerous but equally tough contests: "It's goin' to be mighty hot skirmishin' to find a dollar these days" (109) one says.

Garland inserts this brief conversation, in fact, between two moments of narration that happen at exactly the same time: the paragraph ending "it was nearly two o'clock" quoted above is followed by this statement of new economic hardships, only for the narration to return to the train's arrival at the station once more. Now, however, the approximation of time—that "nearly two o'clock"—is replaced with something more precise: "The station was deserted, chill, and dark, as they came into it at *exactly* a quarter to two in the morning" (110, my emphasis). It is odd that Garland specifies the time like this when he has already told us it is "nearly two," a level of accuracy that sits more convincingly in a story of war-weary men on a long journey home in a pre-standardized-time 1865. Such precision of timekeeping becomes a conspicuous detail in the context of the story: "quarter to two" local time or railroad time, the time on the men's watches—presumably set back in New Orleans—or on the station clock?

This temporal indeterminacy is underlined by the way time is dealt with throughout the rest of the story. The return to a rural life also sees the return to a more relaxed and natural sense of time: "She don't hev dinner usually till about *one* on Sundays" (113, emphasis in original) a local man says, immediately followed by another stating that "I'll git home jest about six o'clock" (113). The earlier narrative precision is lost in this gestural, conversational sense of time. Where the train prescribed a precise timekeeping determined by timetables and economic need, rural Wisconsin seems to adhere to the cyclical rhythms of an older form of time awareness. This notion of cyclical time is subtly underlined again when the elderly Mrs. Gray complains, to the amusement of her young listeners, that "[g]irls in love ain't no use in the whole blessed week." Starting on Sundays, girls "can't think o'nothin' else" except their suitors, a state-of-mind that then affects them all through the week: "Thursday they git absent-minded...Friday they break dishes...Saturdays they have queer spurts o'workin'...An' Sunday they begin it all over again'" (119). Used to comic effect here, the direct link between cyclical temporal arrangements and rural life is being directly made.

The story itself ends, significantly, on this note. Garland uses the notion of cyclical time, something he has explicitly associated with a more natural and agrarian life, to suggest that the traditional patterns of Wisconsin farm life will outlast the historical disruptions of war: "The common soldier of the American volunteer army had returned. His war with the South was over, and his fight... with nature... was begun again" (126). An underlying narrative that seems to valorize the temporal rhythms of rural life is briefly compromised by the exact piece of timekeeping at the station, itself determined by the very symbol of modern life, the train, that the story uses to signal its intentions. Writing from the early 1890s, Garland's narrative reveals the social and psychological coincidence of standardized railroad time and prestandardized localized time.

Other moments in the collection explore and reveal similar anxieties. When Robert Bloom and his family take a train ride from Chicago to the small Wisconsin town of Bluff Siding in "God's Ravens," the journey is notably marked by a concern with time. The passage begins conventionally enough: "It was a lovely day in late April when they took the train out of the great grimy terrible city. It was eight o'clock..." (195). The retreat to the countryside from the "terrible city" (Garland cannot resist the pastoral cliché) begins, quite precisely, at eight o'clock. City time, and train time, are posited in rigid terms. But as the journey progresses away from the city environs and out into the midwestern prairies, the precision of clock time loosens its hold: "All day they rode. *Toward* noon they left the sunny prairie-land of northern Illinois" (195, my emphasis). The day is still regulated and experienced according to clock time, but there is no longer the need for the same accuracy. Advancing into Wisconsin, time is now drawn in vague periods: "As evening drew on, the hylas began to peep from the pools" (195). In other words, as the Bloom family move from the city into the country, Garland charts their journey in terms of its relation to a changing sense of timekeeping. Where "The Return of a Private" discloses the interpenetration of modern and traditional modes of timekeeping, "God's Ravens" strives to separate them out again in order to signal the experiential differences between contrasting types of space.

This geo-temporal move is something to which Garland also alludes in *Rose of Dutcher's Coolly* (1895) when the eponymous Rose rides a train to Chicago. Earlier in the novel, a train journey to Madison is conspicuously absent of any mention of the time at all—in fact, the whole episode is oddly timeless. It is all the more significant, then, that the chapter describing Rose's train journey to the city, a chapter pointedly called "Chicago," should open with the line "Almost 6 o'clock, and the train due in Chicago at 6:30!" (180). Rose's trepidation on entering the city is marked again by an awareness of time and timetables that was missing in the gentler rural journeys of her past. The temporal imperatives that distinguish city life, imperatives literally taken to the countryside by the city-regulated train, are also apparent in the flustered friend who meets Rose at the train station: "O, here you are! I got delayed—forgive me" (184). The passing reference to a delay takes on a particular significance because in that apologetic excuse for lateness a whole underlying psychopathology of time consciousness can be heard. Ostensibly, rural life is governed by a sense of temporal organization that differs from the city, but the incursion of technological modernity into the rural landscape—in this case, the train—begins to flatten out that difference. A nationally shared and regulated experience of time oscillates with a more geographically localized one, so that these moments in Garland's fiction open up to the complex heterogeneity of the period's temporal organization.

* * *

While the consciousness of a new train time plays an important role in many of the rural fictions I examine, one aspect of the train's relation to subjective experience seems to provoke more literary interest than any other: the visual. I opened the chapter with the passage from "Up the Coolly" partly because it illustrates perhaps the most ubiquitous narrative device to be found in Gilded Age representations of rural space—the view from a train carriage. Whereas issues of capitalist flow and temporal organization are primarily concerned with the train *in* and *on* the rural landscape, notions of vision and visuality move the emphasis inside: how is rural space represented *from* the train? Tied up in this question are a host of ideas that I will bring back at the end of the chapter to a further discussion of the train's ability to "make literal" the lines of urban-capitalist expansion. For now, however, it is worth dwelling on the idea of the view in its own right.

At the start of "Up the Coolly," as Howard McClane sits back in his train carriage and looks out across the midwestern landscape, several visual points are invoked: the concatenation of "past lakes, groves of oak, past fields of barley being reaped, past hay-fields" not only suggests the scrolling movement of the landscape outside the window, but also reduces that landscape to a series of generalized rural sights. Similarly, "a panorama of delight" and "down a sudden vista lakes open" insist on the specifically visual nouns "panorama" and "vista" to secure the landscape as at once distant and visually manageable, as if the expanses of rural countryside are predisposed to aesthetic contemplation. "Panorama," in particular, links the view from the train window to other forms of nineteenth-century mass culture, namely the public displays of painted panoramas and dioramas that had been so popular during the middle of the nineteenth century. As Ana Parejo Vadillo and John Plunkett have pointed out, such analogies were common at the time and popular visual entertainments such as the panorama would sometimes explicitly liken themselves to the visual experience of rail journeys (45). Likewise, Kirby talks at some length about the "panoramic perception" the train instilled in passengers and how this is itself a precursor to the intimate connection between the train and early cinema (a point I return to later). Garland's story perhaps comes too early to make any convincing links between Howard's view and the influence of cinema, but even if only unconsciously the story seems to gather some of its descriptive material from those popular forms of nineteenth-century visual entertainment.

There is an implicit suggestion of the picturesque here, so shifting the focus to a more general discussion of the unique way the train mediates between the viewer and the world outside, and commenting on the reduction of particular landscapes to something spatially generic, Mark Seltzer's evocation of painterly terms seems apposite: "The transport of still persons across landscapes converts landscapes into the arrested and unrooted nature of the still life. That is, the panoramas in perspective, seen through the glass frame of the window, reduce motion to the shift of the gaze, and the shift of the gaze reduces landscape to 'scenery'" (18). Seltzer is himself building on the suggestive short chapter on rail travel in Michel de Certeau's *The Practice of Everyday Life*, where he argues that the view from a train constitutes a distinct form of visual experience. "The windowpane is what allows us to *see*, and the rail, what allows us to *move through*," he writes (112, emphasis in original), pointing out that we are both distanced from the contemplated landscape by the windowpane and compelled to leave it behind by the motion of the train. What results, he says, is "an imperative of separation which obliges one to pay for an abstract ocular domination of space by leaving behind any proper place, by losing one's footing" (112). The experience of looking from a train window transforms our relationship with rural space from one of subjective engagement to one of objective contemplation.

Furthermore, this aestheticized notion of landscape implicates the politics of viewing that Raymond Williams summarizes: "[a] working country is hardly ever a landscape. The very idea of landscape implies separation and observation" (*Country and the City*, 149). The landscape in this specific meaning is a curiously labor-less space, somewhere emptied of the signifiers of real human toil in favor of a happy vision of contented and easy activity. The viewing subject, moreover, is separated from the landscape that is being observed; it implies the leisured point of view of someone not part of the rural scene or connected to the industry of agriculture. Viewing the world from the train is an activity loaded with the conditions of urban-capitalist modernity, one of which being the invisibility of the exploited workforce who make possible those very conditions. In *Human, All Too Human* (1878) Nietzsche talks of the "partial and false sight and judgement" brought about by the nineteenth century's "enormous acceleration of life," a situation likened to people who only ever get to see a country from a railway carriage (150). Such partiality of vision is the premise of "landscape" as a critical term; the train-based views of landscape found in rural fiction frequently operate to undermine any realist or naturalist impulse to reveal the conditions of agricultural life, and instead serve as set pieces that make room for moments of romantic pastoralism.

These series of connotations can be brought back to what Howard McClane sees when he looks out at the landscape from his place in the train carriage. The description of the view suggests those visual notions that Seltzer and de Certeau recognize, as well as the more politicized assertions of Williams: "The farming has nothing apparently petty about it. All seems vigorous, youthful, and prosperous" ("Coolly" 42–43). Labor is still visible, but it has been incorporated into the landscape as another aspect of the idealized scene. Howard's view is heavy with the complexities of landscape: the "apparently" and "seems" signal an awareness of the illusory quality of such a view, subtly qualifying the more assertive generalizations—"The farming" and "All"—that open the sentences. The general argument here—that the language of rural representation reveals the altered conditions of rural life under urban-industrial modernity—is underlined by something as apparently everyday as looking from a train window.

Some of these issues connect with the generic shifts and slips taking place in rural fiction that I highlighted earlier. Staying with Garland for a moment, such points are illustrated during Rose's journey to Madison in *Rose of Dutcher's Coolly*. The view from the train window operates, this time, not as mere scenery but as a kind of pathetic fallacy. It first echoes her own excitable mental state, so that a romanticized rural landscape of "fields and farms" is described as "whir[ling]" by in "dizzying fashion" (90)—interestingly, another use of the word "whirl" to describe the sensation of viewing from a train (see the opening paragraph of "Up the Coolly"). The speed of the train matches Rose's own excitements. However, when she is confronted by a lascivious brakeman—labeled, perhaps a touch melodramatically, as a "sex-maniac" (90)—she is reduced to a timid wreck. Now the view from the train loses its idyllic pastoral glean, becoming a series of "queer rocks" and land "covered with wild swamps...out of which long skeletons of dead pines lifted with a desolate effect" (90). The distancing effect of the train window, that conversion of landscape into scenery, here transforms a pastoral landscape into a gothic vision of alienation and fear.

It is important to recognize, however, that the alienated and purely scenic apprehension of the world outside the train has a basis in the physical experience of rail travel itself. From the 1830s onward, discourses surrounding the railway emphasized the effect on vision; the speed of a train carriage, it was often suggested, meant the foreground was moving too rapidly to be properly seen or comprehended.[8] The passenger has to ignore "the portions of the landscape that are closest to him, and to direct his gaze on the more distant objects that seem to pass by more slowly" (Schivelbusch 56). The train therefore altered the mode of observation, as existing ways of seeing (i.e., the visual experience of traveling in a horse-drawn carriage, or by foot) were no longer viable.

Illuminating parallels can therefore be drawn between the visual experience of the train journey and that of the city streets. Georg Simmel's discussion of urban experience in his classic 1903 essay "The Metropolis and Mental Life"[9] is developed by film historian Ben Singer, who argues that on one level at least the visual demands of urban space manifest themselves physiologically: "the things we are conditioned to pay attention to, the strategies we use in scrutinizing those things, and the sense we make of them, can and do change as we adapt to different environments" (110). The sense of visual comprehension that Seltzer and de Certeau discuss is developed if we take into account the pre-railroad experience of vision. The shift is from slower, horse-drawn modes of transport that meant the foreground (and the ground itself) could be viewed and experienced as part of a full comprehension of the space through which one was traveling, to the train that, in its relatively smooth and rapid movement and distancing of the traveler from the world outside, is the "different environment" that the passenger finds themselves in. This different environment, furthermore, actually reinstalls a sense of landscape that is associated more with a midcentury romantic vision, so that ways of seeing associated with distinctly modern experiences often serve to translate rural space into an idealized vision secured in a premodern past. Howard's view from the window of his train carriage, in other words, is a view of rural space modified by a distinctly modern, even urbanized, mode of perception; he is returning to his childhood home, after all, from a life in the city. In examining how the views of rural landscapes are described from the train, the actual process of perceptive adaptation unveils itself as embedded in the descriptive strategies of literary texts.

As I mentioned before, these descriptions of the subjective experience of train travel are more common to literature from later in the century, but one exception pertinent to this discussion comes in William Dean Howells's first novel, *Their Wedding Journey* (1871). Following Basil and Isabel March on a day's leisurely "railroading" (just the beginning of the eponymous journey), and "an hour after leaving the city" (83), the protagonists find themselves "quite comfortable in the common passenger-car, and disposed to view the scenery" (83). Placing the action in the passenger car, and stating that the March's are now "disposed" to "view the scenery," anticipates Seltzer's formulation of rail travel as the transport of "still persons across landscapes," a process which converts those landscapes into "still life." Such a notion is certainly confirmed as Howells's train passes through some quintessential pastoral scenes: "the great brooding warmth gave to the landscape the charm which it alone can impart. It is a landscape that I greatly love for its mild beauty and tranquil picturesqueness" (83). The narrative reveals a certain modern awareness by placing the landscape at that peculiar train-determined distance from the source of narration, and so reducing it to the picturesque.

But Howells has his third-person narrator convert this captive (and captivated) view of the outside world into a desire to move past the windowpane, and in a passage that somewhat jars with his more familiar realism we leave the train and the Marches behind and stroll through an idyllic rural New England. The passage begins while the action is still on board the train, but any sense of realism is soon replaced by a purely romantic reverie:

> Spaces of woodland here and there dapple the slopes, and the cozy red farm-houses repose by the side of their capacious red barns. Truly, there is no ground on which to defend the idleness, and yet as the train strives furiously onward amid these scenes of fertility and abundance, I like in fancy to loiter behind it, and to saunter at will up and down the landscape. I stop at the farm-yard gates...and am served with cups of buttermilk by old Dutch ladies...I do not complain if the drink is brought to me by some red-cheeked, comely young girl, out of Washington Irving's pages. (84)

The scene from the train is composed of those old topographical clichés, the farm house and the barn, but such a description is interrupted by the "furious" train that the narrator implies is antithetical to an idealized vision of rural life—not to mention the suggestion of its masculine contrast to the feminized, "fertile" landscape. The strange couple of pages where Howells's narrator does his sauntering up and down the landscape are therefore marked by explicitly romantic and antebellum signifiers—figures from Old Europe, or the Europeanized American Irving—that are human (rather than the architecture and flora that are easier to see from the train) but decidedly unthreatening. The personable interaction with the world is imaginatively incommensurable with a narrative based on board the train, yet such a romanticized saunter was only possible to begin with because of the distanced, alienated picturesqueness that the speeding train created.

It is a difficult and not altogether convincing passage, because in rejecting the train for a more intimate walk among individually identified people the narrator ends up romanticizing a scene that the train (now rejected as an antipastoral symbol) had allowed to be romanticized in the first place. Howells has no choice but to step down from the train—his signpost to tell us this is a contemporary narrative grounded in the reality of Gilded Age America—if he wishes to dwell a little longer, and a little more "humanly," in the nostalgic landscape that his protagonists hurtle through. The passage reveals, in the end, the train's inherent incompatibility with a detailed, place-based apprehension of the rural space it traverses.

Their Wedding Journey comes, as I mentioned, early in the period I am concerned with here. Later narratives are often more consciously aware of the particularly "modern" mode of perception the train instills, and Jewett's "Going to Shrewsbury" illustrates this in a pertinent way. Following the opening line quoted earlier, the train departs and the elderly Mrs. Peet strikes up a conversation with the anonymous narrator of the story. Gazing from the window, she casually describes her view of the landscape in a way that encompasses many of the issues of distance, time, and vision at stake in the discussion here:

> "There looks to be plenty o' good farmin' land in this part o' the country," she said, a minute later. "Where be we now? See them handsome farm buildin's; he must be a well-off man." But I had to tell my companion that we were still within the borders of the old town where we had both been born. (702)

The world outside the carriage, insinuated in the explicit use of "looks" and "see," is idealized (the farming land is "good" and the buildings are "handsome") from within the train. More than this, however, it is made anonymous: Mrs. Peet has only been traveling a minute, and is still within the village she has lived her whole life, yet she does not recognize it. The train has reduced the landscape outside to anonymous scenery.

What makes this passage particularly intriguing is that the reader's own vision is focalized through Mrs. Peet, the landscape reported rather than described. Instead of Howells's problem of having an omniscient narrative voice unable to reconcile the speeding train with a desire to make a tangible contact with the landscape, here the first-person narration means we read less about the view itself and instead see the effect of that view on a perceiving subject. The intimate, grounded visual apprehension of the world that older forms of transport allowed collides here with a new form, and in a telling phrase Mrs. Peet even anticipates forms of the future: "Ain't it jest like flyin' through the air? I can't catch holt to see nothin'" (702). The speed of the train unsettles Mrs. Peet's view of the "place" she has inhabited all her life and so reduces it to mere "space," forcing her traditional mode of perception to confront a "different environment"—a confrontation that Singer, via Simmel, sees as a paradigmatic urban experience.

Between Howells's and Jewett's fictional treatments of the view from a train carriage there is, I am suggesting, a developing historical consciousness that impacts on modes of writing and representing rural space. Where Howells displays an apparent inability or unwillingness to reconcile the train journey to a mode of representation still enmeshed in the romantic idea of the narrator's exultant vision, Jewett's later story employs the train journey as a realist signifier that paradoxically allows the narrative to gesture back to notions of pastoral idealism—all of this wrapped up in the way that rural landscapes are viewed through the train window.

* * *

The issues explored in this chapter so far come to the fore most prominently, and in a way that draws them together, in the three texts I turn to now: Stephen Crane's "The Bride Comes to Yellow Sky" (1898), Booth Tarkington's *The Gentleman from Indiana* (1899), and Owen Wister's *The Virginian* (1902). Crane's tale once again opens on board a train, a location that serves to mediate the evocative description of the natural landscape outside the window:

> The great Pullman was whirling onward with such dignity of motion that a glance from the window seemed simply to prove that the plains of Texas were pouring eastward. Vast flats of green grass, dull-hued spaces of mesquite and cactus, little groups of frame houses, woods of light and tender trees, all were sweeping into the east, sweeping over the horizon, a precipice. (79)

"Whirl" is again the verb employed to describe the feeling of traveling forward, here given extra emphasis by the assertion that it is with a "dignity of motion" that the train, and presumably the passengers on board, move through the landscape. This sense of motion is then transferred from the carriage to the landscape itself, which is "glanced" from the window—the rural landscape of Texas appears to be "pouring eastward." As David Halliburton has demonstrated, the language of this opening scene is underpinned by complex poetic techniques—the use of alliteration and assonance, the metrical feet of the prose, and the particular syllabic arrangement—that mean "[t]aken as a whole, the effect is of a movement that, like the movement of the train across the landscape, combines striking regular rhythm with striking rhythmic variety" (230). We are returned to de Certeau's notion that viewing the world from a moving carriage, through a windowpane, allows us both an "ocular domination" over the view but also a sense of "losing one's footing" (112), the still life of scenery transformed into something more transitory and elusive.

This opening scene has other implications, however, that go beyond the visual to incorporate some of the deeper themes of urban modernity. Ben Merchant Vorpahl, commenting on the story's opening scene, has pointed out that while in one sense "the landscape's motion is a merely optical quality," it is also suggestive of otherwise-hidden historical processes: "the fact that the Western setting is 'sweeping into the east' suggests that it is becoming more *like* the east" (199). What Crane effectively does, Vorpahl argues, is to use an "optical illusion to identify reality, [using] an oddly kinetic prairie to define the static fact of time's passage" (199). The falling away of regional difference under the conditions of modernity finds a metaphorical equivalent in the blurring of the landscape outside the train window, so that the train's arrival on this landscape is both a tangible sign of modernization and the vehicle from which Crane can make a literary gesture at modernity's processes.

Such processes are underlined when the attention moves inside the train, and the eponymous bride gazes at the extravagant fittings of the Pullman carriage:

> [H]er eyes opened wider as she contemplated the sea-green figured velvet, the shining brass, silver, and glass, the wood that gleamed as darkly brilliant as the surface of a pool of oil. At one end a bronze figure sturdily held a support for a separated chamber, and at convenient places on the ceiling were frescoes in olive and silver. (80)

The newly married pair that the story centers on have already been marked as rather out of place amid such opulence: they are self-conscious in their smart clothes, have never been in a "parlor car" before, and the bride worries that paying a dollar for a meal is "too much—for us" (79). Crane contrasts the economic situation of the rural pair (Jack Potter, the groom, is the town marshal of Yellow Sky) with the luxurious, urban Pullman carriage. Such carriages aped "the elegance of the major urban hotels" (Gordon 179), and to be aboard one "was to be in a rarefied world of urban elites...isolated from the dust and heat of the great western plains" (Beaumont and Freeman 28). More abstractly, the alienation of the pair from their fellow passengers—various other people in the carriage watch them with some amusement, even "stares of derisive enjoyment" ("Bride" 80)—mirrors the atomized relationships associated with modern urban living: "railroad...cars were also part of an expanding sphere of anonymous social relations associated with the nineteenth-century city" (Richter 14). While the landscape outside is marked by a topography of rural life (the mesquite and cacti, the "frame houses") and yet metaphorically connected with the growing dominance of an urbanized and monied East, the main protagonists are similarly both surrounded by an urban, middle-class vision of modernity and remain apart from it.

Crane also uses the new temporal imperatives of train travel to distinguish the town of Yellow Sky from a more modernized America. Some of that timekeeping precision surfaces again when Jack tells his bride that "[w]e are due in Yellow Sky at 3:42," a detail that means she produces her new silver pocket watch—her wedding gift from her husband—to announce that the time is currently "seventeen minutes past twelve" (80). The specificity of these times feels conspicuous, the train timetable inducing a precision of time awareness between the two newlyweds that signals their effort to conform to a modern system of temporal organization, and in turn announce themselves as modern individuals. The contrast between this exacting attention to time and the social life of the ranching community in Yellow Sky is given more obvious expression at the beginning of the second scene; the action has now shifted to the town itself, but the opening line seems to be an echo from a more time-constrained place: "The California Express on the Southern Railway was due at Yellow Sky in twenty-one minutes" (82). By naming both the train and the line on which it is traveling, Crane contextualizes the imminent arrival as something that belongs to a wider, corporatized network—it is not simply "the train," which it surely would be to the residents of Yellow Sky, but a more specific component within a national system of privately owned railroads. That gesturing at a wider urban-industrial consciousness continues in the further precision of the "twenty-one minutes" until arrival time.

Yellow Sky is explicitly set apart from this world by a shift in the narrative register, described in a way that emphasizes its adherence to a different level of temporal detail: six men are drinking at the bar of the "Weary Gentleman saloon" (82), and the rest of Yellow Sky "was dozing" (83). The action that carries the rest of the story—Scratchy Wilson's threat to the newly returned marshal Jack Potter, and the deflated drama of a shootout that never happens—turns this contrast into a moral one, so that the traditional legal codes of Yellow Sky are frustrated by the emerging modern sensibilities of a town marshal (just returned, by train, from the city of San Antonio) who refuses to fight. The tension between an emerging new order and the vestiges of an old one, essentially what the confrontation at the end of the story plays out, has already been established as a governing theme by the explicit use of the train as a herald of modernity.

The train orders and gives shape to the opening of "The Bride Comes to Yellow Sky," first in the experience of the people on board and then in the community it is traveling towards. As a stable material entity whose purpose is to traverse time and space, the train has the capacity to both embody and symbolize the multiple geographies of modernity, the heterogeneous scales of space—here, relations between metropole and province, as well as nation and locality—as well as the story's investment in a contrast between the rural landscape and the processes of change that modernity brings. As Halliburton comments, "[w]herever it appears in Crane's fiction, the advent of the train is associated...with challenge and change" (228). The story, through its use of the train, works to highlight the intimate connection between these fluid states and serves to record, both stylistically and thematically, the process of their unfolding.

In Booth Tarkington's first novel *The Gentleman from Indiana* we find a more overt and prolonged use of the train journey in a rural narrative, concerned again with the unique visual relationship that the passengers on board have with the landscape. In an opening that by now feels like something of a cliché, the novel begins with a long passage describing the landscape of Indiana as seen from the window of a train. It encompasses so many of the themes already discussed about the relationship between rural space, the train, and visual perception that it is worth quoting at some length here:

> There is a fertile stretch of flat lands in Indiana where unagrarian Eastern travelers, glancing from car-windows, shudder and return their eyes to interior upholstery, preferring even the swaying caparisons of a Pullman to the monotony without. The landscape lies interminably level: bleak in winter...hot and dusty in summer.... The persistent tourist who seeks for signs of man in this sad expanse perceives a reckless amount of rail fence; at intervals a large barn; and, here and there, man himself, incurious, patient, slow, looking up from the

fields apathetically as the Limited flies by. Widely separated from each other are small frame railway stations—sometimes with no other buildings in sight, which indicates that somewhere behind the adjacent woods a few shanties and thin cottages are grouped about a couple of brick stores. (5)

What is immediately striking about this description is how it is both similar to and yet crucially different from the opening of Garland's "Up the Coolly." As in Garland's story, a traveler from the East looks out at the midwestern landscape as the train hurtles through it, picking out particular details—barns, farmers, the buildings of rural settlements—as he does so. What marks it out, however, is the total absence of any pastoral romanticizing: the "unagrarian" viewer of the scene (even the "tourist") can barely look at the "monotony" of the "interminable" scene outside, preferring the rich comforts of the Pullman carriage[10] to the rather forlorn rural workers scattered in the fields.

John Stilgoe has commented on the opening of the novel in these same terms, arguing that "Tarkington understood...that to the observer on the train everything beyond the window is so much spectacle," the result being that the farmers glimpsed outside are viewed "not as individuals but as a type, or even worse, as quasi-human stereotypes" (253). By opening the narrative on a train, Tarkington is able to create the same kind of impressionistic description of rural life that Garland attempted, this time to adopt in more negative terms the same distanced subjective stance that romanticized landscapes infer. Whereas workers are written out of romanticized conceptions of rural landscapes as an act of forgetting that allows nature to be re-enchanted, here they are part of a grim panorama that confirms the economic superiority of the privileged viewer.

The Gentleman from Indiana uses train journeys to structurally bookend the narrative, so that the impressionistic vision of the midwestern countryside that the train facilitates becomes symbolic of the personal and somewhat sentimental journey that the novel's hero, John Harkless, undertakes during the course of the story. He arrives in Plattville, the small town that serves as the setting for the majority of the story, as an out-of-place easterner, but by the novel's conclusion he is a pivotal member of the intimate community he has found—and, of course, betrothed to a local girl. Traveling back to the town at the beginning of the final chapter, the view from the train window is now the enchanted vision of someone fully awakened to the apparent beauty of rural life:

John looked out over the boundless aisles of corn.... [W]here the train ran between shadowy groves, delicate landscape vistas, framed in branches, opened, closed, and succeeded each other...and the intensely blue September skies ran down to the low horizon, meeting the tossing plumes of corn.

It takes a long time for the full beauty of the flat lands to reach a man's soul. (347–48)

Now transformed into "delicate landscapes" that are "framed" by trees, the midwestern countryside has metamorphosized into the picturesque and labor-less visions found in "Up the Coolly" and *Their Wedding Journey*. The interminable flatness of the landscape that had been so objectionable in the opening vision is now something precious and alluring: "[t]he fields, like great, flat emeralds set in new metal, were bordered with golden-rod" (349). John, viewing the landscape through the eyes of a stranger at the beginning, had preferred the luxurious interior of his Pullman carriage; now, fully cognizant of rural life, he can recognize the line of sycamores that trace the path of "Hibbard's Creek," smell walnut and the "hint of coming frost" on the air (350), and admires the haystacks "garnered to feed the industrious horse who had earned his meed" (351). The novel's investment in a romanticized idea of rural life, an idea central to the sentimental trajectory of the plotline, finds no more conducive home than the neatly packaged and comfortable vision of Indiana's landscapes uniquely possible on board a train.

In *The Gentleman from Indiana*, perhaps more so than in any of the texts examined here, the effect of the train on the perceiving subject is directly employed as a narrative contrivance that is both a sign of the text's realist intent—a ubiquitous and markedly modern form of transport—and the means by which a distinct way of viewing the landscape can be converted into thematic and aesthetic literary material. The panoramic and distanced apprehension of the countryside that the view from a train compels allows for the kind of impressionistic literary descriptions found at the beginning and end of the novel. These in turn can be inserted in the narrative to neatly summarize and symbolize the personal and psychological state of its protagonist. A resolutely and complexly "modern" form of experience is transferred into the substance of literary representation, so that rural life can continue to be treated in generalized and distanced terms: the uniformly bleak and toilsome landscape at the beginning, or, swapping one stereotype for another, the idealized and picturesque pastoral vision of the novel's conclusion. Rural fiction, at these moments, often underlines inherited notions and attitudes toward rural life in the very act of its intimate immersion in modern experiences. The train window frames not just the visual composition of the rural landscape, but converts that composition into ideologically charged "scenes" that can emphasize or destabilize a text's generic identity.

Turning finally to Wister's *The Virginian*, I return to a theme discussed at the beginning of this chapter: the role of the train in the commercial incorporation of rural America. Melody Graulich has pointed out just how immersed in the networks of capital the novel is, and particularly how the railroad comes to signify those networks. She shows, for example, how the narrative discusses the "flow of capital into the West" that "connects the region to the global economy" (38) and how the railroad signals those connections in ways which inflect the novel's representation of, among other things, race and gender. My focus here is more specifically on the way the novel deals with narrative point of view in connection with the train, relevant not least because it opens, yet again, on board one. This time the narrator does not hurtle through the landscape but in fact looks out at a detail of local life as his stationary train waits to pull into the station:

> Some notable sight was drawing the passengers . . . to the window. . . . I saw near the track an enclosure, and round it some laughing men, and inside it some whirling dust, and amid the dust some horses, plunging, huddling, and dodging. They were cow ponies in a corral. . . . Through the window-glass of our Pullman the thud of their mischievous hoofs reached us, and the strong, humorous curses of the cow-boys. (11)

Whereas the train has so often had a distancing effect on the rural communities outside the window, transforming them into picturesque scenes or emphasizing the relative hardship compared to life on board, here the narrative begins by placing the narrator on board a stationary train so that he can be presented with a vignette of the life he is about to enter into. The physically demanding work of ranching (though enjoyable—the men are laughing) is what now becomes apparent, with even the sounds of that work, something lost on a moving train, audible to the passengers.

Furthermore, to return to a point I briefly mentioned earlier, the situation described here—male and female passengers crowded around to gaze through a rectangular glass window at a short scene taking place on the other side—would have unmistakably evoked the new medium of cinema that, by the time the novel was published in 1902, was beginning to emerge as a popular form of entertainment. Indeed, the cultural invention of the "Wild West" at the end of the nineteenth century, something that *The Virginian* played an instrumental role in, was also a favorite subject for pioneering filmmakers. In the 1890s, famed producer William K. L. Dickson would make numerous short films of performers from Buffalo Bill's Wild West Show, focusing on exactly the kind of skillful displays that Wister's opening scene evokes.[11] While it is usually the experience of the moving train carriage that has led critics to draw an analogy between rail travel and film,[12] Wister halts the train so that the details of the action outside can be fully comprehended. Nevertheless, the connection is one worth making here as it implicates the opening of the novel within the new perceptual paradigms of urban modernity: the view from a train becomes analogous to the "urban medium and art form" (Kirby 133) of early cinema, which in turn underwrites the structure and form of the opening scene. The emergence of a modern urban consciousness frames a world tied to more traditional orders—the ranching activity outside the window—so that the novel's opening scene records their coexistence within that particular historical moment.

The anonymous narrator is, however, portrayed as a reluctant tenderfoot in these opening pages, and the train serves to act as a psychological umbilical cord back to the "civilized" East from which he has traveled. Alighting at the station and angry to find that his luggage has been lost, the narrator wistfully watches another train depart the station:

> [T]he East-bound departed slowly into that distance whence I had come. I stared after it as it went its way to the far shores of civilization. It grew small in the unending gulf of space, until all sign of its presence was gone.... Medicine Bow seemed a lonely spot. A sort of ship had left me marooned in a foreign ocean; the Pullman was comfortably steaming home to port, while I—how was I to find Judge Henry's ranch? Where in this unfeatured wilderness was Sunk Creek? (15)

The ranching lands of Wyoming are strange territory for a narrator more used to the urban busyness of the East, and the train is metaphorically transformed into another form of transport—the ship—in a way that accentuates his sense of isolation and the apparent featurelessness of the landscape. In these opening pages the train is identified quite explicitly as a civilizing presence, a literal connection to the modern world, while also symbolizing more generally the processes of modernization that, throughout the novel, begin to creep into the community.[13]

It is the Virginian's own arrival into modernity, however, that the train finally signals. At the novel's conclusion we learn that "the railroad came, and built a branch to that land of the Virginian's where the coal was. By that time he was an important man, with a strong grip on many various enterprises" (327). The positioning of the narrator at the beginning of the novel—the view of ranching life comfortably couched within a modern viewpoint, and the recognition of the train as an instrument of change—finally comes to underpin the story's narrative arc. The Virginian, for all his rough-hewn heroism and archetypal cowboy antics, is by the end a capitalist entrepreneur who has made his money because the railroad has tied his land into a commercial network of coal production. The novel invests much of its descriptive and dramatic efforts into a gritty vision of Wyoming ranch life that seems at odds with a vaguely effete and decadent urban East, yet ultimately the narrative opens and closes in a way that acknowledges the irresistible processes of modernization that the railroad heralded—the same "sweeping into the east" highlighted by Crane. The representation of nineteenth-century rural life is framed, once again, by a modern vision firmly grounded in an urban-industrial and commercialized consciousness that, in the case of *The Virginian*, seems more at home in the newly arrived twentieth century.

It is not surprising that of all the examples of modernization addressed throughout this book, the train is by far the most conspicuous, by far the most frequently described, in the rural literature of the late nineteenth century. It provides an obvious physical link to the expanding urban world—being simultaneously a cause and a symptom of that very expansion—while being a life-altering presence in rural communities themselves, both intrusive and emancipatory. Literary representations of rural space, reflecting the importance and ubiquity of the train in the daily lives of Gilded Age Americans, also provide a window into the altered conditions of both communal and personal experience, registering in their thematic interests and generic composition the adjustment to new modes of experience even in the midst of their happening.

CHAPTER 2

Commerce and Carnival at the Canvas City: Traveling Circuses

Few occasions in Gilded Age America generated the same level of excitement as the arrival in town of a traveling circus. Circus day in Tarkington's *The Gentleman from Indiana*, for example, meant that the "air was full of exhilaration; everybody was laughing and shouting and calling greetings." A previously quiet country village is now the focus of a convivial invasion: "Carlow County was turning out, and from far and near the country people came" (90–91). So, too, in Hamlin Garland's *Rose of Dutcher's Coolly*: "It was the mightiest event of their lives," the narrative grandly informs us, while the distribution of the colorful advertisements meant the "whole county awoke to the significance of the event and began preparation and plans, though it was nearly three weeks away" (41–42). Some twenty years before Tarkington and Garland, Jewett also highlighted the importance of the circus to the country locales of her first book *Deephaven* (1877) when the narrator, a visitor from the entertainment-rich Boston, states that "Kate and I looked forward to a certain Saturday with as much eagerness as if we had been little school-boys, for on that day we were to go to the circus" (59). And, a final example, when William Dean Howells discusses circus day in his memoir of 1890, *A Boy's Town*, he recalls that "[f]or a fortnight beforehand they [the boys in the village] worked themselves up for the arrival of the circus into a fever of fear and hope, for it was always a question with a great many whether they could get their fathers to give them the money to go in" (776).

This chapter considers the ways in which the circus is represented in rural fiction, partly because of its obvious significance in the culture of everyday life for rural America, but also because it offers a particularly resonant synecdoche for the period's wider industry of commercialized mass entertainment. By exploring both how the experience of circus day is represented as a disruption to ordinary daily life in rural areas and the spectacular, illusory, escapist nature of the performance itself, this chapter addresses two related strands: how forms of mass entertainment bring a distinctly modern set of experiences to rural space, and how this set of experiences deeply effects and destabilizes the generic and aesthetic strategies of rural fiction. As a space where many of the underpinning tenets of respectable society were challenged, the circus in some ways typifies notions of carnivalesque excess and romantic freedom. In other ways, however—as a prime form of commercialism, a venue for innovative technologies, and as an arena for highly orchestrated and meticulously planned performances—the circus reinforces and exemplifies processes of rationalization and urban-industrial organization. I therefore begin by outlining the series of complex connotations and associations the circus evokes, and giving more consideration to the theoretical tools most useful in explicating these associations, before moving on to some case studies of circus representation in rural fiction that develop and expand on these points. I ultimately argue that in representing the circus, rural fiction of this period faces distinct challenges that not only mirror the highly ambivalent and paradoxical space of the circus itself but also point to the radically altered perceptual conditions of urban modernity.

* * *

By the time Jewett published *Deephaven* in 1877, the traveling circus was a well-established fixture on the calendar of amusements in country districts. It was in fact an American, Joshua Purdy Brown of Delaware, who had pioneered the traveling circus back in 1825, "thereby paving the way for a fully peripatetic circus which was free to leave the expensive city amphitheaters...and travel into often entertainment-starved rural areas" (Stoddart 22). Key to the sheer ubiquity of the traveling circus in the nineteenth century was the financial sense it made to the owners now that road travel, and later on rail travel, made rural towns viable stopping points. It would be after the Civil War, however, that the circus as a truly large-scale undertaking came into being. Following his partnership with W. C. Coup and Dan Castello in 1871, P. T. Barnum would later establish a circus company with the other circus magnate of the age James A. Bailey, their names eventually combining with the Ringling Brothers to form a virtually monopolistic circus empire. But my interest here is how the circus as a form of entertainment came to represent something distinctly modern, how it is in some ways the materialization of a series of social and economic conditions indicative of a burgeoning urban modernity in Gilded Age America.

What is striking when looking at how the Gilded Age circus is described, both in nineteenth-century journalism and in subsequent scholarly works, is the prevalence of urban and industrial metaphors. The circus "was often received as a model of industrial discipline" (Adams 165) at the time, an example of finely tuned and rationalized efficiency. Typical contemporary accounts certainly bear this view out in their choice of language: the *Boston Daily Globe*'s admiring piece on Barnum's circus in June 1887, for instance, reported that "[i]t is a perfect system, maintained by the most rigid discipline.... Every man has his particular piece of work to do, just the same as in a great factory" (qtd. in Adams 189–90). The London *Times*' 1889 report of Barnum's "Greatest Show on Earth" similarly describes the scene as "some vast factory, with its endless spindles and revolving shafts and pulleys," and American journalist Cleveland Moffett, writing in *McClure's Magazine* in 1895, called the circus a "kingdom on wheels, a city that folds itself up like an umbrella" (qtd. in Harris 275, 240). It is also clear from recent critic Janet Davis's language that the scale of the Gilded Age circus invites urban metaphors: a "nomadic city" (39), a "magical, movable city", or a "canvas city" (46) were common descriptive tags for the circus. Gregory Renoff reveals how the huge crowds that gathered in towns on circus day were also often understood in explicitly urban terms, citing a newspaper report from 1875 describing circus day in Rome, Georgia: "Broad Street, Rome, had the appearance of Broadway, New York," the reporter grandly states (91).

In fact, the complexity and size of the traveling circus, something which grew to astounding proportions after the Civil War, is in some ways a prime form of the move to rationalization that I outlined in the introduction. It was, after all, a precisely calculated undertaking, a necessarily efficient and goal-oriented process that could unpack and erect Barnum and Bailey's 1894 circus (consisting of over a dozen tents, the biggest more than 400 feet in length) in just half an hour (Davis 47). As Neil Harris points out, "the circus became a symbol of administrative coordination in an age that venerated...executive skills" (240). Its utilization of improved means of transportation, commitment to commercialization, and need to remain in touch with technological advances meant that the circus became a site where the transformations of urban-industrial modernization could be read and understood in unique ways.

As a symbol of modern efficiency, then, the circus invited comparisons to the more complex systems of modernity that typified the age—both the factory and the city. Yet the circus does depart from, challenge, and even disrupt these modern forms in crucial ways. Its organization and implementation may require all the strictly organized timekeeping of an industrial age, but the experience of the audience, the actual spectacle of the performance, is a strange, jarring mix of temporal and spatial dislocation. I return to some of the conceptual notions that this evokes—in particular spectacle and the carnivalesque—later; for now it is worth dwelling on how the circus represented a disruption to ordinary daily life in rural communities. Circus day itself was a brief window when normal routines would simply stop, when "shops closed their doors, schools canceled classes, and factories shut down" (Davis 2). Amid these unsettled routines the circus seemed spontaneous and rebellious, so that the parades of ornately dressed performers and cages of wild animals gave spectators a feeling that "the entire world [had] appeared on Main Street," while inside "the crowded tents, time also seemed in abeyance as spectators tried to comprehend three rings, two stages, and an outer hippodrome track of constant, relentless activity" (Davis 52). The rhythms of daily time certainly become confused on circus day for the residents of Plattville in *The Gentleman from Indiana*: the town clock-keeper, caught up in the excitement of the circus parade, is suddenly "reminded that it was getting on toward ten o'clock, whereas, in the excitement of festival, he had not yet struck nine." Rushing to the clock tower to amend for his forgetfulness, he strikes the hour—"and, in the elation of the moment, seven or eight besides" (Tarkington 105).

The circus reinforced a sense of geographical specificity and place-based identity (a tangible site that appeared in villages according to a strict itinerary), and yet its content purposefully suppressed the contingencies of time and space in order to present a repeatable performance of transnational and transhistorical spectacle. To the residents of country towns and villages across America, circus day offered a curious mixture of mythical, stereotypical, romantic, and fantastic scenes, ranging across the world and across history. Lewis Atherton recognizes what a potentially radical challenge, both politically and morally, such spectacle may have posed: "[Circuses] overwhelmed the imagination of townsmen with their glitter and pageantry. Knights rode on Main Streets in a land committed to the ideal of a classless society. Roman chariots raced within view of Protestant church steeples" (132). There are obvious social and cultural tensions here, the circus offering as it does both a potent example of rationalized industry and commercialism and yet operating as a site that subverts cherished nineteenth-century values. An anecdote recounted by cultural historian Bluford Adams illustrates the point: when the Adam Forepaugh Circus arrived in the Pennsylvania town of Easton in 1883, the local cotton mill refused to close to allow the workers to visit the attraction. In protest at missing out on what they considered a "holiday from the factory," four hundred of them went on strike. For all its transitory commercialized charms, the circus still represented a cherished moment of real escapism, a genuine invocation of the carnivalesque. "[T]he Easton operatives still found something liberatory in one of the nation's most heavily capitalized culture industries" (190), Adams concludes.

The circus clearly embodies several conflicting connotations, a site of industrial rationalization, urban-like sensory complexity, and an escapist, ludic festivity. As I have already suggested, the last of these connotations evokes and bares close resemblance to the well-worn notion of the Bakhtinian carnival, a familiar critical term that is nevertheless helpful here in conceptualizing some of the representational complexities that the circus poses. "Carnival celebrated temporary liberation from the prevailing truth and from the established order," Bakhtin writes in his famous definition, "it marked the suspension of all hierarchical rank, privileges, norms, and prohibitions" (10). The carnival (a broadly conceived event, a time and a place that is also a general sensibility) is a disruption of normality that becomes a site apart from social expectations—and, in the more narrowly literary terms at play here, prevailing generic expectations as well. But as I have pointed out, the circus did not simply represent an escape into some utopian realm; as a successful commercial product, it also operated much like the event Bakhtin offers as the counterexample of carnival, the official feast. Here "the existing pattern of things [is] reinforced," an event which serves to emphasize "the existing hierarchy, the existing religious, political, and moral values, norms and prohibitions" (Bakhtin 9). Both these strands seem paradoxically combined in the Gilded Age American circus. While it offers both a place and a time apart from the normal daily life of rural America, its presence is also indicative of the incursions of rationalized capitalism into that life.

Pushing the theoretical implications of this a little further, we naturally enough encounter the more specifically visual notion of "spectacle." In the Marxian sense of the word that Guy Debord's work established, spectacle is "a massive *internal* extension of the capitalist market—the invasion and restructuring of whole areas of free time, private life, leisure, and personal expression" (Clark 9, emphasis in original). It is summarized in the phrase "the colonisation of everyday life," the condition whereby everyday culture (leisure time, the media, public space) becomes ordered and commodified—and, crucially, the individual becomes an increasingly passive consumer of fetishized products. In Debord's own words, the "spectator's alienation from and submission to the contemplated object" is the defining characteristic, the spectacle itself becoming something external to the "acting subject" (23).

To think of these series of points in terms more suited to my discussion here, it is worth bearing in mind the kind of transformation in circus performance that P. T. Barnum and others pioneered in the 1870s and that became widespread during the period. As the commercial scale of the circus grew after the Civil War—from one to two to three rings, from audiences in the tens to audiences in the thousands—so it became truly spectacular. Neil Harris's discussion of Barnum's circuses even evokes those Debordian terms; contrasting Gilded Age circuses with their antebellum forebears, it was in circuses later in the century that "slapstick and pantomime replaced verbal sallies. Intimacy was lost, along with certain kinds of interactions between performers and spectators" (241). The audience became "passive prisoners" as Barnum's commercial productions "permitted more passive spectatorship. This was artifice caught up in its own splendor and profusion; onlookers had nothing more to do than sit back and enjoy" (244–45). This peculiar stance, implicating circus goers in a carnivalesque defiance while simultaneously securing them as passive Debordian spectators, is one that Jonathan Crary sees as indicative of the wider field of late nineteenth-century popular entertainment. Appropriately, it is Georges Seurat's painting *Parade de Cirque* (1888) that Crary examines in exactly these terms, arguing that it occupies a "social" and "imaginary position that coincides neither with dreams of subjective freedom nor effects of power" (152).

Such an elaborate cultural form poses questions for literary representation, especially in a historical moment that saw realist aesthetics in the ascendancy. In Helen Stoddart's discussion of the circus in Charles Dickens's fiction, for instance, she suggests that "as a form of live, predominantly mute, body-centered entertainment, [the circus] issues a radical challenge to literary representation" (115). Nancy Bentley has more recently discussed a similar issue through the frame of Gilded Age literature, provocatively arguing that mass cultural forms like the circus presented a variety of experiences that seemed diametrically opposed to the act of reading the high literary novel itself. The latter "favors an individual mental concentration that...[excludes] other somatic and social realities," whereas circuses and other forms of popular entertainment "seek to multiply objects and stimuli." "In their very excess such sites open out to multiple zones of experience and feeling, zones to which the high cultural novel has no imaginary access," Bentley claims (38). The visual and aural stimulation of the circus, which in the three-ring tents would have been considerable, offers a challenge not just to the operation of literary aesthetics but also to the place of literature in the wider cultural scene. The sheer number of simultaneous demands on the senses, and not least the nature of the performances themselves, work to destabilize the "subtle and cumulative" (Bentley 44) narrative operations of literary realism in a way that prompts writers to hark back to some of the flowery excesses of romanticism, while at the same time inducing them to anticipate modernism's effort to find an aesthetics commensurate with the fractured and overstimulated subjectivity of modern life.

These paradoxes and contradictions lie at the heart of much of the discussion that follows. What does it mean to rural fiction, with its uneven mix of generic registers, to represent a cultural phenomenon that is simultaneously modern, citylike, industrial, unstable, idealized, romantic, carnivalesque, and, on some level at least, unrepresentable? Through close attention to passages of circus representation in Sarah Orne Jewett, Hamlin Garland, Mark Twain, Alice Brown, and Booth Tarkington, I build on some of the themes and issues raised here, exploring the ways in which the circus unsettles not just literary representations of rural space but also notions of rural space itself.

* * *

Sarah Orne Jewett's first book, *Deephaven*, is neither a novel nor a collection of short stories, but a series of interconnected sketches or chapters, some of which had been published previous to 1877 (as early as 1873, in fact) in *Atlantic Monthly*. They center around one summer in the Maine coastal village of Deephaven, where Helen Denis (the narrator) and her friend Kate Lancaster, both from Boston, come to enjoy a leisurely extended holiday in the old house left by Kate's recently deceased great-aunt. Early on, Kate explains to Helen what the appeal of such a holiday might be, and it becomes clear that for these two urban visitors the trip represents not just an escape from the city but also an escape from an adult present:

> "It might be dull in Deephaven for two young ladies who were fond of gay society and dependent upon excitement, I suppose; but for two little girls who were fond of each other and could play in the boats, and dig and build houses in the sea-sand, and gather shells, and carry their dolls wherever they went, what could be pleasanter?" (8)

Such a statement, spoken early on, provides a key to how much of the rest of the narrative should be understood, not least the visit to a circus that forms one of the book's central episodes. Deephaven seems to be an escape from the city for these young women, one justified by the opportunity it offers for a temporal escape back into childhood—an escape from the responsibilities of their adult lives in the city into a more subdued rural life that evokes the historical and personal past. In other words, the central characters appear on one hand to be treating their summer retreat in a way that mirrors the romantic equation of spatial types with vaguely drawn historical moments (the city with the present and the country with the past).

In regionalist terms, it can also be seen as placing the book itself into a touristic economy that seeks to construct a "mentally possessable version of a loved thing lost in reality" (Brodhead, *Cultures* 120), a piece of escapist fiction designed to be consumed by a cosmopolitan readership. As Sandra Zagarell has persuasively argued, however, *Deephaven* frequently unsettles any such designs, with one of its operations being to deliberately disrupt "established regionalist formulas like the urbanite's replenishing country sojourn" (641). Following Zagarell's reading of the text, I consider how the ambivalent depiction of rural life is both underlined and troubled by the chapter "The Circus at Denby" (something Zagarell largely overlooks), and how this, in turn, implicates the way forms of modern entertainment help to structure a broader geographical imagination. The use of the circus as a narrative episode is an attempt to accentuate the kind of romantic construction that, because of the circus's complex place in a modern commercial economy, ultimately proves to be incompatible with a truly successful romantic escape. Not only does it undermine Helen and Kate's geographical-temporal summer escape, but in doing so it reveals the intimate spatial, economic and cultural interpenetration of urban and rural life in the Gilded Age.

The chapter in question opens with the book's familiar themes being restated. Helen claims that she and Kate are looking forward to the event "as if we had been little school-boys," (an intriguing and characteristic slippage in a story that never allows gender to settle as a straightforward category)[1] and when some "dashing young men" come and put up some advertising posters—"amazing pictures" according to Helen—she is stirred by thoughts of circuses she had visited as a girl: "I thought I had lost my childish fondness for circuses, but it came back redoubled" (70). The telling point here is that these excitements are stirred not by the circus itself but the advertising that precedes it. Advertising was a vital part of the commercial enterprise of the circus, an aspect that became increasingly sophisticated after Barnum entered the business in 1871 (Davis 42). The posters that were put up to alert local populations to the coming attraction were perfect examples of the kind of alluring images and exaggerated claims typical of Gilded Age advertising. Essential for the creation of advance hype, "circus billposters marked the landscape, claimed it, and transformed it months before the actual onslaught of crowds, tents, and animals" (Davis 45). The advertising in *Deephaven* certainly stirs its residents, and come the day of the circus the entire village seems to be making its way by carriage (there is no railway station) to the town of Denby, eight miles away inland. In fact, the circus posters have created such anticipation that, as one resident exclaims, "I wonder the folks in the old North burying-ground ain't a-rising up to go to Denby to that caravan!" (73).[2] The promises the "amazing pictures" seem to hold have persuaded everyone to make their way to the circus—and for Helen and Kate, at least in their own imaginations, to further align their summer vacation with a lost childhood.

The women travel to Denby with Mrs. Kew, an old woman who has lived in Deephaven all her life, but the party finds only disappointment when it gets there. They visit the accompanying menagerie first: "I cannot truthfully say that it was a good show; it was somewhat dreary, now that I think of it quietly and without excitement," Helen narrates, commenting that the animals look "tired," "old," and "shabby," as if they "were miserably conscious of a misspent life" (73). The excitement that had built up before the circus's arrival quickly dissipates, and Jewett quite deliberately implicates the advertising as the reason for this uncomfortable disconnection between the imagined circus and the real one:

> There was a picture of a huge snake in Deephaven, and I was just wondering where he could be, or if there ever had been one, when we heard a boy ask the same question of the man whose thankless task it was to stir up the lions with a stick to make them roar. "The snake's dead," he answered good-naturedly. (74)

The advertising posters, with their gaudy pictures of the attractions to be seen at the circus, are revealed as exercises in persuasive but untrustworthy marketing. The picture has created an idealization of the circus, both for Helen and the boy, which the reality does not coincide with. The narrative acknowledges the commercialism of the circus but, by extension, what the circus has been already symbolically and psychologically identified with: if Helen treats the whole summer as an escape from the modern city and a return to childhood, and the circus as a particularly evocative part of that escape, then the distance between the circus's hyperbolic advertising and its weary menagerie analogizes the same gap between the romantic idealization of rural life and its plain, sometimes hard realities.

Helen and Kate certainly treat their rural surroundings as if they were there to be passively consumed. They think it will be "fun enough to see the people go by" (70), listen in to conversations going on around them (74), and once inside the big-top notice the "countless pairs of country lovers [who] we watched a great deal," pleased that the occasion gives them "a grand chance to see the fashions" (75)—an echo of their urban habits that seems out-of-place in the rural village. Their role is observation and, as Michael Davitt Bell has pointed out, this is another indication of the cultural work of the kind of rural writing where "the emphasis is on the vicarious experience of the spectator rather than the reality of rural life" (181). In filtering the descriptions of the rural setting through these urban narrators, the narrative implicitly aligns with an urban vision that then comes to structure and order the reader's relationship with rural space.

But this role is not allowed to rest easily, and nowhere in the book is the notion of viewing and the relationship between observer and observed more fully implicated than after the circus performance when the three women go in to see one of the sideshows, the "Kentucky giantess." The importance of spectacle is immediate and obvious: they are lured into the tent by a picture outside, finding inside the huge woman sat upon a stage. Once again, however, the reality does not quite match: "Why, she is n't more than two thirds as big as the picture," Mrs. Kew says in a "regretful whisper" (77). At first it is just another disappointing indication of the circus hype. Jewett complicates any simple relationship between the people who have come to gawp and the unfortunate woman on stage—collapses any straightforward construction of a "spectacle" in the Debordian sense—because it turns out Mrs. Kew knows the giantess from years ago. "'Have you been living in Kentucky long?'" Mrs. Kew asks her:

> "No," said the giantess, "that was a picture the man bought cheap from another show that broke up last year. It says six hundred and fifty pounds, but I don't weigh more than four hundred...but you must n't mention it, for it would spoil my reputation, and might hender [sic] my getting another engagement." (78–79)

As a sideshow freak, the woman ostensibly represents all that is most cynical and spectacular about the commercial enterprise of Gilded Age circuses; she has become yet another commodity that can be advertised—falsely, once again—effectively becoming a component in a commercial economy of exchange. Yet that status is undone in the narrative's efforts to humanize her, refusing to maintain her status as the "observed" and giving her a voice: "I believe I'd rather die than grow any bigger. I do lose heart sometimes, and wish I was a smart woman" (79).[3]

The circus episode repeatedly juxtaposes these two apparently antithetical narrative strains: the urban-industrial world of a faceless capitalism (where the visiting women have come from), and the rural community that apparently exists outside such concerns (where the visiting women hoped they would be escaping to). The circus encompasses such contradictions, being both a particularly conspicuous element of a modern commercial economy and yet the site of an imaginatively projected otherness that promises escape from the modern world. When the women leave the tent, any humanity that may have been briefly bestowed to the giantess is replaced by aggressive commercialism: "'Walk in! walk in!' the man was shouting as we came away. 'Walk in and see the wonder of the world, ladies and gentlemen,—the largest woman ever seen in America,—the great Kentucky giantess!'" (79). We witness the crucial incompatibility between a fictionalized version of rural life and the realities of modern commerce, at the same time as we witness the role the former plays in the geographical imagination of the latter.

In the circus episode of *Deephaven*, a hierarchy of observation is unraveled by the refusal of the observed "others"—the giantess most conspicuously, the rural residents more obliquely—to maintain the distance necessary for their imaginative consumption. Zagarell rightly argues that commodity capitalism is one of the book's preoccupations (642), and the ambivalence it displays toward such a system is uniquely concretized in the multivalent signifier that the circus becomes. It operates as a microcosm of rural space's own fluctuating and disorderly relationship with urban modernity, as well as of the position of rural fiction in an urban-capitalist literary economy.

* * *

It is clear that as a mass-cultural form the circus offers a particularly potent symbol of modernity's geographical reach, as well as a symbol of potential resistance to its accompanying experiences. What this lends works of rural fiction is a discrete narrative event that can legitimately appear in any rural town or village, reinforcing the generic expectations of realism while also offering a site of romantic dislocation. Furthermore, this Janus-faced metaphorical capability is something that only seems to attach itself to the circus under the specific economic conditions of Gilded Age society, during the process Alan Trachtenberg called "the incorporation of America." It is interesting to note, for instance, that one of the most significant British novels of the mid-nineteenth century, Charles Dickens's *Hard Times* (1854), organizes itself partly around the metaphorical and social potential of the circus. Rather than being the complex symbol it becomes in later nineteenth-century American fiction, however, the circus operates here as a straightforward site of relief from Gradgrindian utilitarianism and the dehumanizing work of industrial capitalism. Raymond Williams critiques Dickens for exactly this point, seeing the use of the circus in *Hard Times* as too simplistically oppositional: "The Circus can express it [criticism of industrialism] because it is not part of the industrial organization. The Circus is an end in itself, a pleasurable end, which is instinctive and (in certain respects) anarchic" (*Culture and Society* 95).

Yet in the texts under consideration here the circus is an ambivalent historical fact as well as, if not more than, a symbolic device. Culturally speaking, it is the site where a ludic irrationality comes under the auspices of modern rational business. But also, just as the circus allowed *Deephaven* to concretize a set of abstract concerns, it offers a fitting narratological device that literalizes (and so, to some extent, orders) the generic entanglements of rural fiction. Bill Brown has written persuasively about the complex role that entertainments and amusements play in fiction from this period, arguing that it is "as though American realism deploys recreational space to retrieve something of the liberty and intensity of the romance," suffusing "recreational space with...the liminality that traditionally characterizes the forest, the frontier, the sea" (20). Brown's argument—that sites of entertainment enable fiction to spatialize generic problems—is developed by the geo-social issues at play in rural fiction: what Brown calls "recreational space" acts as the particularized site of the tensions that rural space more abstractly, and more problematically, plays host to. From Brown's implicit evocation of a Weberian sense of the translation or "disenchantment" of mythical symbols (those romantic American staples of the forest and the frontier) into their modern rationalized forms (sites of recreation and entertainment), I suggest an added dimension is at play in the rural fiction being examined here. The circus, while providing realist writing with a potent symbol of romantic potential, also acts synecdochally, distilling and embodying some of the contemporary cultural and social issues inherent in the urban/rural relationship—a symbol that, unlike the vanished frontier, would have rung with contemporary credibility.

Such rich narrative potential no doubt occurred to Mark Twain. In his works where the competing impulses of realism and romanticism seem most visible, and where he tackles most obviously the effects of modern civilization on traditional agrarian society, the circus appears in illuminating ways. When Hank Morgan awakes in sixth-century England at the start of *A Connecticut Yankee at King Arthur's Court* (1889), for instance, he is greeted by the sight of a knight fully clad in armor and jumps to an assumption that is noteworthy in the context of this argument: "Get along back to your circus, or I'll report you" (37) Hanks says to him, immediately betraying a late nineteenth-century mindset immersed in everyday cultural references. The knight takes him captive, and as they walk on it dawns on Hank that the knight may not be what he assumed: "we did not come to any circus or sign of a circus" (37), he says, somewhat bewildered. Maybe Hank was a fan of the circus back in the 1880s, as he is still calling the knight a "circus man" when he is taken to Camelot (41), and on seeing King Arthur's round table remarks that it "was as large as a circus ring" (52). Hank even aligns himself with the circus at one point, referring to his tendency toward elaborate displays of emotion as the "circus side" of his nature (129). There are, in fact, eight direct references to the circus throughout the story,[4] and toward the end it even returns in a more oblique sense in Hank's description of the jousting tournament: "Vast as the show-grounds were, there were no vacant spaces in them.... The mammoth grand stand was clothed in flags, streamers, rich tapestries.... The huge camp of beflagged and gay-coloured tents...was another fine sight" (355–56). Transposed from Hank's industrial nineteenth century to the rural society of medieval England, these ironic analogies work to puncture the grand pomposity of feudal ceremonies at the same time as they mark our historical distance from them.

More substantially, in *Adventures of Huckleberry Finn* (1884) Twain uses a brief circus scene to dramatize his critique of Southern agrarian society while also restating the conflict between social awareness and boyish naivety that characterizes Huck. On one hand, he defies the capitalist enterprise of the circus—designed, after all, to make money for the owners—by refusing to pay: "I went to the circus, and loafed around the back side till the watchmen went by, and then dived in under the tent" (191). As he removes himself from the economics of the circus by avoiding its commercialism, he further distances himself from the structures of a modern society he seeks so hard to evade: "I ain't opposed to spending money on circuses, when there ain't no other way, but there ain't no use in *wasting* it on them" (191, emphasis in original). Still implicated in a monetary economy, he nevertheless falls outside its self-perpetuating logic.[5]

Yet he is not fully able to adopt a knowing and removed stance when it comes to the performance itself. Drawn in by the banter between the clown and the ringmaster, Huck is ignorant of the artificiality of their conversation, openly stating his lack of understanding and so ironically reminding the reader of his own naivety: "The ring-master couldn't ever say a word to him but he was back at him quick as a wink with the funniest things a body ever said; and how he ever *could* think of so many of them, and so sudden and so pat, was what I couldn't no way understand" (192, emphasis in original). He is, in this light, the quintessential Barnum-ized spectator. The performance's illusion of spontaneity has him fooled, so although his free entry maintains his distance from a more perfunctory commercialism he fully submits to the magic of its orchestrated spectacle.

His submission to the performance continues when an apparently drunk man tries to get into the ring to ride a horse, Huck gazing in growing wonder as the man rides around the ring with unexpected ease: "He just stood up there, a-sailing around as easy and comfortable as if he warn't ever drunk in his life" (194). The whole thing is staged, of course, but Huck remains in a state of enraptured ignorance. This peculiar distance between Huck and the reality around him is maintained by the telling distinction Twain secures between Huck's narrative "I" and the circus audience. Huck repeatedly refers to them using the collective noun "people": the "clown carried on so it most killed the people"; "Then the people began to holler"; "stirred up the people"; and finally the "whole crowd of people standing up shouting and laughing till the tears rolled down" (192–3). The discrepancy between Huck's view of things and the view of everyone else (after all, Huck is presumably physically as much part of the crowd as the people he describes in this peculiarly unempathic tone) suggests Huck's inability—or perhaps it is refusal—to align himself with the shared social vision of the rural South.

While he personally experiences the circus as a spectacle in the way that Gilded Age productions instigated, the audience around him seems more grounded in the antebellum world of the novel's setting, retaining some intimacy and pantomimic interaction with the performance. The sight of the "drunk" man precariously hanging from a galloping horse confirms this divided sense of spectatorship: "round and round the ring, with that sot laying down on him [the horse] and hanging to his neck...and the people just crazy. It warn't funny to me, though; I was all of a tremble to see his danger" (193). Huck's moral standpoint is still contrary to the nameless Southern mass he shares the grandstands with; he feels sympathy where others merely laugh. Twain turns Huck into a figure who is at once antagonistic to and at home in the modern world of mass entertainment, defying its commercial purposes yet swept up in its artifice. The transformed experience of circus going that characterizes the period in which Twain writes seeps into the representation of a time before that transformation, so that Huck exists simultaneously in both in a way that highlights his distance from either. Twain recognizes the complex symbolic and cultural implications of the circus, and employs it—not in any major, sustained way but as another comic anecdote—to reveal the contradictions of Huck's experience and innocence.[6]

Being one of the primary forms of popular entertainment in Gilded Age America, it is natural enough that the circus should appear frequently in the fiction of the period. A particularly extended example of this, and one that allows for a closer examination of the generic implications of the circus I briefly discussed earlier, comes in Hamlin Garland's *Rose of Dutcher's Coolly*. It tells the story of Rose Dutcher, a determined farm girl from Wisconsin who moves to Chicago to attend university and, she hopes, become a poet. It is Rose's visit to a circus as a young girl, however, that sets into motion the changes that will take her to the city and away from the simple rural life of her childhood. Garland uses the metaphorical and social potential of the circus to form a crucial passage in the novel, but its presence has wider implications for the settings in which the story unfolds and even for the literary genres which the story employs. In the narrative's use of the circus as a crucial plot point, it begins to break down the coherence of its own generic strategies.

"One June day," the chapter titled "Her First Ideal" begins, "a man came riding swiftly up the lanes... [flinging] a handful of fluttering yellow and red bills into the air" (41). Like Jewett, Garland uses the appearance of circus advertising to signal the imminent arrival of the circus—and, like Jewett, the posters offer a vision of the approaching spectacle that seems dubious:

> The whole population awoke to pathetic, absorbing interest in the quality of the posters and the probable truth of the fore-word. The circus was the mightiest contrast to their slow and lonely lives that could be imagined. It came in trailing clouds of glorified dust and grouped itself under vast tents whose lift and fall had more majesty than summer clouds, and its streamers had more significance than the lightning. (42)

The posters are tentatively questioned by the local rural population, but in a hope-filled way the use of "pathetic" signals as ironic. Where the posters in Deephaven had promised animals that turned out not to be there, here they conjure a more general idea of the circus that seems fantastic, romantic, and quasi-mythical.

There is more to say here about that romantic aspect of the circus, and certainly how Garland uses this in the novel, but I want to pause a moment over the posters themselves. In both examples of circus posters alluded to in this chapter, there is an issue at stake that has a particular and quite specific historical resonance. The proliferation of images in advertising brought on (or at least enabled) by advances in printing technology is a phenomenon that, for some historians, has a social equivalent in the visual complexity of America's expanding metropolises. As Jackson Lears has argued, "as society became more urban, more anonymous, what Walt Whitman called 'the terrible doubt of appearances' became more widespread" (55). The notion of "trusting" and "distrusting" the commercial image was something exacerbated by the rise of an advertising industry with little or no regulation. Circus posters, as they operate in the fiction of Jewett and Garland, present exactly this problem: an image of an event that for all its glitzy persuasiveness cannot be reliably trusted. Advertisements, the material debris of a rationalized commercial enterprise, present an image of the circus that obscures its real nature (a money-making exercise) and so cultivates a persistence of what Max Weber would have called "magical thinking."

In fulfilling this role, the posters that precede the circus become part of the spectacle that is the defining aspect of the modern circus experience. Alan Trachtenberg discusses the broader context of such spectacle, a phenomenon he calls the "unprecedented quantity of visual data" in Gilded Age America, and like Lears aligns these new modes of experience with a particular spatial organization: "[v]iewing and looking at representations, words and images, city people found themselves addressed more often as passive spectators than as active participants, consumers of images and sensations produced by others" (122). I would argue that city people were not alone in encountering this change in the experience of visual culture; the circus posters that adorned barns and farmhouses, and that implicated local rural people as both "passive spectators" and "consumers of images," seem an especially fitting example of how such phenomena transcend any geographically delimited notion of modernization.

But that spectacle, for all its commercial apparatus, is also the site of a certain romantic potential. That the posters in *Rose of Dutcher's Coolly* should evoke a cluster of rather grandiose meteorological metaphors—the tents are more majestic than summer clouds, the streamers more significant than lightning—is telling. Garland recognizes that such a grand entertainment is both the capitalist enterprise that produces a flurry of advertising, while at the same time being a place of dislocated romantic experience. Like the parade of knights that Hank Morgan was presumably recalling when he first awoke in Arthurian England, the circus brings something to late nineteenth-century rural Wisconsin that feels historically, as well as geographically, exotic: "For one day each humdrum town was filled with romance like the Arabian Nights; with helmeted horsemen, glittering war maidens on weirdly spotted horses; elephants with howdahs and head-plates of armor" (*Rose* 43). Similarly, when the parade comes down Main Street: "with glitter of lance and shine of helmet, came a dozen knights and fair ladies riding spirited chargers" (48). The sights and sounds the circus brings are clearly evocative of a romantic, idealized image, performing the task Bill Brown saw recreational space performing more generally by retrieving "the liberty and intensity of the romance."

This retrieval is not simply narrated, however; it is enacted on a semantic level. Rose is awestruck by the parade of knights, captivated by the display she has seen; it seems as if "they came from the unknown spaces of song and story beyond the hills" (48). The carefully orchestrated and commercially sanctioned parade evokes a sense of romantic potential that is made ironic by its connection with the capitalist enterprise of the circus. It is a similar pattern that Terry Eagleton has questioned at the heart of Bakhtinian ideas of carnival, where, in an often-quoted passage, he points out that carnival is "a *licensed* affair in every sense, a permissible rupture of hegemony, a contained popular blow-off" (148, emphasis in original). Rather than a radical and transcendent instant of disruption, the carnival (or circus parade, or recreational moment, or however the non-everyday festivity is configured) is an example of the "mutual complicity of law and liberation" (Eagleton 149). The circus parade in *Rose of Dutcher's Coolly* is nothing more or less than men and women dressed up to represent shared myths and ideals about another time and place, all in the hope that the spectators will come to the circus and spend their money. But Garland's language, the voice he uses to narrate Rose's experience of the parade, is itself complicit with the illusion the parade is consciously trying to create, closing the semiotic circuit between the parade going on in front of Rose's eyes and the "unknown spaces...beyond the hills" it apparently signifies.

Such passages depart from the realism more usually associated with Garland's writing in the 1890s, as if the circus is transforming not just the village into a site of romantic imagery but the very language in which it is conveyed. This play of realist and romantic idioms, the literary characteristic of recreational space that Bill Brown discusses and that I have argued characterizes rural fiction in general, is something Garland consciously explores in the novel. He goes to great lengths, after all, to emphasize that Rose's conception of the rural environment she inhabits is mediated through the romantic literature she becomes so attached to. Early in the novel we learn she is a voracious reader, and it is through literature that she awakens to a new perception of her surroundings:

> Scraps and fragments of her reading took curious lodgement in her mind. New conceptions burst into her consciousness with a golden glory upon reading these lines:
>
> > "Field of wheat so full and fair,
> > Shining with a sunny air;
> > Lightly swaying either way,
> > Graceful as the breezes sway."[7]

They made her see the beauty of the grainfield as never before. It seemed to be lit by some mysterious light. (18)

A standard icon of the midwestern rural landscape, the wheat field, is transformed—"re-enchanted" perhaps—from the site of commerce and physical labor into a rhapsodic vision of transcendent nature. The language Garland uses here, the "golden glory" and "mysterious light," suggests less the kind of socially committed realism of *Main-Travelled Roads* and more the florid romanticism of Rose herself. Her idealization of her surroundings, her translation of everyday reality into rarefied aesthetics (the very thing that Howellsian realism rejected so vehemently), reveals a mindset that goes on to instill the circus episode with a particular narrative importance.

It is here that she sees William De Lisle, a male acrobat whose performance awakens Rose to her sexualized adulthood and sets into motion the events that form the rest of the novel. Enjoying a performance that ranges across all the spectacular and exotic elements of the late nineteenth-century circus, from "iron-jawed" women lifting "incredible weights" to "Japanese jugglers" and a baby elephant, Rose is suddenly captivated by the arrival of the male acrobats. One in particular has caught her eye:

> He wore blue and silver, and on his breast was a rosette. He looked a god to her. His naked limbs, his proud neck, the lofty carriage of his head, made her shiver with emotion....
>
> She had seen naked boys, and her own companions occasionally showed themselves naked and cowering before her, but these men stood there proud and splendid. They invested their nakedness with something which exalted them. They became objects of luminous beauty to her, though she knew nothing of art. (55)

The performer becomes a catalyst of sexual awakening for Rose. Just as the poetry she reads imbues her rural environment with a romantic lyricism, here the acrobat is elevated to god-like status, his naked flesh differentiated from the nudity of local boys because it takes on the "luminous beauty" of art.

The display and objectification of the male body would have had a strong contemporary resonance for Garland's readers, one explained in John Kasson's discussion of the fine line that such displays trod among the exacting morals of Victorian America: "To display the unclad male figure...bereft of divine, allegorical, or alien trappings—not as a god, virtue, ruler, hero, exotic figure, or scientific specimen but simply as a person—was to risk falling from the lofty plane of the nude to the shameful one of the merely naked" (21). Rose performs exactly this kind of "artistic" justification, removing the acrobats from the mere nakedness of the local boys and elevating them to the morally sanctioned realm of respectable art. Furthermore, Garland may have had a specific person in mind when he created William De Lisle: the acrobat, actor, and strongman Eugen Sandow. Sandow had made his debut on stage in New York City in 1893, just two years before Garland's novel was published, and soon enough became the most famous male physique in the world. Claiming to represent "an ancient heroic ideal of manhood that had been lost in the modern world," he actually "turned his body into a commercial spectacle and a commodity whose image was widely reproduced and sold" (Kasson 29–30). He did more than any other performer to popularize a hypermasculine ideal, an ideal which appeared to restore subjective agency in a depersonalizing modern society but in fact acted as one of its most fitting exemplars—a vision of perfection that "lay in materially defined, standardized, and repeatable processes" (Kasson 75).

Yet for Rose, the male figure allows her to focus her burgeoning sexuality into an object of desire. Leaving the big top after the performance, the contrast is clear: "Somehow it seemed strange to see the same blue sky arching the earth; things seemed exactly the same and yet Rose had grown older" (58). The circus has been the site of a life-changing event for Rose, one that has been filtered through a romantic and highly aestheticized worldview. She lies in bed the night after the circus thinking of the "splendid and beautiful men, whose naked majesty appealed to her pure wholesome awakening womanhood...with sex and art both included" (59). That "wholesome" reveals a lot: by removing the origin of Rose's sexual awakening from her everyday world, and having the whole experience couched in ornate language, the narrative avoids entering her into a more naturalistic relationship with a biologically framed sexuality and instead places it in the altogether more "wholesome" realm of romance. Eugen Sandow had presented middle-class theatergoers with a vision of naked flesh that they could accept, an object of human sexuality safely placed on the stage for perusal by spectators who could then justify it as elevating art or scientific display. William De Lisle's heroic figure appears in the romanticized space of the circus, allowing Rose to project her passionate sexuality into a safely theatricalized spectacle.

There is something of late nineteenth-century social manners in how Rose is deployed by Garland, and the circus episode serves as a focus for this. The language used throughout the chapter feels so strained and flowery—even the wagon ride to the event is through "some world-old idyl [sic]" that leads to "glory and light" (47)—that it feels like a sustained exercise in *bovarysme* free indirect discourse. For all the progressiveness of Rose's apparent New Woman[8] status, her conception of the world is filtered through a lens that feels somewhat naive. Frequently disrupting this, however, are references to a conspicuously modern culture that fixes the narrative in a contemporary historical moment and adopts a more realist posture—certainly in the way that Barthes saw apparently incidental material referents as a crucial part of realism's "reality effect." The calliope, a steam-driven organ only developed in the mid-nineteenth century, which accompanies the circus parade (49); the dinner at the hotel where they desperately try "to seem citified" by using forks instead of knives to eat their pie, thereby revealing their own self-consciousness about their difference from urban-defined fashions (50); a reminder of the hard commercialism of the circus in the "cries of lemonade, candy and fruit hucksters" in the street, the "brazen-voiced young men" inside the tent "selling, at appalling prices, sticks of candy, glasses of lemonade" (53); and the attendants peddling tickets for a minstrel show after the main performance (57). The circus is replete with such fantastic scenes that it can operate within the narrative as a stark contrast to the plain realities of the village, retrieving some romantic intensity. As a commercial enterprise, however, its description necessarily includes those fragments of a material modernity that nullify the circus's ability to offer escapism.

For all the generic entanglements the circus invokes, it also plays a more direct role in the action of the novel. In *Deephaven* the circus is merely another epistle from a summer's vacation, providing no impetus and having no impact on the plot—perhaps because the "novel" is really just a string of sketches. In *Rose*, however, the trip to the circus has a lasting effect on its main character: she determines to get an education, attend university in Chicago, and then become a writer. The circus, because it offers Rose a site where her romantic ideals are spectacularly manifested, allows her to conceive of a world beyond the rural community she now sees as stifling, and to long for something equal to the rich sensuality of the circus tent. The sheer ordinariness of the Wisconsin countryside is suddenly apparent, even at the moment she emerges from the performance: "The grass, crushed and trampled and littered with paper, and orange peel, gave out a fresh farm-like odor, that helped her to recover herself" (58). After the visual assault of exoticness, and especially after the athletic body of William De Lisle, no amount of genteel idealization will be sufficient to translate her environment into something commensurate with her lofty ambitions. As Lewis Atherton notes, it was "no accident that Garland selected the clean-limbed, acrobatic circus performer as the stimulus which led his *Rose of Dutcher's Coolly* to escape the confinements of rural life and to seek perfection and her destiny in cities" (131). Only urban life can now provide the range of experience, the sheer quantity of sensory data, that Rose craves.

Soon after Rose's trip to the circus, and after she has discussed her move to the city with her mentor Dr. Thatcher, the point is emphatically made:

> She pictured the world outside in colors of such splendor that the romance of her story-papers seemed weak and pale.
>
> Out there in the world was William De Lisle. Out there were ladies with white faces and heavy-lidded, haughty eyes, in carriages and in ballrooms. Out there was battle for her, and from her quiet coulé battle seemed somehow alluring. (81)

It is the fashions, refinements, and amusements of urban life she craves, a world removed from her "quiet coulé." The movement between rural and urban life becomes the keynote of the novel, but the circus has been the mediator convincing Rose to move from one to the other. In a prolonged description of Chicago later in the novel, where Rose has wondered around observing a "ragged newsboy and the towering policeman," "street vermin," and "the curious dress of swart Italian girls" (a typical mixture of class and ethnic stereotypes in nineteenth-century caricatures of the city), the circus provides a simile that, in its evocation of an old life back on the farm, links the two spheres of Rose's geographical imagination: "Their faces were old and grimy, their voices sounded like the chattered colloquies of monkeys in the circus" (205). The circus has equipped the rural girl with a breadth of imaginative vocabulary and reinforced her romantic worldview to the point that only the city now seems sufficient for her.

The circus in *Rose of Dutcher's Coolly* plays a complex narrative role, initiating Rose into an adult world that only the city can satisfy. The conscious employment of the circus as a bridge between rural and urban life, however, serves to destabilize the generic strategies of the novel itself; the circus's own distinct qualities, its simultaneous signification of commercial modernity and timeless festivity, mirrors the narrative's own shifts back and forth between highly romanticized and sentimentalized idioms, and Garland's more familiar realism and naturalism. The intimate connection between geography and genre, and the indistinctness of the lines separating them, is made readable in the Gilded Age circus.

* * *

The capacity of the circus to play host to a variety of seemingly incompatible narrative concerns and generic positions, and the way this capacity can itself highlight the changing place of rural life in a broader geography of Gilded Age modernity, comes even more sharply into focus in Alice Brown's "Strollers in Tiverton" (1895). The final story in her collection *Meadow-Grass: Tales of New England Life*, and published in the same year as Garland's *Rose*, the story is typical of the folksy nostalgia of many rural tales from this period. Centered on a reminiscence of a "very rich year" (278) in the tiny village of Tiverton (no year is specified, although we learn it is sometime after the Civil War), the anonymous narrator tells of the day the circus came to town: "We rose before three o'clock, every man, woman and child of us, to see the procession" (281). Such preemptive excitement among the villagers is matched by their "faint hope" that the circus will bring some remarkably exotic sights when it does arrive: "a blaze of glittering chariots surmounted by queens of beauty,...lazy beasts of the desert sulking in their cages, and dainty-stepping horses, ridden by bold amazons" (281–82). Village life has already been established as quiet and uneventful, so this pointedly heightened moment of exoticized fantasy stands as a very deliberate contrast to daily life. The narrator shifts from reporting the rustic talk of her companions—"You better build a platfoam over that spring! Go hard with ye if 't overflowed!"—to a richer vocabulary suited to an event that is very much not part of the conventional New Hampshire landscape. That momentary move into a semantic domain more redolent of high romance than regional dialect fiction—something akin to what Dorrit Cohn, in narratological terms, calls a "stylistic contagion" (33)—bleeds back into the narrator's description of their own, more unassuming, surroundings: "but as the eastern saffron penciled one line of light and the bird chorus swelled in piercing glory, we grew cross and all unbefitting the smiling morn" ("Strollers" 282). The circus, even before it arrives, provides the lexical conventions through which a plain rural reality can be turned into pastoral idealism.

The realities of rural life are exactly what exert themselves at this moment, however, and the demands of agricultural labor become a higher calling than the possibility of a circus parade:

> The men grew nervous, for milking-time was near, and in imagination I have no doubt they heard the lowing of reproachful kine.[9]
>
> "Well, 'tain't no use," said Eli Pike, rising from the stone-wall, and stretching himself, with decision. "I've got to 'tend to them cows, whether or no!" And he strolled away on the country-road, without a look behind. Most of the other men, as in honor bound, followed him; and the women, with loud-voiced protest against an obvious necessity, trailed after them, to strain the milk. (283)

A communal responsibility (and one that subtly points out the gender hierarchy of the farming business) interrupts the narrative reverie. Gone is the fantasizing about the circus's heroic extravagance, replaced by a return to local dialect and an acknowledgment of the quotidian duties of dairy farming. Moving back and forth between idioms, the story places the circus at the center of everything romantic, and rural life as the disrupting reality that presses in upon it.

It is the circus parade itself that cancels out this simple division. Escaping into a pointedly orientalized spectacle, it also questions the ability of the cynical commercial enterprise to actually offer that escape:

> The circus was approaching, from Sudleigh way.... We were tolerant potentates, waiting, in gracious majesty, to receive a deputation from the farther East. It grieves me much to stop here and confess, with a necessary honesty, that this was but a sorry circus, gauged by the conventional standards.... The circus-folk had evidently dressed for travelling, not for us. The chariots, some of them still hooded in canvas, were very small and tarnished. There were but three elephants, two camels, and a most meagre display of those alluring cages.... Yet why depreciate the raw material whereof Fancy has power divine to build her altogether perfect heights? Here was the plain, homely setting of our plainer lives, and right into the midst of it had come the East. (284–85)

The passage begins with a direct evocation of the exotic "East," but is soon forced to admit that such fantasies cannot be sustained if the parade is judged by "conventional standards" (whose convention, we might ask; presumably the sophisticated reader of 1895). Instead, its paucity and determined lack of spectacle momentarily restores a realistic admission of what, after all, the circus parade actually is: advertising for a piece of commercial entertainment. In turn, however, even the bare fact of the lackluster parade cannot hold off the desire to escape the "plain, homely" rural setting for that same exotic East they began with.

At work here are a series of implied perspectives and geographical imaginaries that vie for narrative authority. Firstly, there is the contemporary fact that the circus's involvement in modern global networks of transport and trade means that elephants and giraffes (to say nothing of foreign performers themselves) can be present in the first place, and yet there is also a closing down of the more troubling aspects of that trade (fears of immigration and imperialist ambitions) in favor of an aestheticized, dehistoricized orientalism. In late nineteenth-century America, after all, the "East" was a vague enough designation to have signified, among other things, both the general cultural vogue for Japonisme and the numerous attempts to restrict Chinese immigration and naturalization.[10] At the same time, the narrator is situated in a more localized but no less ambivalent position: they implicate an acquaintance with the spectacular forms of modern entertainment found in populous centers (hence the jaded disappointment at the "meagre display"), but also a grounding in the relative simplicity and uneventfulness of New England farm life where any form of distraction is welcome. In the midst of a short rural tale that otherwise presents a typical escape from the contemporary realities of its historical context, the presence of the circus breaches the quaint pastoral vision and opens out the frame of reference to a geographically and generically multivalent modernity.

* * *

Plattville, the small town at the heart of Tarkington's *The Gentleman from Indiana*, is an uneventful place. The main square rests "in a shady grove of maple and elm," in the courthouse yard "amongst the weeds and tall, unkempt grass, chickens foraged all day long," and "[h]ere and there a big dog lay asleep in the middle of the road." Main Street, the only street with "the dignity of a name," is unpaved and prone to the weather of the seasons: in winter "a series of frozen gorges and hummocks," in fall and spring "a river of mud," and in summer "a continuing dust heap" (Tarkington 6–7).

The arrival of a circus into this archetypal quiet rural village turns the space into a bustling, crowded chaos of people and noise: "[s]ince earliest dawn they had been pouring into the village.... The air was full of exhilaration" (90–91). Rural space, in other words, takes on the experiential qualities of something more like urban space. Renoff points out that for contemporary newspapers describing circus day in rural villages, "only the throngs that filled the streets of northern cities seemed apt in comparison" (91), while Davis similarly states that the events of circus day meant that "provincial communities became temporary cities, complete with anonymous, pushing crowds" (6). The notion of the crowd as a distinctly urban phenomenon is a link that Mary Esteve subscribes to in her study of crowds in American literature, admitting that her "point of entry is the city crowd" (1), one of the "iconic topos" of "urban modernity" (8)—an assertion that sits uneasily with her broader claim that, as part of the experience of nineteenth-century modernity more generally, the crowd was "a ubiquitous, culturally saturating phenomenon" (2). One effect of the specific equation of crowds with urban space, as well as the more abstract notion that crowds are a kind of metonymic phenomenon of modernity, is to elide rural space from the experience of modernity altogether.

If we take Esteve's point for a moment, however (and, as she points out, figures such as William James and Friedrich Nietzsche also proclaimed the nineteenth century "the crowded age"), then it poses interesting questions about what the appearance of a crowd may mean in spaces that do not normally experience such gatherings. The anonymity and alienation of the urban crowd is, after all, muted in Tarkington's description, replaced by a crowd that is "laughing" and "calling greetings." Where the novel has been careful to present Plattville as a particularly *un*crowded place, this moment of crowdedness is a temporary spatial transformation of the town:

> The Square was heaving with a jostling, good-natured, happy, and constantly increasing crowd that overflowed on Main Street in both directions; and the good nature of this crowd was augmented in the ratio that its size increased. The streets were a confusion of many colours, and eager faces filled every window opening on Main Street or the Square. (100)

While there is something distinctly "urban" about Tarkington's description here, it is still a determinedly "good-natured" crowd bearing none of the hallmarks of atomization and anonymity commonly associated with stereotypes of urban living. The rearranged spatial experience of the town may have broken the intimate bond of community, but it does not yet appear to have installed urban aggression and competition.

Yet this ambiguous change in the sensory experience of the town, what might be called its carnival atmosphere, brings with it an unfamiliar commercialism:

> A thousand cries rent the air; the strolling mountebanks and gypsying booth-merchants; the peanut-vendors; the boys with palm-leaf fans for sale; the candy sellers; the popcorn peddlers; the Italian with the toy balloons that float like a cluster of coloured bubbles above the heads of the crowd…the red-lemonade man, shouting in the shrill voice that reaches everywhere and endures forever: "Lemo! Lemo! Ice-cole lemo! Five cents, a nickel, a half-a-dime, the twentieth-potofadollah! Lemo! Ice-cole lemo!"—all the vociferating harbingers of the circus crying their wares. (101)

It is a familiar space rendered oddly unfamiliar by the event of the circus. Rural space starts to take on some of the characteristics of urban space, but the "iconic topos" that lend it this strange status—the crowds and hard commercialism—are themselves transformed in the midst of circus day. This double movement continues when the parade does eventually arrive and the crowd itself loses its last vestiges of individualism: "Lines of people rushed for the street, and…tossing forward, they seemed like surf sweeping up the long beaches" (108). The crowd as an amorphous and nameless mass is a quintessential urban motif, replete with both dreams of collective power and fears of mob rule, and captured in Henry James's deliciously Jamesian description of a crowd in New York City as a "consummate monotonous commonness" (65). Circus day temporarily induces this classic emblem of urban experience—including strangers, as in the case of the Italian balloon-seller, marked by their ethnic difference—but such events are made strange by their presence in a rural village.

This "making strange"[11] is also present in Rose's experience of the circus in *Rose of Dutcher's Coolly*. Most notably, it occurs when she first steps into the big top:

> Under the tent! Rose looked up at the lifting, tremulous, translucent canvas with such awe as the traveler feels in St. Peter's dome. Her feet stumbled on, while she clung to Carl's hand without knowing it. O, the enormous crowds of people, the glitter and change of it all! (52)

From the exclamation marks to the apostrophic "O," this is not only more free indirect discourse but also a revealing passage in terms of how the space of the circus is constructed within the narrative. There are the "enormous crowds" again, and the unsettling of familiarity (Rose is nervously clinging to Carl's hand), but also the reference to, presumably, St. Peter's Basilica in Rome. The circus is momentarily aligned with a sacred space, a metaphorical connection that renders the apparently vulgar and debased commercialism of the circus in terms equal to the architecture of Renaissance Europe. The geographical and material referents of the past are re-employed just as the description of the crowded space—both here and in Tarkington's street scene—re-imports a sense of the exotic, even sublime, into the site of modern, commercial entertainment. It is also a change in scale, a sense of the monumental or vast (all of Garland's and Tarkington's crowd descriptions emphasize the overwhelming numbers) that the circus embodied; Trachtenberg goes as far to say that the circus was "the very paradigm of changes of scale" (123). Such changes affect both rural space and subjective perception: "Everything seemed inexplicable and mysterious, and roused confusing trains of thought" (52) Garland's narration states.

This defamiliarizing of space can also be the unsettling of what that space traditionally connotes and represents; in the case of rural villages, all those romantic notions of community, togetherness, and civic virtue. Returning to Tarkington's novel, it is this connotative unsettling that happens when a stall is set up by two "swarthy, shifty looking gentleman" (103) in the courthouse yard. They are running a simple shell game,[12] the narrator informs us, that only the "fanciful or unsophisticated might have been pleased to call a game of chance" (103)—a pointed choice of words, particularly when he also emphasizes that the people who have played the game and "won small sums" are "several countrymen" and a "rustic stranger." Their geo-social labels (resolutely rural as they are) mark them out, though presumably they are also the "fanciful or unsophisticated" people who think the game is genuine. The two confidence tricksters continue their game, but just as we are about to see a drunk local man gamble a huge sum of money, the circus parade arrives and interrupts—only for it to be picked up again, a few pages later, once the parade has passed through. The parade itself is the first real moment of the circus's presence in the town, and as the painted cars and the brass band appear it is clear that the increasingly disrupted experience of rural life is being further transformed into something chaotic and unstable. Such a transformation, as Janet Davis points out, was part of the experience of circus day in small towns: "Established bonds of intimacy within watchful communities temporarily dissolved into anonymity, which gave people license to engage in illicit activities" (29). As the crowds obliterate the familiarity of social bonds within the rural community, filling once-empty spaces with out-of-town anonymity, so established codes of behavior are abandoned for a more anarchic, less ordered atmosphere.

It is significant, then, that the parade should happen in the middle of the confidence-trick episode. As soon as the parade passes, we discover that the swindle has been uncovered and that a small crowd has gathered on the steps of the courthouse to confront the tricksters and demand the return of the money. But now a familiar figure of rural writing—the new member of the community—comes into view, both in the form of the novel's hero, college-educated urbanite John Harkless (he has come from a New York City newspaper), and in the redeemed local man Eph Watts. Watts can show the crowd just how the trick works because he was a confidence man himself: "[H]ere's a man we ran out of town once," Harkless says to the crowd, "because he knew too much about things of this sort. He's come back to us again and he's here to stay" (111). Harkless can now address the gathering of local people, standing above them on the steps, in words that reveal his own difference from rural life: "You all see... what a simple cheat it is.... [I]t is because you are greedy that they robbed you so easily.... It's when you want to get something for nothing that the 'confidence men' steal the money you sweat for and make the farmer a laughing stock" (112). In Harkless's admonishment there are echoes of the complex political context in which the novel was written; the reference to the exploitation of farmers evokes the politics of the Populist Party that campaigned to restore balance to agricultural prices and who, in the 1892 presidential elections, had won four states. Such political tensions had been partly exacerbated by a perceived division between urban and rural values, and this moment turns on the same ideas of rural people being "duped" or treated unfairly by outsiders. It is part of a longer passage in the novel that centers on circus day, where the notion of rural and urban space, and the values attached to them, are dislodged, even inverted, by the transformative experience of the circus.

It is revealing, then, that it is exactly this transformed experience of rural life that should illicit Harkless's most positive reaction to his life in the town. "I used to think it was desolate," he admits to his would-be sweetheart Helen Sherwood, "'but that was long ago.'... In his dark cheek was a glow Carlow folk had never seen there; and somehow he seemed less thin and tired" (106). The bustling crowd of circus day, rather than the dusty silence of normal village life, has reinvigorated Harkless. In one of the few critical comments made on the novel, Park Dixon Goist reads the story simplistically as one which "most clearly expresses Tarkington's image of the town as ideal community," an ideal which "means enjoying a sense of solidarity among one's own kind" (15, 17). The veiled suggestion of dubious racial politics in the idea of "one's own kind" is undoubtedly present in the novel—the characterization of kindly Uncle Xenophon is racial stereotyping of the crudest kind—but Harkless himself displays very little of this reactionary impulse, finding in the visual stimuli and social mixture of circus day a welcome change from the claustrophobic nativism of everyday rural life. The circus delivers a vibrant burst of activity, modern spectacle, and secular carnival—in short, of difference—into a tired, forlorn, and homogenous landscape. The transformation of rural space is in fact a repudiation of any claims to its uniqueness: gone are all the signifiers of romantic or pastoral idealism, replaced by a kind of naturalistic logic; gone, too, are the mechanisms by which rural life was romanticized and sentimentalized—it is now a socially forgotten and economically disadvantaged place.

Surprisingly, given the attention paid to the build up, the actual event of the circus does not occupy very much narrative time. A large part of what *is* described is once again concerned with the sensory experience, this time of the events inside the circus tent itself: inside the "enormous white tent" a "hazy yellow light" fills the air, a light "found nowhere in the world except in the tents of a circus" (123). The emphasis falls on the visual aspect of the circus experience, on sights and colors: because children's faces are buried in food, "very often the eyes of them were all you saw," while beneath the white tent and yellow light we get "blue tissue-paper" and "pink crescent[s] of water-melon," (124)—all of this within the first few lines of description. Even a list of people and sights in the tent employs a tightly controlled focalization: "Here swayed the myriad palm-leaf fans; here paraded blushing youth and rosy maiden...here marched sturdy yeomen" (124), and so on, the anaphoric chain of "here's" acting as a kind of narrative finger pointing from one sight to the next in a rapid concatenation of images.

It bears a notable similarity to the same moment in *Rose of Dutcher's Coolly*, when Rose is walking into the circus tent: "She saw the great tigers....She saw the lions rise like clouds of dust....She looked at the elephant...they came to the circus entrance, and then she lifted her eyes again around the great amphitheater" (52–53). The continued emphasis on gazing at the sights before them and, crucially, the protagonists' apparent distance and lack of interaction with those sights, links the circus explicitly to Debord's statement about the "spectator's alienation from and submission to the contemplated object," or Neil Harris's description of circus audiences as "passive prisoners." Not only is the subjective experience of the circus rendered in these explicitly spectacular terms, but the narrative voice itself becomes implicated in the spectacle; it has, in its fidelity to mimesis, no choice but to replicate the hurried visual extravagances it bears witness to. It attempts to keep up with the array of simultaneous stimuli, but the sheer complexity of those stimuli, and their simultaneity, are rendered in the linear terms and grammars of a realist mode whose conventions require detailed description and a stable narrative point of view.[13] Reaching for the excesses of melodrama and romance, and evoking a fractured subjectivity that anticipates modernism, realism falters in the face of the circus spectacle.

The circus, perhaps the most recognizable and frequently the most ambitious form of Gilded Age entertainment, operates as a distinct node within the wider network of modernity. Wedded to the expanded commercial horizons of mature capitalism, its ability to accentuate rationalized industrialism is matched by its ability to momentarily offer a spectacular (if only illusory) counter to that rationalism in the act of its performance. Its presence in these rural fictions highlights not only its cultural reach—something that itself is predicated on the kind of transport infrastructures discussed in chapter 1—but, more importantly, its uniquely destabilizing narrative presence. Reading the modern circus through these rural fictions brings the generic complexities of Gilded Age fiction to the fore, and it does so because of the web of geographical imaginaries that the circus has the capacity to embody. The generic conventions of pastoral, romance, sentimentalism, realism, naturalism, even a kind of proto-modernism, are all occasionally employed within texts that represent a rural life playing host to a similarly unsettled sense of cultural and social modernity and a growing awareness of wider geographical connections.

CHAPTER 3

The Place of Medical Knowledge: Country Doctors

Chapter 7 of Joseph Kirkland's *Zury: The Meanest Man in Spring County* (1887) opens with this description of a midwestern summer morning:

> Summer night—unless fear distort the vision—is beautiful, but summer morning in malarial regions (to the experienced dweller) is positively ugly. All night the world is a lovely, half veiled Danaë; with break of day she becomes a squalid, unkempt, disorderly invalid. A blue, unwholesome-looking haze spreads over every flat space, and the rays of dawn silver its surface with a pale, sickly light.... Ague, like the ghost of a giant snake, crawls visible over the land. (106)

The language used to narrate this unsettling vision—filled with metaphors of sickness and disease, personifying the landscape as it diagnoses it—highlights the intersection of rural space and medicine that is the subject of this chapter. While I concentrate mainly on the figure of the country doctor as the carrier and site of medical knowledge, Kirkland's peculiar piece of description is worth dwelling on, mainly because it restates some of the more general arguments being pursued here. On one hand, the narrative style is steeped in ostentatious rhetoric (the "half veiled Danaë"); but Kirkland also employs a metaphorical register embedded in pseudo-medical terminology—the landscape becomes an "invalid" bathed in "sickly" light. There is even an attempt at specific diagnosis, the "ague" related to, and sometimes used synonymously with, the "malaria" already mentioned at the beginning of the paragraph.

Even to describe the midwestern landscape as "malarial" reveals the text's historically specific medical awareness. It seems to be a reference to the miasmatic theory of disease, generally accepted by the lay population before the Civil War until the popularization of pathogenic theory in the later nineteenth century discredited it. Miasmatic theory held that disease was spread through the air, postulating "that disease-laden air—often called miasma or malaria—was produced by particular landforms [and] climates" (Szczygiel and Hewitt 708). Although the theory was largely dismissed in the scientific community, the idea that the landscape itself could be responsible for disease remained popular among pockets of the general population until at least the 1880s. Furthermore, the term "malaria" had rather more expansive associations in the nineteenth century than it does today. William Rothstein points out that "quinine became a panacea for all ills in the 1870's and 1880's" because physicians saw that it reduced fever in most diseases, an observation that led in turn to a hugely expanded application of "malaria" as a diagnostic label: "reasoning backward from quinine's therapeutic uses, physicians assumed that these other diseases [pneumonia, typhoid, yellow fever, etc.] could be classed as malarial" (188). Kirkland's description of the midwestern rural landscape as "malarial" would, it seems, have evoked a more generalized understanding of sickness to contemporary readers who had a semblance of medical knowledge.

By thinking about the relationship between Gilded Age medical history and rural fiction along the lines suggested here—that is, through close attention to the historically specific medical context, and by equally close attention to the generic strategies employed by the text in question—this chapter will move the argument of this book into somewhat more abstract territory than has been covered so far. Rather than centering on a specifically material synecdoche of modernization, like the train or the circus, this chapter relates the highly contested arena of late nineteenth-century medicine to the figure of the country doctor. Such a figure immediately evokes two particular and ostensibly separate strands, of course: the status of "country" will prove crucial to the broader arguments being made here about the interrelatedness of urban and rural space, while the status of "doctor"—which, as I will discuss, is far from stable—will link those geographical considerations to the medical context in question.

I therefore begin by outlining how the medical profession underwent a process of modernization in the Gilded Age, particularly through its ever-increasing attention to scientific method. As will become clear, however, such metanarrational accounts of modernization do not tell the whole story, and important here is the continuing existence, especially in rural areas, of older, alternative, and usually scientifically discredited forms of medical knowledge. The figures of the herbalist and the patent medicine salesman are discussed in this light, before I turn to more developed discussions of works by Mary Noailles Murfree, Jewett, and Elizabeth Stuart Phelps that take country doctors as their protagonists. I end the chapter by considering how Harold Frederic's *The Damnation of Theron Ware* (1896) and Alice Brown's short story "Horn o' the Moon" (1899) bring together the themes of the discussion through their concern with the role of urban and rural space in the development and distribution of medical modernization. Underpinning these discussions throughout are two distinct arguments: firstly, that the modernization of orthodox medicine is an urban-centered, and therefore urban-legitimated, process, and secondly, that by engaging with this medical context all the texts discussed here reveal the generic instabilities that country doctors provoke within rural fiction.

By way of illustration, such a discussion might well turn to two figures who embody and bookend the dominant narrative of medical history being traced here. The first is the French physiologist Claude Bernard, who in 1865 published the seminal *An Introduction to the Study of Experimental Medicine*. "It is...clear to all unprejudiced minds that medicine is turning toward its permanent scientific path" (1) Bernard announced, arguing that such a path can "be established only by experimental means, i.e., by direct and rigorous application of reasoning to the facts furnished us by observation and experiment" (2). Following the revolutionary impact of Pasteur's germ theory, first published in 1861, Bernard's approach exemplifies a belief in scientific method that would come to govern orthodox medical practice in the late nineteenth century. Looking back on that same period in 1901, William Osler—a Canadian born to British parents who dominated medical education in the United States during the 1880s and 1890s—would also characterize the nineteenth century as a period when scientific medicine (especially the fields of pathology, anatomy, and physiology) would usurp the purely theoretical or superstitious thinking of the past. "The study of physiology...within the past half-century has done more to emancipate medicine from routine...than all the work of all the physicians from the days of Hippocrates" (223–24) he told the Johns Hopkins Historical Club. One story of late nineteenth-century medicine, as framed by the figures of Bernard and Osler, is the story of the triumph of scientific principles.[1]

This context, I also want to suggest, is profoundly connected to an urban-centric notion of modern medicine. In *The Archaeology of Knowledge*, Michel Foucault has nineteenth-century doctors specifically in mind—"statutorily defined" figures whose role is "an intermediary in the diffusion of medical knowledge" (59)—when he discusses the geographical location of medical discourse. His assertion, familiar enough by now, is that it is generated at "institutional sites"—he lists them as the hospital, the private practice, the laboratory, and the library—that in turn form that discourse's "legitimate source and point of application" (56).[2] Those sites are, of course, and especially in the nineteenth century, predominantly urban-based institutions. The eminent nineteenth-century surgeon John Shaw Billings commented in 1875 that "[w]e have in our cities...physicians...[who] take good care to be supplied with the best instruments, and the latest literature," physicians who he claimed were "the patrons of medical literature...the men who are usually accepted as the representatives of the profession" (qtd. in Rothstein 205). In the same year as Billings's statement Thomas Eakins would exhibit *The Gross Clinic* (1875), portraying the eminent surgeon Samuel Gross attending to an operation on a man's thigh bone, while fourteen years later he produced *The Agnew Clinic* (1889), depicting a different surgeon, and a different operation (a mastectomy), but with a similar attention to close painterly realism. As documents of medical history these paintings show the deferential aura that surrounded figures like Gross and Agnew, chart a development of increasingly hygienic practice between 1875 and 1889, and, indirectly but crucially, show the kind of sites where pioneering medical work was taking place—Jefferson Medical College and the University of Pennsylvania, respectively, both situated in the heart of Philadelphia. Billings's comments and less obviously Eakins's paintings attest to the urban-centric nature of scientific medicine in both the professional community and in the wider cultural imagination.

The city, after all, "provided an essential cultural milieu as well as ready access to the background work on which scientific activities are based" (Dierig et al. 15). Materially, a modern, scientifically grounded and institutionalized medicine finds its home in the city simply because the city provides the density of people most conducive to developing bodies of knowledge, allowing for a "continual exchange of ideas, practices and objects" (Dierig et al. 15). In the process of communicating that knowledge into provincial and rural areas, however—a process embodied in country doctors—the city ceases to be a spatially delimited object and becomes the centrifugal center of Lefebvre's urban fabric, the originating site of an increasingly incorporative and nationalized standard of medical knowledge. Scientific development, which professional medicine increasingly aligns itself with in the Gilded Age, is a practice profoundly implicated and embedded in the urban context from which it emerges.

How was this growing sphere of urban-located medical knowledge and discourse transmitted into rural space? And, more importantly for this study, what does the urban-centric nature of modern medical knowledge mean to the representation of medical figures who do not speak or operate from those privileged sites? These questions inform this chapter's attention to the representation of medical figures in rural narratives, something that ultimately illuminates the sometimes hidden geographies of modern medical practice.

* * *

While the term "country doctor" may well have designated a medically qualified individual in the formal sense, it was also a somewhat ambiguous term that could extend the idea of a doctor to someone who simply administered to the sick and injured. In fact, one of the features of the field of medicine in the Gilded Age was the increasing formalization of the term "doctor"; around midcentury, the right to call yourself a doctor was by no means limited to individuals who held professional qualifications. K. Patrick Ober points out that it was "an era of unregulated medical practice" where "licensure laws were virtually nonexistent, and any citizen who wished to do so was allowed to practice medicine" (11). Ann Anderson similarly claims that, even in the decades after the formation of the American Medical Association in 1847, "you were a doctor simply if you said you were" (30). The increasing formalization of the doctor's role is invested in a host of other related issues—authority, professionalization, and specialization in particular—and I expand on these as the chapter progresses. For now, however, it is worth addressing the figure that most obviously embodies a field of medicine seemingly at odds with these modern shifts in the field, a figure that keeps alive a notion of medicine that increasingly comes to be seen as unscientific: the herbalist.

While such figures are carriers of beliefs about the efficacy of various botanical and superstitious remedies, in late nineteenth-century America they also provided a link back to the more coherent (if scientifically unfounded) craze of Thomsonianism. Sweeping the country in the antebellum period, and taking its name from the methods advocated by Samuel Thomson in his huge bestseller *New Guide to Health*,[3] first published in 1822, the movement believed in forms of treatment that consisted mainly of "steam baths and botanical remedies" (Duffy 110). Essentially a more expansive and pseudo-scientifically sanctioned form of disparate and localized folk medicine, in the words of one historian it "epitomized the influence of rural botanical medicine" (Rothstein 129). Thomson's plea for well-informed and self-reliant individuals to reclaim medical treatment from the professionals—their motto was "to make every man his own physician" (Anderson 29)—appealed to the Jacksonian spirit of mid-century. Even by the time of the Civil War Thomson's ideas had been dismissed by the orthodox medical profession, but their impact on popular notions of medicine could still be felt, especially in rural areas. The herbalist as represented in Gilded Age fiction embodies these connotations, their frequent appearance in rural fictions often serving to provide a rural antagonist to modern, city-based medical professionals. As I will argue, however, the historically complex stratification of medical knowledge that such figures operated within not only complicates a crude urban-rural geography of medical knowledge, but also poses problems for the generic logics of the fiction that sought to represent them.

As with the other topics explored in this book, references to botanical and folk medicine are common occurrences in rural fiction. In Kirkland's *Zury*, for instance, the competing sense of authority between folk medicine and more modern developments in medical treatment are succinctly revealed in a dialect-heavy conversation between two midwestern women about the ailing health of the local blacksmith's wife:

> "Physic don't seem t'take no holt on her. Blacksmith 'llaows 't ef she lives till th'change o'th'moon she may git well, but ef not, why he hain't much hope o'her ever bein' any better."
>
> "Hev the'tried the slipp'ry ellum peeled in th'dark o'th'moon?"
>
> "Slipp'ry ellum! Why the've had the new doctor, 'n'real store drugs! *They'd* a pulled her threw ef anythin'could." (287, emphasis in original)

The blacksmith's desperate hope that his wife's health may improve with the cycles of the moon gives rise to the suggestion of a particular botanical remedy, slippery elm,[4] which in turn is deemed inferior to commercial drugs that, rightly or wrongly, were associated with scientific legitimacy. The course of the conversation charts a hierarchy of treatment, from an essentially superstitious faith in the lunar cycle, through a more empirically based belief in botanical compounds, to an apparently modern faith in the science of man-made medicine. Such a hierarchy acknowledges the growing authority and effectiveness of modern medicine at the same time that it reveals the residual authority of those older, more traditional forms—especially in the novel's rural setting.

This notion of competing discourses of medical knowledge, and the geographical dimension of their authority, is also found in Eggleston's *The Hoosier School-Master* in the form of Granny Sanders, an "old and shriveled hag whose hideousness gave her a reputation for almost supernatural knowledge" (84). That knowledge, flagged immediately as unscientific, nevertheless means she is a "doctress" who "collected and disseminated medicinal herbs" (84). Eggleston's crudely stereotypical characterization of the local herb doctor as an "old and shriveled" (not to mention "hideous") woman living alone in a ramshackle cabin underlines a suspicion of her medical knowledge that the use of "supernatural" only confirms. Yet her methods are, oddly, not simply dismissed: "In the matter of her medical skill we can not express an opinion, for her 'yarbs' are not to be found in the pharmacopœia of science" (84). The elderly spinster (a stock character in rural fiction) is not someone readers can criticize because they cannot apply the criteria of science to judge her form of knowledge—the two are, in the strict sense of the word, incommensurable.[5] The difference, simply put, is between a form of subjective knowledge invested in an individual's idiosyncratic adoption of shared superstitions, and a form of consensual knowledge officially sanctioned by professional institutional practice.

It is worth pausing here to explain how close readings like this one help to engage with the broader theoretical points in which this chapter is anchored. I alluded to Foucault earlier on, and although summarizing and restating his arguments here would serve little purpose, I do want to expand on his key notion of "medicalization" by evoking again the late nineteenth-century shift to a modern, scientifically grounded idea of medicine.[6] As Deborah Lupton explains, within medical sociology the idea of an "orthodox medicalisation critique" refers to how "[modern Western] medicine...despite its alleged lack of effectiveness in treating a wide range of conditions and its iatrogenic side-effects, has increasingly amassed power and influence" (95). In contrast, a Foucauldian perspective nuances an understanding of modern, clinical, scientific medicine by suggesting that "[t]here is not a single medicine but a series of loosely linked assemblages, each with different rationalities" (100). Rather than affirming the epistemological dominance of the kind of clinical medicine exemplified by Claude Bernard and William Osler, this approach emphasizes the ongoing existence (and potentially subversive nature of) "subjugated knowledges," "knowledges that tend to be buried and disguised beneath more dominant, often more 'scientific' or 'expert' knowledge" (Lupton 104). Bringing this back to the context of my argument here, the residue and continuing presence of subjugated knowledges, especially in the rural areas where modern clinical medicine was less firmly established, helps to explain the complex place of medical figures in rural fiction. Granny Sanders's folk remedies are a form of medicine that, to a cosmopolitan and informed reader, represent a discredited—a "subjugated"—form of knowledge.

This tension expresses itself in Eggleston's narrative both in terms of the ongoing plot and the generic strategies of the text itself. The professionally trained Dr. Small, the laconically detached villain of *The Hoosier School-Master*, is the figure who embodies modern science. A crucial moment of the story comes when he goes to see Granny Sanders, ostensibly to talk about medicine but actually to plant a detrimental rumor about the novel's hero, Ralph. Dr. Small sits silently in her cabin while she tells him all about the various folk remedies and methods she employs (consisting mainly, it seems, of draining the blood of various unfortunate animals).[7] Dr. Small, attempting to ingratiate himself with Granny Sanders, asks at one point how old the hen was whose blood she used; it's an insincere inquiry, of course, in that he clearly inhabits a professional world where such concerns would seem absurd, but Granny Sanders takes him at face value and proudly exclaims, "There you showed yer science, doctor!" (87). Eggleston's point is clear enough: recognizing the authority that the professional doctor has over the "quack," he illustrates Dr. Small's manipulative malevolence by showing how he exploits his position of medical superiority, the old woman imagining that his question signals that her knowledge is somehow commensurate, somehow on an equal scientific footing, with his.

But while such a hierarchy of medical authority reflects the sociohistorical situation which the text is representing and within which it operates, it in fact poses problems for the narrative's generic expectations. We have already been positioned as readers who cannot judge Granny Sanders's folk methods because we inhabit a social position sympathetic to modern, professional science, but such a positioning now effectively identifies us with the voice of modern science in the text: the villain. The narrative's effort to distance the "hideous" rural figure from the reader means that its plot line—the dastardly Dr. Small's cunning abuse of the old woman's naivety—loses its dramatic and moral thrust. The ongoing, uneven, and incomplete nature of that medical paradigm shift, the social and historical reality that world views do not neatly and progressively replace each other but reside simultaneously and problematically within the sociolect, means that even as the narrative strives to align our affinities with modern forms of medical knowledge, it morally invests itself in the nonscientific knowledge we would presumably discredit. The vacillating shift from "traditional" to "modern" forms of medical knowledge exerts a narrative pressure that undermines the dichotomously simple moral universe needed for Eggleston's melodramatic story to comfortably operate.

Rural fiction's generic instabilities in the 1870s and 1880s are exacerbated by a story's employment of medical figures, the representations of whom, in turn, reveal the evolving and fractured nature of medical knowledge in the period. There is a direct link here between the generic currents—in particular the move toward realist and naturalist aesthetics—and the move toward scientific medicine. Lawrence Rothfield, while not suggesting any overly schematic mapping of literary form and medicine, has argued that realism as practiced in the literary-aesthetic sense shares a connection with the increasingly clinical nature of medical practice. Capturing reality means, after all, "maintaining faith" that details and particularities are typical and shared "in the same way that medical diagnosis assumes that signs and symptoms will resolve into cases of disease" (148). Equally, Rothfield adds, "realism's sincerity is analogous to the disinterested benevolence claimed by the medical profession" (148). As realism became the preferred generic choice among a professionalized literary elite during the Gilded Age—a process that, in its contested and incomplete influence, mirrors the uneven nature of modern medicine's rise—so its fundamental aesthetic strategy of situating the author in the position of objective reporter found a counterpart in medical practice's own shifts. The depersonalization of narrative voice in literary realism distances the reader from the origin of production, in the same way that one of the dominant shifts taking place "between the 1870s and the early 1900s is that the social distance between doctor and patient increased" (Starr 81).

A brief illustration of this is Sarah Orne Jewett's depiction of a herbalist in her best-known work, *The Country of the Pointed Firs* (1896). Mrs. Todd is a fundamental part of the community in Dunnet Landing and plays a crucial role in the fictional world Jewett creates around the tiny Maine fishing village. While I do not want to oversimplify her as a character, the passage where she and her home are first described in *Country* is relevant to this discussion in the way it encapsulates her uneasy position within both the rural community and the narrative itself:

> At one side of this herb plot were other growths of a rustic pharmacopœia.... There were some strange and pungent odors that roused a dim sense and remembrance of something in the forgotten past. Some of these might once have belonged to sacred and mystic rites, and have had some occult knowledge handed with them down the centuries; but now they pertained only to humble compounds brewed at intervals with molasses or vinegar or spirits in a small caldron on Mrs. Todd's kitchen stove. They were dispensed to suffering neighbors... bringing their own ancient-looking vials to be filled. (*Pointed Firs* 6)

The passage ranges from an emphasis on our temporal distance from Mrs. Todd's medicine ("forgotten past," "down the centuries," "ancient-looking"), through the archaic and superstitious nature of its methods ("sacred and mystic rites," "occult knowledge"), to a careful placement of the narrative voice within a modern register that makes Mrs. Todd a primitive, albeit sympathetic, figure: "*now* they pertained only to humble compounds" and the ironic detail of that "small caldron." All the indications secure the narrator-reader in a privileged position that insists on the difference between Mrs. Todd's form of medical knowledge and our own. Mrs. Todd comes to be the embodiment of Dunnet Landing while being fundamentally distant—literally, temporally, and epistemologically—from us: "her distant figure looked mateless... and at last I lost sight of her as she slowly crossed an open space... and disappeared again behind a dark clump of juniper and the pointed firs" (101) the narrator states as she leaves Dunnet Landing behind at the novel's conclusion.

The focal dissonance between the first-person narrator and the character being described is more sharply defined than in the third-person narration of Kirkland's or Eggleston's work, so that Jewett's form of realism is noticeable for its "disinterested benevolence" (Rothfield's term for the modern medical profession) toward the character of Mrs. Todd. A modern form of medical knowledge only becomes widely ascendant at the turn of the century, when its "truthfulness as a science and its ethical attractiveness" (Rothfield 148) become affirmable. This cultural and social affirmation means that the implicitly modern medical standpoint of Jewett's narrative is an increasingly accepted position among an urban readership.

* * *

It is clear that while medicine shifted toward a more scientific and clinical basis in the Gilded Age, preexisting and "subjugated" alternatives still existed—albeit ones that found their credibility increasingly undermined. Before I move onto the idea of a "country doctor" as a figure who becomes increasingly enmeshed in the growing net of modern medicine's authority, however, I consider a form of medicine that in many ways bridges the gap between the herbalist and the professional physician. Patent medicines (or proprietary medicines, or even "nostrums"; the terms are often synonymous) were huge business in nineteenth-century America, "one of the first successful industries in the United States" (Anderson 31), and as with herbalists and professionally trained doctors, the use of and belief in patent medicines is something directly implicated in both the social experience and literary representation of rural space.

Kirkland's *Zury* again offers a way into the discussion, illustrated in a conversation between two old village residents:

"I've often wondered why them big town doctors don't put up a mixter of all the strong med'cines, 'n' put in what's good fer everythin'– not leave aout a single complaint — 'n' send it aout inter the kendtry ter save the lives of their feller-creeters. It'd have a big sale, I tell ye!"

"Wal, naow, ther wuz a man he come by with suth 'n' o' thet kind—a pannersee he called it—thet'd cure every mortial thing.... I tuk the pannersee 'cordin' t'directions, but" (here she sighed) "I never see's it done me much good." (This with an air of resigned melancholy at the well-recognized fact that her case formed an exception to the general experience of humanity.) (113)

Once we have maneuvered through Kirkland's punctilious attention to dialect, it is clear that notions of urban and rural-based medical practice, and the place of patent medicine in that relationship, underpin the logic of the conversation. The statement that "big town" doctors could just mix a series of strong medicines together and "have a big sale" reflects the general state of (and attitude toward) patent medicine manufacturing in America at the time. As Anderson points out, patent medicines were frequently a seemingly random mixture of numerous ingredients, put together in the belief that a kind of "buckshot" approach was the best route to a remedy: "blast the target with multiple pellets and perhaps something will hit the bulls-eye" (32).

The popular belief in such remedies, however, meant that many patent remedies were indeed a "big sale." Paul Starr recounts the story of William Radam, who in the 1880s (when Kirkland's novel is set) "promoted a Microbe Killer that played upon public misunderstandings of the recent discoveries of Pasteur and Koch. Consisting nearly entirely of water— except for traces of red wine, hydrochloric and sulphuric acid—Microbe Killer was supposed to cure all diseases by destroying germs inside the body" (128). By 1890, Starr reports, Radam's "medicine" was so popular that seventeen factories were producing it. The justified and growing belief that modern medical knowledge was a rarefied, specialized, and elite pursuit meant that patent medicine manufacturers were able to financially exploit a general public bewilderment in the face of complex scientific terminology.

The positioning of *Zury* in this knowledge economy is clearer in the respondent's comments, where a traveling patent-medicine salesman's wild promises about his "pannersee" (panacea)—it will "cure every mortial thing"—are ironically placed in the position of unimpeachable truth by the parenthetical interjection of the narrator. The linguistic contrast is clear enough, but the narrative also distances itself from the character by implying that the two rural people having the conversation believe in the efficacy of these patent medicines—a belief that the condescendingly overblown language of the narrator signposts as naive. The geography of this complex stratification of trust and authority is clearly centered in an urban-rural divide: the patent medicine salesman and manufacturers are city-based, and as such come from the authoritative seat of modern medical knowledge. Just as patent medicines exploited the lack of understanding of new scientific ideas, they also exploited their position as urban "outsiders" within a rural community. *Zury* depicts this particular social and historical phenomenon, but its uneasy sense of its own generic positioning means that the narrative operates both as *representing* the medically "naive" rural setting and as *representative of* a more knowing and medically informed urban outsider.

Read in this way, the passage from *Zury* quoted above demonstrates the peculiar place of patent medicine in the geo-social arrangement of Gilded Age America. At the same time as it acknowledges the self-administering spirit of rural communities, it also acknowledges the capitalist nature of commercial medicine, and the assumed authority of urban scientific practice. This conflicted social context then manifests itself in the generic problems it causes for rural representation. Looking toward a realistic representation of rural life, it employs such cultural references to secure its historical footing and imbue its narrative world with some recognizable markers of contemporary life. Patent medicine's place within that context, however, disrupts the unequivocal morality of the often sentimental and melodramatic storylines of rural fiction by occupying an ambivalent and indeterminate position.

Hamlin Garland takes up the subject of patent medicine more extensively in "Uncle Ethan Ripley." It tells the tale of the eponymous protagonist's agreement with a passing salesman to paint a sign for "Dodd's Family Bitters" on the side of his new barn. In return for advertising the stranger's wares, Ethan gets twenty-five bottles for free. Reluctant at first, when the salesman explains that Ethan could sell the bottles for a dollar each, keeping five to treat his own ailments and still making a cool twenty dollars, he agrees—much to the displeasure of his wife, who returns home to find "DODD'S FAMILY BITTERS—Best in the Market" painted in black lettering on the side of their barn. Ethan, visiting nearby farmsteads to sell the bitters, soon realizes that the anonymous salesman has been pulling the same trick elsewhere: he is greeted by his neighbors trying to sell him their own surplus of the bitters and barns adorned with the same sign. Ashamed and annoyed at being duped, Ethan eventually, and rather sheepishly, abandons the worthless "medicine" and repaints his barn.

It is a gentle, comic tale—far lighter than some of the other stories in *Main-Travelled Roads*, the collection in which it appears—but offers a deft illustration of the impact of a new, mercantile medical world on an unsuspecting rural community. What the unscrupulous salesman peddles to Ethan is exactly the kind of generic, homely cure-all that patent medicines promised. In an exchange between Ethan and the salesman, we see both the appeal of the medically ecumenical potion, and the modern presumption that any medicine claiming an authoritative scientific position would be highly specialized:

> "Here's what it cures," pursued the agent, pointing at the side, where, in an inverted pyramid, the names of several hundred diseases were arranged, running from "gout" to "pulmonary complaints," etc.
>
> "I gol! she cuts a wide swath, don't she?" exclaimed Uncle Ethan, profoundly impressed with the list.... "What's its speshy-*ality*? Most of 'em have some speshy-*ality*."
>
> "Well—summer complaints—an'– an'– spring an' fall troubles—tones ye up, sort of." (181)

A medicine for all seasons, it seems. Ethan is wary because he knows that anything claiming such a broad application (and in such broad terms) is generally associated with a nonscientific medical world, yet in the end the salesman's appeal to exactly this "old-fashioned" type of remedy is what wins Ethan round. It also highlights the intriguing place that patent medicines held within a developing capitalist economy: they clearly represent a prime example of the shift to consumer capitalism in their utilization of modern advertising and marketing techniques, yet their appeal is predicated on an earlier, producer-oriented form of economic exchange. Both the scientific and the economic connotations of patent medicines, in other words, are bound up in their ambiguous geographical dispersion.

Garland, however, is keen to emphasize the gap between the cynical sale of patent medicines and the apparently different—presumably more honest—values of rural life. The salesman reveals a critical gap in his knowledge when he compliments Ethan on his crop: "[g]ood piece of oats," he admiringly tells him, only to have it pointed out that it is in fact barley. "So 'tis. Didn't notice," the salesman replies (180). It is a small mistake, but a telling one, betraying the stranger's lack of agricultural knowledge. He is further established as a figure out of touch with rural life by the advertisement he paints, a stark signal of modern capitalism in its own right. It "disfigured the sweet-smelling pine boards" (183) of the barn—itself a quintessential piece of rural topography—and when Ethan "stepped out into the yard next morning that abominable, sickening, scrawling advertisement was the first thing that claimed his glance—it blotted out the beauty of the morning" (187). The trend of using the authoritative status of urban-located scientific medicine to make money from the general public literally "disfigures" rural space.

Patent medicines had a curious cultural life in Gilded Age America. They tended to sell well in the general stores of rural communities, partly because they appealed to the "self-directed approach to medical therapeutics" (Ober 61) that isolated rural residents often necessarily embraced, yet interest in them was generated by utilizing the nationalized networks of publishing and communications. They were, according to historian Thomas Schlereth "the first national brands that country store owners stocked" and became popular with "customers who had read about them in the agricultural, religious, or regional press." "Drake's Plantation Bitters or Radway's Ready Relief," for example, "were also promoted by the extensive publishing network of free 'medical' almanacs sent to country merchants every November" (144–45). Nationally distributed patent medicines employed a pseudoscientific vocabulary on their products to mystify potential customers, and particularly targeted the sectors of society who were likely to be less educated in scientific terminology—the working class and rural poor—to sell their product. The salesman in "Uncle Ethan Ripley" seeks to exploit this same lack of medical knowledge and generate a recognizable brand identity by monopolizing local consumption of his patent medicine. The presence of patent medicines in rural communities becomes a key signifier of the growing spatial reach of a centralized urban-capitalist economy, so that these scenes from the rural fiction of the time implicate rural life in a geography of medical knowledge from which they are excluded even as they become its target market.

***

While folk and patent medicines were crucial elements in the expansion and modernization of medical knowledge in the period, it is the figure of the trained physician that most directly embodies those changing knowledge systems. Before turning to more detailed discussions of how those figures operate in rural fiction, it is important to outline how the key notion of authority plays into their representation: which way of practicing medicine is believed to be the most "correct" or the most effective, and which generic mode seems to have authority within a given text. In terms of the medical context, such uncertainties were clearly a source of social and cultural anxiety in the Gilded Age; Ober suggests that nineteenth-century medicine was a confusing assemblage of competing voices, a field "splintered into sects and fiefdoms" (3). One way in which the orthodox medical profession reacted to this uncertainty was to develop areas of specialization, something that not only secured a degree of authority for the professional classes but also secured urban space as the prime arena for medical knowledge. "The new order of urban life and industrial capitalism generally required people to rely more on the complementary skills of others and less on their own unspecialized talents," Paul Starr points out, so that "[p]rofessional medicine drew its authority in part from the changing beliefs people held about their own abilities and understanding" (142). As clinical science achieved an ever-greater hold over the actual practice of medicine, so the field of knowledge expanded, specialization could arise, and fewer people could hope to have a truly comprehensive knowledge of medicine.

Moreover, this move is economically reliant on both the concentrated populations of cities—"urban population aggregates had to become sufficiently large to support a specialist in the practice of his speciality" (Rothstein 207)—and the class stratifications that accompany urban life: specialization "assisted the strong post–Civil War reaction among the cultivated classes against the alleged excesses of the democratic revolution.... [Specialists] were detaching themselves from a loosely structured, nontheoretical, community-based culture of Jacksonian America" (Higham 9). The idea of an earlier "community-based" culture aligns with popular republican notions attached to rural life, so that specialization becomes only one indicator of the much more generalized shift in medical knowledge to centralized, institutionalized, and professionalized practice. Such a geography of medical knowledge has profound implications for the country doctor, as their necessarily unspecialized knowledge, coupled with their rural location, means they are both epistemologically and literally removed from the modernization of medicine. As I will show, however, the divide was not that simple, and literary narratives reveal an ongoing cultural negotiation between residual and emergent forms of medical knowledge.

One such example comes in Mary Noailles Murfree's story "The Romance of Sunrise Rock," included in her collection *In the Tennessee Mountains* (1884). The story centers on the character of John Cleaver, a physician who has moved from the "fine social position" of his upbringing in an unnamed Western city (including an expensive medical education in Paris) to the "wilderness" of the East Tennessee mountains. Murfree is careful to accentuate the stark difference between Cleaver and the "uncouth surroundings" he now inhabits, pointing to the "terribly poor" populace (185–86)—one of whom, the first local character we encounter, being described as a "hairy animal" (183)—and especially the contrast between different spheres of medical knowledge. Riding past an isolated inn, Cleaver offers a young girl sitting outside a "pretty cluster of ferns and berries which he had gathered in the forest":

> "Air they good yerbs fur somethin'?" she asked.
>
> A quick comprehension of the ludicrous situation flashed through his mind. She evidently made no distinctions in the healing art as practiced by him and the "yerb-doctor," with whom he occasionally came into professional contact. And the presentation of the "yerbs" seemed a prescription instead of a compliment.
>
> "No,—no," he said hastily, thinking of the possibility of a decoction. "They are not good for tea. They are of no use,—except to look at."
>
> And he rode away, laughing softly. (187)

Cleaver, imagining himself to be a gentleman (not to mention a flirt), makes a gift of flora to a young woman on the presumption that such things have "no use...except to look at." His leisured and privileged understanding of the exchange-value of objects does not coincide with the woman's own, however, who inhabits a social position where the same plants have a use-value; they are not aesthetically pleasing items to be contemplated for their own sake, but botanical ingredients for traditional herbal medicines. As far as the young woman is concerned, Cleaver's status as a professional doctor imbues the transaction with certain assumptions, yet it is exactly Cleaver's educated middle-class status that preconditions his own notions of exchange value and honorable behavior. The bouquet becomes a porous signifier capable of symbolizing the disconnections and miscommunications that initially underpin the plot: between different forms of medical knowledge, and between urban and rural life.

Such disconnections continue to trouble Cleaver, who becomes increasingly dissatisfied with the lack of urbane culture and even the vernacular eccentricities of life in rural Tennessee: "he felt that every concession to the customs of the region was a descent toward the level of its inhabitants" (189), and he worries to his friend Trelawney that "it won't do for us to spend our lives here. We must turn about and get back into the world of men and action" (191). It is a crudely anthropological or Social Darwinistic logic that informs Cleaver's anxieties—rural Tennessee becomes a society, replete with its own "customs," that is lower down on Cleaver's hierarchy of civilization—and that desire to return to urban life is grounded in a concern that his professional status is suffering by being so removed from the "world of...action"; he claims to be, after all, "vowed to science" (205). At this moment, the text's generic sympathies might seem naturalistic; the evocation of Darwinism along with Cleaver's stated fear that his friend is "degenerating" (189) by being in such an environment locate the text firmly in naturalism's philosophical logic.

With such a generic stance established, and the fairly standard tension between a modern outsider and a local rural community firmly in place, however, the story takes an intriguing turn. The nameless recipient of Cleaver's bouquet contracts diphtheria, and by the time he is called to attend to her it is too late; she dies, whereupon Cleaver discovers that the woman had long harboured deep and unspoken affections for him: "He had no name for a certain vague, mysterious thrill which quivered through every fibre whenever he thought of that humble, tender love that had followed him so long, unasked and unheeded" (208). The effects of this knowledge, a mixture of guilt and regret, cause a kind of nervous disorder in Cleaver, a mental disturbance that reaches a critical point "one misty midnight" (208) a few days later when he is riding home. He sees a ghostly apparition of the dead woman by the side of the road, a hallucination powerful enough to make him believe that she actually gets into the carriage with him. Cleaver's rational scientism has vanished, and the narrative shifts gears into something approaching gothic melodrama: "Like the wind they sped together through the mist and the moonbeam, over the wild mountain road, through the flashing mountain waters" (209).

Shaken, the incident drives Cleaver to a "furious" episode of self-analytical writing, a response that encapsulates not only the story's titular "romance" but brings it back to the world of scientific medicine:

> So cleverly did he analyze his own mental and nervous condition, so unsparing and insidious was this curious introversion, that when his treatise on the "Derangement of the Nervous Functions" was given to the world it was in no degree remarkable that it should have attracted the favorable attention of the medical profession; that the portion devoted to hallucinations should have met with high praise in high quarters; that the young physician's successful work should have brought him suddenly to the remembrance of many people who had almost forgotten poor John Cleaver. No one knew, no one ever knew, its romantic inspiration. (210–11)

Restored to mental stability and a degree of fame within his profession, Cleaver returns "to his accustomed and appropriate sphere" (211) of an urban practice; it now seems petty and snobbish, however, and he pines for the simplicity of rural life and the "towering splendors of Sunrise Rock" (212). Having reversed Cleaver's geographical sympathies, the story ends with a curious sense of the triumph of rationalism over superstition: "As to that vague and tender mystery, the ghost that he saw, it had been exorcised by prosaic science" (212).

What makes "The Romance of Sunrise Rock" such a remarkable story in the context of this chapter is the way it binds issues of medical knowledge and authority into a self-consciously unsettled sense of literary genre. At the outset, Cleaver is the carrier of modern medicine and the center of the story, and likewise the narrative point of view tends toward a realistic depiction of isolated rural folk and their distinct dialect—and, as I pointed out, strongly implicates the philosophical worldview that came to be associated with literary naturalism.[8] The "romance" of the story's title comes from the apparent tragedy of a woman's unrequited love, which in turn dislodges Cleaver's—and the narrative's—generic perspective, replacing it momentarily with a gothic episode of ghostly hallucinations. It is this episode, however, that restores the centrality of scientific thinking—it spurs Cleaver into writing a paper that returns him to urban prominence. The story's arc, therefore, is one that shifts between a rational realism (narratologically and scientifically) and a resolutely irrational gothic romance in a way that makes those mutually exclusive perspectives in fact mutually reinforcing. Medical knowledge seems neatly hierarchical in Cleaver's first encounter with a rural resident, but by the end a "superior" scientific medical knowledge has been generated by the very social and cultural milieu it seeks to disavow. Mirroring the geographical and epistemological oscillations the story creates is the generically unsettled narrative voice itself. This all amounts to a story that enacts, thematically and aesthetically, the multiplicity of medical knowledges, geographical cultures, and literary genres that constitute the fabric of its historical moment.

That works of fiction can serve as a point of coalescence for these various cultural, spatial and intellectual currents is important to an understanding of the two novels I turn to next: Phelps's *Doctor Zay* and Jewett's *A Country Doctor*. As a pairing, they have been described by Nina Baym as the "two best-known ... novelistic treatments of women physicians" in the late nineteenth century (184)[9] and as such have tended to be examined through a feminist critical lens.[10] The focus here is more on the geographical dynamics at play in the novels, not as a way to refute the existing feminist readings, or to deny that issues of gender and sexuality are central to Phelps's and Jewett's concerns, but to recast what is often seen as the novels' attention to the historical role of male and female sexuality as, instead, an attention to the historical role of rural and urban space. The following section therefore pursues two distinct lines of inquiry: the dialogue these novels have with the medical context of the time, and the generic implications that arise from that dialogue. It is, I suggest, the geography of modern medicine's production and legitimation that unites these stands.

Doctor Zay tells the story of young Bostonian Waldo Yorke, who on a trip through the "gentle fields ... [and] pastures" (11) of rural Maine has a serious horse-riding accident and comes into the care of Dr. Zaidee Atalanta Lloyd—Dr. Zay, as she is known in the village she serves. Almost from the moment Waldo awakens from his short coma, his vulnerable position becomes clear to him and an ingrained suspicion of country doctors surfaces: "The thing which worried him most was the probable character of this Down-East doctor upon whose intelligence he had fallen.... [H]e thought of some representatives of the profession whom he had met in the mountains, and at other removes from the centres of society" (38). Waldo is, in these early sections of the novel, established as a stereotypical urban dweller, viewing the rural landscape through touristic eyes but resisting provincial medical standards. What is more, that distrust is based around the assumption that rural villages like this one will lack the modern medical fashions and techniques he demands:

> "I suppose there is n't a homœopathist short of Bangor?"
> "Our doctor is homœopathy," said Mrs. Butterwell, instantly on the defensive; "but you need not be uneasy, sir, for a better, kinder"—
> "My mother will be so glad!" interrupted the young man, feebly. He gave a sigh of relief. "She would never have been able to bear it, if I had died under the other treatment." (38–39)

Phelps undercuts the urban man's wariness of rural medical practice by defying his assumptions, placing a practitioner of a popular medical fashion in a rural setting. The passage hints at the geographical element of a particular contemporary concern: the controversy surrounding homeopathy had, by the 1880s, reached its zenith (Rothstein 246).[11] Homeopathy became fashionable among a wealthy urban clientele, mainly because its less-invasive methods appealed to the delicate sensibilities of the Gilded Age middle classes: "By the end of the century, approximately 10,000 homeopaths—about eight percent of all practitioners—practiced throughout the nation. The homeopaths were concentrated in the urban states like Massachusetts, New Jersey, and Illinois" (Rothstein 235).

Waldo, coming from a wealthy Boston family, is clearly meant to represent this group of homeopathy's followers. He is more concerned with the method of his treatment than with its actual effects, and his mother seems to care less about whether her son lives or dies and more about the vogue of his treatment. The conversation, entwined in the cultural uncertainty about the nature of the various medical treatments on offer to Gilded Age Americans, is predicated on a not-unreasonable assumption that such remote rural areas would not have a practicing homeopath—the nearest one, Waldo assumes, would be in the city of Bangor. Dr. Zay turns out, of course, to defy this assumption—an unlikely occurrence in rural Maine, especially because homeopaths only constituted 8 percent of all practitioners in the first place. While this links her to the kind of unorthodox medical practice that would eventually lose cultural credibility, it is a tie, not to the kind of folk medicine associated with rural backwaters, but to modern medical fashions (and specialisms) that are predominantly associated with urban practice. In one sense, Dr. Zay unsettles any city-country binary by providing an epistemological bridge between the two.

She has been educated in cities, after all: first by following her father (also a doctor) around the laboratories of Bangor (87), and then in her formal education which took place "[a]t New York, Zürich and Vienna" (74). Her wider scientific interests also signal a particular modern consciousness, as when she discusses the "spontaneous movements of plants" with Waldo: "I have some books that you may like," she says to her patient, "one of Darwin's especially" (103). It is a pointed reference, probably to Darwin's *The Power of Movement in Plants* (1880), published two years before Phelps's novel. While Dr. Zay's homeopathic methods link her more to the urban arena of modern medicine than to any lingering influence of traditional folk medicine, her professional training and awareness of current trends in scientific thought secure her as a figure whose medical authority is derived at least in part from the legitimatizing knowledge economy of urban institutions.

In crucial ways, then, Dr. Zay is a country doctor whose medical legitimacy must be affirmed elsewhere, a figure who resists some aspects of orthodox medicine's march but who nevertheless finds her professional status reliant on modern urban networks. In an effort to balance the "country" aspect of Dr. Zay's position as a "country doctor," Phelps counters this urban-looking tendency with a somewhat romanticized connection between Dr. Zay and the rural locale she inhabits. I return to the generic implications of this in a little while; for now it is enough to cite a passage from the novel where the medical implications of such contrasts are implicitly present. One evening, Dr. Zay's rustic assistant and stableboy Handy observes her through her office door:

> Doctor Zay was sitting by her office table. A half-open drawer showed surgical instruments. Rows of vials exhibited mysteries of white pellets and powders. Medical books lay open underneath her hat and gloves.... But Handy regarded these points with the apathy of familiarity....Doctor Zay, who drove the

fastest horse in Sherman, who always knew by an awful omniscience whether you missed a pailful or shook the oat-measure... was bent and bowed over her office table, her face crushed into her resolute hands, as if she had been stricken down by a power that no man could see. (116–17)

Phelps constructs Dr. Zay as a detached, professional doctor, signposted by the instruments and medical books, who also displays attributes apparently at odds with that status: traditional agricultural know-how and the emotional vulnerabilities of womanhood.[12] This characterization has led some critics to suggest that Phelps effectively posits a synthesis of modern scientific medicine with a sympathetic, nurturing femininity, so that the novel "imagines a spiritualized, deeply compassionate, feminized medical practice" (Baym 185). The novel's cultural operation, in this interpretation, is to offer "an important antidote to the narrow thinking of modern science" by using "the wit of romantic comedy to underscore the unimaginative language of medicine" (Browner 165).

What critical accounts such as these tend to perpetuate, however, is the same binary that the novel itself constructs: an apparent gulf between modern medicine and a more humane, sympathetic impulse. In whatever ways such oppositions may be read as gendered, the novel is just as intent on delineating this contrast as one located in a geographical divide: the urban character of the medical profession, and the "rural virtues" of humane sympathy. In other words, both literary critics and Phelps herself reimport a pastoral sensibility—what Raymond Williams calls a "romantic structure of feeling" (*Country and the City*, 100)—that seeks to temper the assumed impersonality of urban medicine by championing the community-based intimacy of rural life. Such a construction is firmly grounded in a literary tradition—an issue I turn to in a moment—but its application to a late nineteenth-century medical context feels, in the face of the geographically indiscrete flows taking place between urban and rural space, anachronistic and naive. Phelps recognizes that, within the social context of the 1880s, Dr. Zay needs to be part of a fundamentally urban-based knowledge economy if her status as a modern, professional doctor is to be legitimate and believable. Such a recognition, however, undermines the romantic associations and implicit ethical binary of an urban-rural divide. The city is no longer simply the site of a corrupted inversion of organic country life: the two are entwined by their systems of material exchange and increasing cultural simultaneity. The historical moment in which the novel is grounded invalidates its apparent investment in a dehistoricized divide between city and country.

The intersection of geographical and medical issues is further developed in Jewett's *A Country Doctor*. The novel tells the story of Nan Prince, an orphaned girl in the village of Oldfields who is taken under the wing of local physician Dr. John Leslie, and who eventually trains to become a doctor herself. The text's awareness of the geographical dimension of medical knowledge (signaled first and foremost by its title) has been picked up in numerous critical discussions, but often only as a way to implicitly restate the romantic urban-rural associations just mentioned. Marjorie Pryse therefore reads Nan's teacher, Dr. Leslie, as epitomizing "the juxtaposition of the premodern in 'country' and the professional in 'doctor'" (220–21); from this perspective, Nan's choice to also become a country doctor similarly "reflects the intermingling...of country and city, of the premodern and the modern" (228). Stephanie Browner sees the novel in an antimodern light, stating that *A Country Doctor* offers medicine as a cure to the "intellectual mediocrity, spiritual emptiness, and moral vacuity" of modernity, so that it "bridges the opposites that mark Jewett's fictional world—new and old, city and country...the individual and the community" (170). Hypostatizing the terms of their analysis, these accounts also tend to read Jewett's novel uncritically on its own terms.

Considering it instead through the framework established here, we get a clearer understanding of the problematic conjunction of literature, geography, and medicine. In writing a novel about a country doctor that celebrates the legitimacy of rural medical practice, Jewett cannot help but record and acknowledge the source of that legitimacy: the modern expansion of an urban-centered knowledge economy. The contemporary social context of medicine that frames Jewett's narrative, like Phelps's before, disrupts the attempt to imbue Dr. Leslie and Nan with dehistoricized "rural virtues," so that the city's installation as the "essential cultural milieu" of scientific progress prescribes any attempt to represent a country doctor in late nineteenth-century fiction.

This is not to say that *A Country Doctor* does not construct some overt differences between urban and rural life and the ways in which these differences inflect constructions of medical knowledge. On the surface at least, the novel centers its moral compass in the rural way of life it represents; the pastoral setting of Nan's childhood becomes directly indicative of her sympathetic impulse to heal. Elderly village stalwart Mrs. Meeker, for instance, describes Nan's surprisingly mature girlhood activities: "I [saw her] yesterday, and one of the young turkeys had come hoppin' and quawkin' round the doorsteps with its leg broke, and she'd caught it and fixed it off with a splint before you could say Jack Robi'son"

(44). Nan is later described as having an "aptness" (109) for medicine; as a child "she had been nicknamed 'the little doctor'" (109). Passages like these evoke, of course, a standard romantic construction of the intuitive child of nature, and do so in a way that echoes the communal, humane connotations of folk practitioners. The origin of her medical knowledge is therefore implicitly situated, not in the institutional sites of urban scientific medicine (what Foucault calls the "legitimate sources"), but in her subjective rural intuition.

Such an alignment becomes a defining narrative tension. In a conversation between Dr. Leslie and his well-traveled colleague Dr. Ferris, the latter lightheartedly warns Leslie about introducing Nan to too much scientific theory: "You surely aren't going to sacrifice that innocent creature to a theory! I know it's a theory; last time I was here, you could think of nothing but hypnotism or else the action of belladonna in congestion and inflammation of the brain" (71). While Jewett recognizes the tendency for medical theories to quickly become discredited as medical science advances in the period, the pejorative use of "theory" here suggests a certain suspicion toward the apparent growth of orthodox medical knowledge to begin with. Along with the suggestion that Nan's innocence would be "sacrificed" to these theories, the statement posits a romantic desire for the intuitive child untouched by the corruptions of overcivilization. When Dr. Leslie describes Nan sitting and reading one of his old medical dictionaries, a similar point is raised:

> I couldn't help looking over her shoulder as I went by, and she was reading about fevers...as if it were a story-book. I didn't think it was worth while to tell her we understood things better nowadays, and didn't think it best to bleed as much as old Dr. Rush[13] recommended. (72)

Nan's youthful curiosity (not to mention precociousness) brings her to reading material that seems appropriate for a science-minded child, yet the status of that science as modern is nullified by its obsolescence and trivialization as a "story-book." Laying the foundation for a plot that must legitimate and valorize Nan's eventual status as a country doctor, the child is presented as a figure well-read in medical sources and yet preserved as essentially innocent and antimodern by the distancing of those medical sources from contemporary scientific debates.[14] The narrative constructs Nan as "scientific," but also as connected to some innocent essence beyond the impermanence of science. The sense of medicine's uneven and contested progression toward a more scientific basis is therefore something the novel seeks to evade in its efforts to install a simplified contrast between rural and urban knowledge spheres: it irons out the intricacies and complexities of medical authority by constructing a science-sympathy divide that aligns with an urban-rural divide.

Yet the novel cannot finally escape the fact that by the 1880s medical knowledge and medical authority were things profoundly connected to the growing urban world. Jewett attempts, like Phelps, to construct a country doctor who is also a legitimate medical figure, but recognizes that that legitimacy requires an engagement with a knowledge economy that is based beyond the rural setting. Sources of knowledge are therefore city-based, transmitted into rather than emanating from the countryside: a new book Dr. Leslie is reading at one point, "a stout French medical work of high renown" (84), has been sent from New York; trips to Boston are a necessary pleasure because there he can "visit the instrument-makers' shops, and some bookstores," or the "Athenæum library" (102); and when the issue of Nan's medical education arises, he acknowledges that the two of them are "[s]eparated...from the groups of men and women who are responsible for what we call the opinion of society" (121). Even after Dr. Leslie has taken Nan to her medical college in Boston and begins the lonely ride home, he is content that he had "provided himself with some most desirable new books" (130). The "high renown" of that French medical work and the desirability of the books he picked up in Boston point not only to the centrality of the urban arena in the physical exchange of medical material, but the geographical reach of an urban-based system that sanctions modern medical knowledge.

These all suggest the material reasons urban medical practice is the defining site of medical legitimacy, underlining the point made earlier about the city allowing for a "continual exchange of ideas, practices and objects." On a more abstract level, however, the modern scientific medicine of urban practice serves as a metadiscourse underwriting any claims to medical authority; even Dr. Leslie, who seems dedicated to his country practice, had only taken up the post "somewhat unwillingly" and now relies on a network of knowledge exchange that links him to urban medical practice. He studies alone in his quiet country village, but the medical research he performs is only validated by its recognition in the wider medical community: "little by little he gained great repute among his professional brethren" (65), urban colleagues who "thought it a pity" that he should "be burying himself alive" in "provincial life" (65).[15] Jewett suggests that rural-based medical research can also be respected as modern and professional, but the historical circumstances in which she was writing dictated that the status of "modern knowledge" could only be bestowed by the urban-based medical profession.

Dr. Leslie's recognition of urban institutions as an increasingly necessary site of authorization means that he must maintain a dialogue with his urban colleagues to ensure a legitimate career path for Nan: "For her sake he had reached out again toward many acquaintances from whom he had drifted away, and he made many short journeys to Boston or to New York" (127). It is, as well, to an urban medical school that Nan must travel—Wegener suggests that Jewett had Boston's New England Female Medical College in mind (255n)—in order to finally fulfill her "natural" talent: "she must enter the medical school to go through with its course of instruction formally, and receive its authority to practice her profession" (128–29). The point is finally made explicit here: for all of Nan's folksy medical abilities, for all of her romantic characterization, her position within the medical profession is only secured or made tenable by submitting to the authoritative processes of modern, scientific, urban-based medicine.

The connections between literary genre and geo-medical issues are not easy to trace, but there is a crucial element to this argument that brings these strands together and illustrates, not just the historical conditions outlined so far, but also why literary texts offer a distinct way of coming to terms with them. A good way into such a discussion are the descriptions of the Maine countryside found at the beginning of *Doctor Zay*, when Waldo's gentle horse ride is described in particularly heightened literary rhetoric:

> Forest and sea vied to win his fancy.... He became, perforce, a worshipper in Nature's cathedrals.... Galleries of wonder beckon you on.... Sketches which Nature seems to have begun, but never cared to finish, unfold before you, vast, imperfectly interpreted, evanescent. Music, sweet from the now unseen birds in the deserted forest, sad from the waves upon the untrodden beaches, pulsates through the vivid air.... Motionless cattle in the pastures, stray, solitary children on the fences... pass him by rhythmically. (9–11)

The heavily romanticized language of this passage is clearly embroiled in a complex relationship with the position of both the character being narrated and the narrative voice itself: Waldo seems to achieve a sublime oneness with a personified nature, yet the elevated register in which the passage is narrated—the rest of the novel, mercifully, does not keep up this torrent of gush—clearly indicates that such a vision of nature is knowingly exaggerated. There is clearly a geographical element at play here, in that Waldo is implicated as yet another urban tourist who romanticizes the scenery of rural Maine (his comeuppance arrives in the form of a near-fatal riding accident), and in the process the narrative positions itself to imply a default realist standard from which Waldo's position is being judged.

Such generic positioning is hardly unusual for 1882, and certainly not in a novel set in contemporary times representing a modern professional at work—a classic realist subject. As I argued earlier on, the shift to realism and the shift to disinterested medical professionalism share some revealing parallels, but as the opening of *Doctor Zay* vividly suggests, both of these apparently linear narratives of change are far from the whole story. Just as orthodox scientific medicine existed simultaneously (and often antagonistically) with other, competing forms of medical knowledge, so realism was merely the most privileged generic mode among others operating within the fiction of the 1880s.

There is a coming together here, in other words, of the three crucial elements of this argument: the Gilded Age medical context, the geographical element at play in that context, and the intimate connection of these two things to the literary strategies of the works in question. The passage I quoted earlier in which Handy observes Dr. Zay in her office reveals that, at times, all three elements are present at the same moment. The material signifiers of Dr. Zay's modern professional status—the surgical instruments, the anonymous medicines, and the medical textbooks—are described by the omniscient narrator of self-conscious realism. The focal shift to Handy's point of view, however, is a shift to a subjective characterization, narrated in adjective-heavy language, which emphasizes Dr. Zay's rural status: she drives the "fastest horse" in the village, has an experienced knowledge of country customs, and is stripped of her professional veneer by her human vulnerability. The oscillation between sentimental, romantic, and realist idioms is linked to the unsettled medical context that frames the narrative, that in itself is imbued with a geographical element that feeds back into those same generic shifts.

Even the structure of *Doctor Zay* is implicated in these issues. Cynthia Davis points out that from midcentury on there was a growing belief in the need for an "empirical and non-reciprocal" (14) relationship between doctor and patient, reinforcing Paul Starr's point quoted earlier about the increasing social distance between doctor and patient in the period—a problematic context for a story whose plot works in exactly the opposite direction. That realist-medical mastercode, therefore, has to give way as Dr. Zay and Waldo become emotionally closer. The first half of the novel is mainly concerned with Waldo's treatment, and contains the most medically oriented parts of the plot as well as a repeated emphasis on the professional distance between the doctor and her patient. Half way through, however, the tone changes; now we have a fairly standard love story, emptied of most of the medical descriptions that mark the first half and ending in the inevitable union of doctor and former patient in their idyllic village setting. While the novel superficially appears, as Michael Sartisky claims, to adhere to the Howellsian realism of the 1880s (261), the truth is something less straightforward. The "realistic" representation of a country doctor in this historical context entails an acknowledgment of not just an increasingly complex medical profession, but an increasingly complex relationship between medicine and urban-rural interaction; it is that acknowledgment, however, that threatens to undermine the generic stability of the text itself.

In the end, *Doctor Zay* cannot quite reconcile this tension, so that what Nina Baym sees as Dr. Zay's "deeply compassionate...medical practice" is really Phelps's attempt to marry two incommensurate things: the increasingly urban character of medical knowledge, and the romantic associations of a pastoral setting. The novel's interest in literary-historical terms lies in this formal conflict, because deeply embedded in these issues are traces of the ongoing, uneven, and incomplete transitions of modernity itself; it is testimony, in its very failure, that there are no simple narratives to tell of the medical, geographical, and literary transformations of the Gilded Age.

A Country Doctor reveals the same fundamental generic and formal problems. In a much more overt way than Phelps, Jewett evokes a literary pastoralism as a way of linking her principal character, Nan, to a romantic vision of childhood:

> [T]he young girl quickly crossed the rude stile and disappeared among the underbrush, walking bareheaded with the swift steps of a creature whose home was in some such place as this.... [T]he birds which she startled came back to their places directly, as if they had been quick to feel that this was a friend and not an enemy, though disguised in human shape. At last Nan reached the moss-grown fence of the farm and leaped over it, and fairly ran to the river-shore.... [where] the old cedar held its many branches above her and around her. (111)

Nan's innate connection to the rural landscape is emphasized at the same time as that landscape is romanticized: the "rude stile," the personified birds, the "moss-grown fence," and the cedar are quintessential touches of pastoral scene setting. In creating an idyllic rural origin for Nan, Jewett is securing her in a position that will soften her later medical status—attempting, in other words, to imbue the rational scientism of Nan's professional career with the humane connotations of her rural upbringing. The novel nods toward a romantic aesthetic, represented most typically by the figure of an innocent child, while its frames of reference and idiomatic register—the medical context quoted earlier—are invested in a realist one.

Jewett constantly tries to represent Nan as grounded simultaneously in both an idealized, community-oriented rural life and the progressive world of scientific, professional medicine, a meeting (to put it another way) of a literary sensibility with a historically specific medical context. When Dr. Ferris talks of his distaste for "book learning" because it takes "one to more theory and scientific digest rather than to more skill," we are aware once again of the confluence of medical, geographical, and literary spheres that compete within this complex vision: "It is all very well to know how to draw maps when one gets lost on a dark night... but hang me if I wouldn't rather have the instinct of a dog who can go straight home across a bit of strange country" (74). Modern scientific medicine, in Dr. Ferris's characterization, gives rise to a series of new theories and textbooks that all vie for authoritative status. One answer to this confusion is to rely not on the objective bodies of knowledge posited by medical education, but on subjective and intuitive instinct. Dr. Ferris's contrast is, tellingly, between a cartography that seeks to mimetically represent an external, objective reality—the ostensible aim, and the ultimately doomed project, of realism—and the reliance on instinct to navigate through space that is essentially "strange"—a move that gestures at romanticism. The novel replicates on a generic level a point made earlier about its thematic content: it wishes to retain the legitimacy of scientific realism, but also retain some connection to a romanticized nature that insures against the vicissitudes of a modern medical profession.

These novels operate within a particular historical situation: the coming into being of a scientific medical orthodoxy that focuses its legitimating institutions in urban settings, even as the standardizing influence of those institutions extends the notion of "the urban" beyond its physical boundaries. It is this context, I argue, that constricts these novels on both a thematic level—the source of medical legitimacy, and therefore the legitimacy of the characters themselves, lying beyond the idealized connotations of the story's setting—and a generic one: the need for a return to romantic motifs and idioms within narratives striving for realistic representation. It is these problems, however, that register the complexities of Gilded Age medical and literary history in a way that destabilizes simplistic historical narratives.

* * *

As a way of concluding this chapter, I want to briefly discuss the use of medical figures in two final texts: Harold Frederic's *The Damnation of*

Theron Ware (1896) and the less well-known (virtually unknown, in fact) "Horn o' the Moon" (1899) by Alice Brown. These serve as a suitable end point not just because they chronologically cap the period, but because they also foreground the difficulty of ascribing too rigid an end point to that period in the first place. Written at the turn of the century, both texts mobilize medical figures in an explicitly geographical frame, and do so in a way that implicates the various narratives of medical history that precede them. In the difficulties and complexities such figures induce, they allow us to read those texts in a way that undermines simplistic narratives of medical, geographical, and literary history.

In a classic passage in *The Damnation of Theron Ware*, the eponymous protagonist looks down from a hillside at the small New York town of Octavius:

> [A]t one end half-hidden in factory smoke, at the other...an oddly incongruous suggestion of forest odors and the simplicity of the wilderness....Nearer at hand, pastures with grazing cows on the one side of the road...and the racecourse on the other, completed the jumble of primitive rusticity and urban complications characterizing the whole picture. (206)

In one encompassing vision, the uneasy meeting of capitalist development—in the form of the factory—is positioned next to the idealized vision of a rural idyll. The town becomes an archetype of late nineteenth-century geo-social concerns, an awkward melding of "primitive rusticity and urban complications." As Stephanie Foote comments, "[t]he town of Octavius does not merely embody the constitutive tensions of rural and urban; it produces a tension between the 'timelessness' of the pastoral...and the radically future-oriented world of modernity" (*Regional Fictions* 58). Foote sees this contrast as the novel's thematic key, positing the town's intellectuals—Dr. Ledsmar, a medical doctor and scientist, among them—as the agents of modernity that challenge and finally uproot the traditional worldview of Theron Ware. Robert Myers has similarly pointed out that Theron's principal antagonists all act as spokesmen for "some aspect of contemporary thought" (53) that destabilize his beliefs and bring about his final "damnation." These interpretations are, generally speaking, shared by most critics of the novel.[16] While I do not offer any wholesale rereading of Frederic's novel here, my intention is to question the straightforward notion that Dr. Ledsmar embodies one of those aspects of contemporary thought or represents the disruptive presence of a "future-oriented world," by exploring how he actually comes to be an embodiment of the deeply contested and conflicted medical context of the period.

The characterization of Ledsmar certainly points to contemporary trends and general currents within the period's medical field. At one point, Theron asks Ledsmar if "he might not be a doctor of something else other than medicine":

> "Oh, yes, it is medicine," replied Ledsmar. "I am a doctor three or four times over.... In some other respects, though, I should think I am probably less of a doctor than anybody else now living. I haven't practised—that is, regularly—for many years, and I take no interest whatever in keeping abreast of what the profession regards as its progress. I know nothing beyond what was being taught in the 'sixties." (63)

Surprised by Ledsmar's lack of enthusiasm for modern medical developments, Theron says that he "had always supposed that Science was the most engrossing of pursuits" (63), to which Ledsmar dismissively comments, "But that would imply a connection between Science and Medicine!... My dear sir, they are not even on speaking terms" (64). Ledsmar voices an oddly archaic perspective, refuting one of the overarching movements of Gilded Age medicine (its increasingly scientific status) and overtly positioning himself as out of touch with contemporary medical developments.

Shunning the contemporary field of medicine, professional and modernizing, Ledsmar pursues instead the inclusive, experiment-driven science of the amateur gentleman. Yet he is also more aware of contemporary scientific affairs than he claims, and for Theron he represents exactly the modern face of science that is threatening to dismantle his own theological belief system. Theron's initial admiration of Ledsmar as a "scholarly man" with "the most marvellous collection of books" in his house (97) elicits a comment from a local resident that gives us a flavor of the kind of character Ledsmar is: "He is a trifle queer about some things. He lives there all alone, for instance, with only a Chinaman for a servant.... He isn't a practicing physician at all, you know. He is a scientist; he makes experiments with lizards—and things" (97). Ledsmar's own protestations that he is a doctor of medicine who hasn't practiced "for many years" and does not keep up with medical progress is underlined by what the townspeople think of him: not a physician but a rather vague "scientist," and one who conducts his own essentially amateur experiments (on, among other things, the exoticized "Chinaman") outside a laboratory setting.

This uncertainty about Ledsmar's status as a scientist is only exacerbated when Theron pays him a visit at his house on the edge of town. Taking a tour through the house, the two enter a conservatory filled with plants. Theron wonders if Ledsmar is fond of flowers: "They have their points," he said briefly. "My work is to test the probabilities for or against Darwin's theory that hermaphroditism in plants is a late by-product of these earlier forms" (211). Theron sees the flowers as something that may be attractive from a decorative point of view, but for Ledsmar they serve no purpose except the scientific—he "sees nature merely as an object of scientific inquiry" (Myers 59). For a man who has already claimed to be a doctor of medicine, and stressed the division between science and medicine, these resolutely scientific experiments in botany seem further evidence of his attempts at a broad scientific learning. His "amateur gentleman" status feels, anachronistically, to be a hangover from the antebellum period, yet he represents for Theron a voice of rational scientism that speaks from a "future-oriented world."

My larger point here is one that Richard Hofstadter helps to elucidate. Ledsmar appears to be someone who simultaneously harks back to a pre-Jacksonian America when a "patrician elite...moved freely and spoke with enviable authority," and yet is, in quite a radical sense as far as Theron is concerned, modern: "the coming of Darwinism, with its widespread and pervasive influence upon every area of thinking, put orthodox Christianity on the defensive" (121). When Theron first meets the trustees of his new church, for instance, they tell him that "our folks don't take no stock in all that pack o' nonsense about science.... Why, they say some folks are goin' round now preachin' that our grandfathers were all monkeys. That comes from departin' from the ways of our forefathers" (27). Frederic needs a figure whose authoritative utterances on the matter of medicine and science will contribute toward the dismantling of Theron's belief system, so that his depiction of Dr. Ledsmar must refer back to the settled hierarchies of authority associated with an antebellum scientific profession, and yet at the same time immerse his character in a modern scientific world that gnaws at the certainties of religious worldviews.

Ledsmar himself becomes an extension of those same complex mixtures that made up the view of Octavius (a passage that appears in the novel, significantly, when Theron goes to see Ledsmar): the early agrarian republic of patrician authority, and the modern urban-industrial world of scientific development. Even the description of Ledsmar's house invokes a now-vanished agrarian vision: an "old-fashioned" house that "men of leisure and means built for themselves while the early traditions of a sparse and contented homogenous population were still strong in the Republic" (206). A truly modern doctor, Frederic realizes, would be both too associated with urban practice and too unstable in authoritative status. In a sense, this endlessly conflicted and conflicting character, unstable even in his proclamation of apparently stable knowledge systems, embodies less the teleological notion of a "future-oriented world of modernity" and more the vacillating and contested path that medical knowledge trod in the Gilded Age.

That contested path also comes to govern the characterization of Mary Dunbar, Brown's central protagonist in "Horn o' the Moon" (a story from her collection of 1899, *Tiverton Tales*). Set in the remote hills of New England an unspecified number of years ago, the story places Mary into the medical hierarchies of both its own setting as well as the contemporary moment of the anonymous narrator. Mary is the closest the area comes to a doctor—"the good nurse we all go to seek, in our times of trouble" the narrator states (103)—and the plot focuses on her treatment of Johnnie Veasey, a recently returned seaman who becomes paralyzed following a fall. It is the explicit distance the narration sets up between itself and Mary at this moment, however, that brings together many of the strands woven through late nineteenth-century medicine:

> Mary put her patient "to-rights," and set some herb drink on the back of the stove. Presently the little room was filled with the steamy odor of a bitter healing, and she was on the battlefield where she loved to conquer. In spite of her heaven-born instinct, she knew very little about doctors and their ways of cure. Earth secrets were hers, some of them inherited and some guessed at, and luckily she had never been involved in those greater issues to be dealt with only by an exalted science. Later in her life, she was to get acquainted with the young doctor... and hear from him what things were doing in this world. She was to learn that a hospital is not a slaughter house incarnadined with writhing victims, as some of us had thought. She was even to witness the magic of a great surgeon; though that was in her old age, when her attitude toward medicine had become one of humble thankfulness that, in all her daring, she had done no harm. Today, she thought she could set a bone or break up a fever. (117–18)

The historical and geographical narratives of Gilded Age medicine crystallize here in a way that neatly encapsulates the concerns of this chapter. Mary is another of the traditional (and female) purveyors of botanical remedies in a rural village, someone with an "instinct" for medicine, and initially the tone is warmly celebratory of her innate abilities. Those abilities become somewhat quaint, however, when compared with the "greater issues" of "exalted science," and it is here that the historically privileged position of the narrator is asserted over the temporally distant knowledge of the character being described. The attitude Mary held toward hospitals "back then" is made to seem absurdly naive when compared to the epistemological territory that the narrator and, presumably, the implied reader, now occupy. That distance between our own supposedly superior position and the archaic methods of the past govern the representation of Mary by the end of the passage, at which point her "doctoring" is less an instinctual gift and more a potentially dangerous interference. Situating itself in a self-consciously modern moment (the very end of the nineteenth century), the narrative looks back to the beginning of the Gilded Age to project the progress of medical knowledge that has taken place, and grounds that notion of progress in the geographical shift—from folksy rural medicine to the modern surgeons and hospitals of urban life—that accompanies it.

What is clear from Brown's story, as from all the texts discussed in this chapter, is that reading the medical history of the period through the representation of rural space destabilizes unilinear narratives of medical modernization—it points, in other words, to the fact that modernization itself is a unevenly distributed process, both geographically and epistemologically. Read against the broader vectors of geography and modernization that underpin my argument, these texts suggest, yet again, a diachronic approach to an understanding of literary and social history. In the medical issues they embody, and not least in the thematic and generic instabilities they provoke, country doctors stand as significant coordinates in a geography of medical knowledge that helps to map the transformed cultural and spatial relations of Gilded Age America.

CHAPTER 4

A Government of Men and Not of Laws: Lynch Mobs

Bret Harte's "Tennessee's Partner" (1869) revolves around the capture, trial, and execution of a casual laborer called Tennessee who is accused—rightly, the story suggests—of highway robbery. For an event with such grave consequences, however, Tennessee's trial is recounted by a somewhat flippant narrator whose account of proceedings dryly emphasizes the absurdity of its legal pretensions:

> The trial of Tennessee was conducted as fairly as was consistent with a judge and jury who felt themselves to some extent obliged to justify, in their verdict, the previous irregularities of arrest and indictment. The law of Sandy Bar was implacable, but not vengeful. The excitement and personal feeling of the chase were over [*sic*]; with Tennessee safe in their hands they were ready to listen patiently to any defense, which they were already satisfied was insufficient.... Secure in the hypothesis that he ought to be hanged, on general principles, they indulged him with more latitude of defense than his reckless hardihood seemed to ask.... The Judge—who was also his captor—for a moment vaguely regretted that he had not shot him "on sight," that morning, but presently dismissed this human weakness as unworthy of the judicial mind. (51–52)

The evocation of legalese is, of course, laced with a darkly comic irony. The presence of a "judge and jury" seems like a mockery of due process, installed to create the impression of legal fairness where none exists.¹ The fate of the "defendant" is already decided; the assembled jury is "secure" in its belief that he "ought to be hanged"—an execution that in its lack of legal legitimacy is more like a lynching. Furthermore, Harte's use of the word "ought" here implies a whole undercurrent of legal theory (however crudely formulated) that owes more to moral absolutism than it does to a codified and relativistic legal structure. Not that the Judge believes himself to be operating arbitrarily: his regret at not having shot Tennessee straight away is dismissed as a "human weakness" that is incompatible with a "judicial mind," something presumably operating above such mutably subjective standards.

It is important to realize, therefore, that this scene is not simply a comic dramatization of law's absence or a depiction of men existing in some Hobbesian state of nature. The trial is, in the eyes of those conducting it, the very model of judicial process, a sign of their modern, liberal-democratic status. Lawrence Friedman explains that extralegal activity like this, what he calls "lawless law," is better understood as "the action of individuals or groups (or mobs) who seize for themselves the state's role as enforcer of law." "[E]qually important," he goes on to say, "is the idea that it is law that one is taking into one's hands—not vengeance, not whim, not personal opinion, but law" (*Crime and Punishment* 182). Even legal thinkers at the time saw lynching in this curiously ambivalent light; Walter Clark, an associate justice on the supreme bench of North Carolina, stated in the *American Law Review* of 1894 that "the cause of lynching is not a spirit of lawlessness. As a rule the men who participate in it wish to enforce justice" (qtd. in Richard Maxwell Brown 168).

To modern sensibilities, placing lynching within an explicitly legal spectrum seems like a perverse contradiction, but such an approach is crucial if we are to get a properly historicized grasp of the wider legal debates that were ongoing through the late nineteenth century. According to historian Michael Pfeifer, there was on the one hand an understanding of criminal justice (held in the main part, he suggests, in rural and working-class communities) that "sought harsh retribution closely supervised by the community," and on the other hand, urban middle-class reformers who "stressed the role of the state as neutral guarantor of justice, the observance of the forms of law, fairness...[and] decorum" (94). Read in this light, the trial scene in "Tennessee's Partner" can be seen as an attempt to mock "rough-justice advocates" (Pfeifer's term) and their efforts to bestow legitimacy on themselves by adopting and acting out the formalities of due-process law. The narrative weight of the scene lies not in any anarchic absence of what we recognize as law and order, but in the laying bare of the rational logic that can sometimes lie behind collective notions of justice.

Maintaining the structure and approach developed in previous chapters, here I use the act of lynching as a provocative synecdoche for the controversial role of popular justice in the narrative of Gilded Age legal modernization. In a more direct way than any of the other subjects tackled in this book, of course, lynching demands a set of analytical terms that pay due attention to its racialized history; equally, however, it is important that the understanding of lynching being articulated here not be oversimplified into a matter of white-on-black racist violence. As such, I include the vital discussion of African American experiences of lynching within a focus on legal culture as a subject in itself: stories by Charles Chesnutt and Paul Laurence Dunbar sit alongside those by Constance Fenimore Woolson, Eggleston, Garland, and Owen Wister as a way to integrate a racial understanding of lynching into the more familiar set of geographical concerns that animate this book. The existence of lynching in a period that saw radical changes in legal philosophy and criminal justice lead me to read these literary lynchings through the lens of legal modernization and to consider how the narrative "event" of a lynching in rural space serves to lay bare the convergences and contradictions of a multifaceted and sometimes paradoxical legal culture. In short, this chapter explores how rural fiction's foregrounding of geography and popular justice illuminates the fractious development, centralization, and implementation of a modern legal system.

It is particularly noteworthy, for instance, that the description of the lynching scene in "Tennessee's Partner" so explicitly expresses the generic issues—linked, as they are, to the historical and spatial context from which they emerge—that have been part of my ongoing discussion:

> How he met [his death], how cool he was, how he refused to say anything, how perfect were the arrangements of the committee, were all duly reported, with the addition of a warning moral and example to all future evil-doers, in the Red Dog Clarion.... But the beauty of that midsummer morning...the awakened life of the free woods and hills, the joyous renewal and promise of Nature...was not reported, as not being part of the social lesson. And yet, when the weak and foolish deed was done, and a life...had passed out of the misshapen thing that dangled between earth and sky, the birds sang, the flowers bloomed, the sun shone, as cheerily as before. (Harte 54)

The local newspaper reports the events calmly, if approvingly, and with a certain commitment to factual reportage, appending an editorial to the story that celebrates the whole episode as an "example." The narrator, on the other hand, takes a very different line: in by far the story's most sincere moment, standard pastoral signifiers are invoked (the "beauty" of the morning, the life of the woods and hills, the "promise of Nature") to sentimentalize what is, after all, a fairly horrifying scene. The lynching itself is not described, and is commented on in relatively mild terms—it is a "weak and foolish deed," hardly a ringing condemnation—that dilute its moral significance. The perfunctory tone of the newspaper's reportage is contrasted with the romantic rhetoric of the American landscape, each in its own way, an evasion of the reality of lynching itself.

In the light of these narrative strategies, it is significant that advocates and apologists for lynching suggested their actions were "rooted in a rejection of the purportedly lenient and 'sentimental' approach of middle-class reformers, who sought to ... ameliorate the death penalty through humane reforms" (Pfeifer 14). The *New York Times*, for instance, suggested in July 1880 that slow-moving courts promoted a "morbid sentimentality" that could have the effect of investing the accused with "a spurious kind of heroism" (qtd. in Waldrep 91). The idea that the judicial process was sentimental, somehow open to emotional manipulation and therefore not upholding of the strict letter of the law, motivated those who turned to violent expressions of popular justice; anger was considered the proper public response to serious crime. The oblique way in which the lynching is described in "Tennessee's Partner" engages with the unambiguous and verbally straightforward way the newspaper tacitly approves of the lynching, employs an idiom that gestures at disapproval, and yet also hints at the romantic heroism of Tennessee himself—the coolness and silence with which he meets his death. As Tara Penry has suggested, the narrative voice in "Tennessee's Partner" "sometimes sympathizes with, and sometimes disdains, the story's subjects" (148), refusing "to stake out a single position" (160). Such narrative equivocations, unwilling as they are to give narrative license to a particular moral or legal standpoint, begin to suggest the immense difficulty literary representation had in coming to terms with the visceral violence, and cultural implications, of lynching.

Enmeshed in Harte's story, to put it another way, are many of the issues and implications of a changing legal culture, as well as literature's representational and formal response to that change. And it is geography, yet again, that serves to accentuate and symbolize those issues: Harte's habitual location for his fiction was the mining and ranching communities of California, the kind of setting that was not only popularly associated with notions of "frontier justice" but that had become imaginatively connected with the emerging genre of the western. Lynching was not restricted to those locations, of course, just as it was not restricted to the genres of popular mass fiction. In Theodore Dreiser's short story "Nigger Jeff" (1901), key naturalist signatures—the forces of environment and the brutishness of the human animal—come to the fore when an urban journalist is dispatched to cover a lynching in rural Missouri. June Howard argues that the story occupies an important place in Dreiser's development of a naturalist aesthetic (*Form and History* 106), while Jean Lutes has more recently cited the same story as a powerful example of the mutually defining relationship between professional journalism and a masculinized literary realism in the late nineteenth century (468–72). Whatever generic categorizations may be assigned to these works, however, they all share a deep connection between their representation of lynching and a dramatization of the antagonisms between rural and urban life.

My own choice of texts here reflects the fact that lynching actually took place over a much greater geographical spread than the image of "frontier justice" or "Southern racism" suggests; as well as the far West and the South, I also look at texts set in the Midwest and the Northeast. The kind of questions I am asking of these texts, however, remains the same: how does a distinctly modern sense of law and justice, a sense that emerges from and originates in the legal institutions and social sensibilities of urban life, manifest itself in spaces that are physically distant from that life? Lynching as an extralegal act poses a brutal challenge to a modern understanding of the rule of law; how does fiction reflect and make sense of these anxieties and, more importantly, what can lynchings in fiction tell us about Gilded Age legal culture that other types of history cannot?

The history of lynching as a field of study in its own right has grown in prominence in the last few years, and it has, quite rightly, tended to emphasize the racist dimension of the violence: the stark fact is that the overwhelming majority of lynchings were perpetrated on racial and ethnic minorities by mobs of white people. For Jacqueline Goldsby therefore, in her recent study of the cultural responses to lynching, the term is "interchangeable" with "anti-black mob murders" (11), a definition she shares with many recent historians of lynching.[2] Ken Gonzales-Day issues an important corrective to this conflation of lynching to "white racism against blacks" by pointing out that in the west, California specifically, Native Americans, Latinos, and Chinese were also victims (12). However, E. M. Beck and Stewart E. Tolnay's analysis of lynching in the South suggests that "mob violence was not always a racist affair"—two out of ten victims of lynching, they claim, "were killed by mobs of their same color" (149)—while Christopher Waldrep points out that in the 1870s "few of the killings contemporaneously called lynchings involved black people" (85). A common use of the term "lynching," particularly in the immediate post-Civil War years, was simply the "punishment of criminals outside the law," a sense of extralegal activity that did not necessarily involve racial or regional elements (Waldrep 9). It is clear that the history of lynching, and even the word itself, is a highly contentious and sensitive area,[3] and while this chapter can only hope to brush the surface of lynching's well-researched history, it does bring the notion of rural fiction and modernity into direct conversation with the rich body of scholarship that informs and underpins it.

The approach taken here, then, might well see its starting point in Robyn Wiegman's deceptively simple assertion that "[l]ynching is about the law" (81). Her interest is in how categories of race and gender cannot be extracted from an understanding of law in the first place, of course, but as Michael Pfeifer recognizes, discussing lynching through an explicitly legalistic vocabulary runs the risk of suggesting "that lynchers were acting out an understanding of law" and therefore "confer[ring] their actions with legitimacy" (8). He offers instead an account of the social impetus behind lynching that directly ties it to the geographical concerns central to my own understanding:

> Lynching in postbellum America was an aspect of a larger cultural war over the nature of criminal justice waged between rural and working-class supporters of "rough justice" and middle-class due-process advocates. Lynchers failed to assimilate conceptions of an abstract, rational, detached, and antiseptic legal process that urban middle-class reformers wrote into statutes. (2–3)

While Pfeifer does not ascribe a simplistic geographical rationale to the divided attitudes he identifies (the city is a divided and contested space in itself, often along class or ethnic lines), there is an implicit suggestion in his analysis that rural communities tended to be those where "rough justice" held much greater sway than in the middle-class areas of cities. Similarly, in his discussion of the geography of lynching in the Gilded Age South, sociologist W. Fitzhugh Brundage underlines the sense that lynching was predominantly a rural phenomenon (104–5). Such a formulation is quite true, of course, but it can tend to oversimplify lynching history into the old city-country stereotype: rural space as the site of communal, irrational, and traditional notions of law; urban space as the site of modern, rational, progressive legal thinking. The rural narratives examined here, I argue, complicate this binary by revealing how rural space could play host to a particularly contested and violent meeting of differing attitudes toward justice.

**

Morton Horwitz has argued that a strong current in Gilded Age legal thinking was the "tendency to generalize and systematize fields of law that had previously been conceived of as a series of special cases and particular rules" (14).[4] In this sense, law shares some of its modernizing characteristics with the medical context outlined in the previous chapter; both sought to derive their knowledge bases from a scientific and disinterested approach to a core set of data. It is, likewise, a tendency that Pfeifer identifies in middle-class urban reformers who sought to move toward a rationalized system of law, an impulse that itself arose as an attempt to satisfactorily encompass the social diversity of a newly reunified United States. The abstraction and codification of law that took place in order to meet the demands of an "increasingly interdependent and organizational society" (Horwitz 4) clashed with preexisting localized political structures wherein notions of law and justice were differently configured. Brook Thomas brings literary considerations into this broad frame of reference, arguing that nineteenth-century legal change is a particularly "compelling story...about the conflict between the demands of individual freedom and the need of society to be governed by rational, impartial laws" (201), a view shared by Kieran Dolin, who points out that during the nineteenth-century "literary texts repeatedly construct an opposition between individuality and a legal philosophy which stresses the letter at the expense of the spirit of the law" (27). Thomas and Dolin both employ an individual-versus-society model to understand the relationship of law to literature, something fundamentally rooted in a Romantic sensibility and a foundational model in the exceptionalist American mythos.

While this individual-versus-state model of legal process plays an important role in this chapter, equally crucial is the particular historical tension between different *forms* of state, between what might roughly be understood as "populist democracy" and "liberal nationalist democracy" (Esteve 139). A persistent concern in the Gilded Age, primarily among the middle and upper classes, was that a tyranny of the majority might result from the Jacksonian expansion of popular suffrage—a fear that finds voice in some of the pro-lynching tracts from the time. Thomas Dimsdale, in *The Vigilantes of Montana, or Popular Justice in the Rocky Mountains* (1865), sought to acknowledge the positive existence of legal progress while seeing in acts of popular justice an admirable expression of foundational American values: "Let the civil authority...gradually arrogate to itself the exclusive punishment of crime," he said. "That is what is needed, and what every good citizen must desire; but let the Vigilantes...stand ready to back the law....Peace and justice we must have...through the courts, if possible; but...if they fail, the people, the republic that created them, can do their work for them" (267–68). Dimsdale looked to a future where formal institutions would enforce order but located beneath those institutions a spirit of popular sovereignty ready to enact the will of the community if they should fail. Similarly, in *Lynch-Law: An Investigation into the History of Lynching in the United States* (1905), James Cutler claimed that, in a democracy, "[t]he people...make the laws;...To execute a criminal deserving of death is to act merely in their sovereign capacity, temporarily dispensing with their agents, the legal administrators of law. [T]his is the spirit exhibited...toward the law, which seems particularly to pervade the United States" (269). To dispense with the "legal administrators of law" is to dismantle the hierarchies of formalized authority built into bourgeois culture, and the works of Dimsdale and Cutler stand as telling examples of a continuing social unease around political power in the Gilded Age. Such unease is important in the context of this argument because it speaks of fundamental tensions in American legal culture that are, in turn, integral to the status and significance of the act of lynching.

This conception of the general tendencies underlying legal thought and practice should not become an oversimplified model of historical change, however. The period's legal development can be told as the story of the gradual subsuming of individualism to society, popular democracy yielding to liberal democracy, or, in terms legal philosophers would recognize, "natural" law giving way to "positive" law,[5] and this before-and-after conception can also be ascribed its geographical correlative in the form of the rural-urban binary. Although such neat configurations are tempting, and not entirely inaccurate, it is important to recognize that the course of Gilded Age legal culture was never a wholly progressive one. Goldsby's account of lynching provocatively argues that it should be considered not as a throwback to premodern savagery but as congruent with the more general development of late nineteenth-century modernization. By frequently characterizing lynching as a purely Southern and/or purely racist phenomenon, Goldsby suggests, the true extent of its troubling relationship to otherwise "progressive" narratives of modernity have been masked (5). In a similar if more generalized way, Elizabeth Dale posits "an alternative history of criminal justice in the nineteenth-century" that accounts for the fact that rather than the full establishment of a nation-state, America saw weak local governments, unable to "implement the certainty of a rule of law," leading to a criminal justice system that "rested on popular passions and pragmatic practices as much as on legal doctrine" (134). Outside of court-centered histories, these important works contend, one can trace a history of law and justice that unsettles narratives of progress and places extralegal violence at the heart of American modernity.

There is a spatial dimension at the heart of these concepts. Indeed, as Nicholas Blomley states, a major current in histories of legal modernization is the "centralization narrative": "the trajectory of modern legal development ... has been one of a continued disembedding of legal practice and legal knowledge from the locality, and a centralization of legal authority" (107). The late nineteenth-century trajectory is geared to this same shift, the formation of a "unitary legal system" that "begins to moderate and ultimately excise legal differences between places" (Blomley 107). Such narratives would suggest, then, that another tension at work in the processes being traced here is between a legal system that sought to centralize authority and flatten out local variation, and those vestiges of popular justice that still exercized authority in particular geographical locales. In the same way that the previous chapter demonstrated the complex geographical dispersal of medical knowledge in the period, so the centralization of legal institutions and jurisprudential thought also installs urban space as the centrifugal origin of modern law.

* * *

Edward Eggleston's *The Hoosier School-Master*, in its explicit evocation of lynching as a tool of justice, captures much of the complex legal-cultural moment it emerges from—in particular the specter of violence behind the representation of legal proceedings in the novel. The central plotline concerns Ralph Hartsook being falsely accused of committing a robbery, for which he ends up going to court and being tried, and conflicting ideas of justice (however broadly conceived) are a key thematic preoccupation throughout. When the children in Ralph's school play a trick on him by hiding a puppy in his desk, they wait in anticipation for his "outburst of wrath": "For they had come to regard the whole world as divided into two classes, the teacher on the one side representing lawful authority, and the pupils on the other in a state of chronic rebellion" (21). Ralph is established as the representation of "lawful authority" in a place that would otherwise be in a state of "chronic rebellion"; but rather than turning to violence as the mechanism of that authority Ralph chooses to maintain a restrained approach to managing his pupils and simply makes an embarrassing joke at the perpetrator's expense. Ralph's insistence on using his wits, rather than corporal punishment, to control his class meets with a certain amount of skepticism once the village learns of his approach. Pete Jones, for one, complains that the schoolmaster "[d]on't thrash enough. Boys won't larn 'less you thrash 'em.... Lickin' and larnin' goes together. No lickin,' no larnin' " (24).

In a way that serves the novel's main drama later on, Ralph is venerated as a civilized and humane influence to elicit the reader's affection, and in doing so the narrative perspective implicitly sides with a modern understanding of legal punishment that anti-lynching protestors in particular were keen to promote. Rather than enact physical retribution, Ralph becomes representative of the trend that Foucault spends much of *Discipline and Punish* discussing. The reduction in penal severity that takes place over the course of the eighteenth and nineteenth centuries means, in a quantitative sense, "less cruelty, less pain, more kindness, more respect, more 'humanity,'" and for Foucault signals a shift in the objective of punishment itself: "the expiation that once rained down upon the body must be replaced by a punishment that acts in depth on the heart, the thoughts, the will, the inclinations" (16). In the moral simplicity of the novel's early scene, positing rural space as the home of an older, more violent approach to penal justice, a narrative position is assumed that corresponds with a modern, middle-class logic.

It is this implicit stance that underwrites the portrayal, later in the novel, of Ralph as an agent of a modern judicial sensibility. Falsely accused of robbery, and refusing to flee the town despite a mob threatening to tar and feather him, he attempts to circumvent the threat of lynching and "surrender himself to the law," insisting that he undergo a proper trial in the nearby town of Clifty. Not only this, he also refuses legal help and represents himself; he is, compared to the mob rule that surrounds him, literally the spokesman for modern legal processes. It is after the trial and Ralph's acquittal, however, that the novel presents the most overt moment of contrast between Ralph's sense of correct legal procedure and the locals' sense of violent retribution. Dr. Small, leader of the gang that actually committed the robbery, is captured by a mob of townspeople:

> Nothing can be more demoralizing in the long run than lynch law. And yet lynch law often originates in a burst of generous indignation which is not willing to suffer a bold oppressor to escape by means of corrupt and cowardly courts. It is oftener born of fear. Both motives powerfully agitated the people of the region round about Clifty as night drew on after Ralph's acquittal.... I must not detain the reader to tell how the mob rose. Nobody knows how such things come about.... But, at any rate, a rope was twice put around Small's neck during the night, and both times Small was saved only by the nerve and address of Ralph, who had learned how unjust mob law may be. (217–18)

It is a curious passage in the novel, maintaining Ralph as the rational voice fighting "unjust mob law," yet seeing in the expression of popular justice a "burst of generous indignation" that understandably stirs local people when faced with "corrupt and cowardly courts." It still insists that the narrative sympathies lie with Ralph as the modern figure resistant to violent retribution, but will not totally condemn the form of law that Ralph prevents. The novel, in these moments, seems to express a tentative and ambivalent sympathy with the motivations of lynchers who were, according to Michael Pfeifer, "impatient with the inevitable delays of legal process and disdainful of the alleged leniency of legal solutions" (3).

Yet the local people in Clifty have just sat through a trial played out according to all the formal trappings of law that the novel takes three chapters to narrate and that results in cheering crowds in court—hardly an impatient or disdainful reaction to legal solutions. At work in the logic of the plot, then, is the modern judicial mindset I outlined before, yet the events it narrates undermine that logic: it equates rural space with a regressive and violent approach to justice, epitomized by the threat of lynching, yet also makes rural space the arena in which procedural justice prevails. *The Hoosier School-Master* records the simultaneous existence, within the same social and cultural moment, of antagonistic and opposed approaches to criminal justice—and does so because it is a narrative of rural life.

Eggleston allows his episode of popular justice to pass off bloodlessly, but there is no such good fortune for the eponymous protagonist of Constance Fenimore Woolson's "Peter the Parson." Originally published in *Scribner's Monthly* in 1874 and appearing in her first collection of stories *Castle Nowhere: Lake Country Sketches* in 1875, it is set in the far north of Michigan on the shore of Lake Superior and concerns an Anglican minister named Herman Peters (mockingly called Peter the Parson by the locals) who comes to the isolated mining village of Algonquin to recruit members for the church. Ostensibly a story of frustrated love between the minister and a local girl, it is the setting of the story, and the violent events that transpire there, that dominate the plot. Emptied of any semblance of idyllic rural life, the story takes place over a few grey November days in a place seemingly removed from civilized America altogether: "Algonquin remained a lawless mining settlement, whose inhabitants believed in nothing, and whose children hardly knew what Sunday meant, unless it was more whiskey than usual" (Woolson 69). The drama of the story's closing pages revolves around the discovery by the local people that the identity of the thief who has been plaguing the town for months is a popular local preacher, Brother Saul. Dragged to the edge of town by a mob of enraged men, Brother Saul is beaten and is about to burned alive when the Parson intervenes and pleads with the men to stop—only to be struck down dead himself by a piece of iron ore thrown by someone in the the crowd.

It would be fair to describe the tone of the story as rather bleak, but in its depiction of popular justice it offers an interesting comment on the legal culture of its historical context. The most overt engagement with notions of justice comes in the passage where the narrative attempts an explanation for the violent indignation it is about to recount:

> On the border, the greatest crime is robbery. A thief is worse than a murderer; a life does not count so much as life's supplies. It was not for the murderer that the Lynch law was made, but for the thief. For months these Algonquin miners had suffered loss; their goods, their provisions, their clothes, and their precious whiskey had been stolen... [their] fury increased tenfold when, caught at last, he [the thief] proved to be no other than Brother Saul, the one man whom they had trusted.... An honest, bloodthirsty wolf in his own skin was an animal they respected; indeed, they were themselves little better. But a wolf in sheep's clothing was utterly abhorrent to their peculiar sense of honor. (85)

There is some of the same equivocation found in Harte and Eggleston here: at the same time as it offers a justification for lynching, the narrative distances itself from those that would carry it out. We are made to feel, by way of various rhetorical flourishes, the wrong that has been committed against the community and the scale of their "loss" (most of what they own, it seems), and also that they have been victims of a particularly invidious abuse of trust. The sympathy for their misfortune this induces is tempered, however, by dashes of irony (the "precious whiskey") and disapproval (the "peculiar sense of honor"). If these moments complicate our identification with the miners, then we are fully distanced from them when they are reduced to something barely human at all; "little better" than wolves. While the narrative establishes its ethical difference from the would-be lynchers, a difference grounded in a modern disapproval of violent retribution, there remains a faint glow of the righteous indignation that sparks the violence in the first place.

The ambiguity of the language in which the attempted lynching is described offers a sense of the deeper cultural ambiguities surrounding the role of popular justice, but other moments in Woolson's story point to the political implications and challenges that lynching posed. A brief exchange in which the Parson beseeches one of the mob to follow the due processes of law acts as a dramatization of the conflicting attitudes toward legal action:

> "If he is guilty, let him be tried by the legal authorities."
> "We're our own legal 'thorities, Parson."
> "The country will call you to account."
> "The country won't do nothing of the kind. Much the country cares for us poor miners, frozen up here in the woods!" (86)

The exchange condenses a complex series of social and political issues that lie at the heart of Gilded Age law. The contrasting understanding of where legal authority is actually vested—in an abstract, distant body or in the local community itself—implicates a particular political viewpoint. The Parson's insistence that the "country" (meaning here the nation) will supersede localized popular justice places power in centralized, anonymous hands, geographically distant but authoritatively present. The miner's cynical rejection of state intervention, however, refuses to recognize federalized power, and he does so, crucially, because its administrative reach is too weak. The story brings a geographical dimension to the historical tension between a modernizing legal system that sought to consolidate Gilded Age society by formalizing its increasing interdependence, and the fractured, localized systems it was in the process of replacing.

The Parson ventriloquizes, much as Ralph did in *The Hoosier School-Master*, a modern jurisprudential viewpoint that emanates from the judicial and political centers of American life, one that contrasts with the rural, local voice of popular justice. The story's bleakness is, then, significant: while it portrays the mining village and its residents as crude and inhumane, it does not seem to hold the Parson in much higher esteem. His death is so perfunctory that it borders on the dismissive: "A fragment of iron ore struck him on the temple. He fell, and died, his small body lying across the thief, whom he still protected even in death" (89). If he has come to be the voice of judicial order in this remote community, his silencing is unceremonious and his resting place—across, pointedly, the thief—seems like a wry comment on how ineffectual modern law's attempts could be to enforce order in the geographically disparate localities of the nation.

In this way, the story's depiction of a violent mob begins to speak to a much wider understanding of Gilded Age legal culture that did not see lynching as a totally taboo act. As Richard Maxwell Brown points out, even respected members of the "legal illuminati" (145) recognized lynching as an understandable, if regrettable, side effect of a nascent legal system. As much as it offends twenty-first-century morals, many Americans at the time—especially those in remote rural areas—saw lynching as a necessary complement to the law. As Brown notes, "some founders of the state bar associations could...be unashamed participants in lynch law" (146). "Peter the Parson" does not sympathize with or advocate the popular justice of rural communities, but neither does it commend a bureaucratic legal system located in urban America; it is, instead, a narrative whose ambiguity reveals the geographical stratum of a nineteenth-century legal controversy.

* * *

It is to a cluster of texts published around 1900 that the rest of this chapter now turns, partly as a way to explore in greater depth how a racial understanding of lynching became increasingly central as the period drew on, but also to show how rural fiction did not always represent lynching as an exclusively racist affair. Charles Chesnutt's "The Sheriff's Children" (1889) and Paul Laurence Dunbar's "The Tragedy at Three Forks" (1900) bring the racial element of mob justice to the fore, while Hamlin Garland's little-known short story "A Lynching in Mosinee" (1896), and Owen Wister's bestseller *The Virginian* (1902) represent lynching purely as an extralegal mechanism. What they share, however, and what I ultimately emphasize here, is a focus on how lynching is a geographically located phenomenon, one that not only makes transparent the imbrications of law, race, and modernity, but that also corporealizes such issues in the contested and developing space of rural life.

Chesnutt's "The Sheriff's Children" does this most emphatically. The plot of the story (set in 1875) involves the murder of a village resident, the attempt by a gang of local people to lynch the "strange mulatto" (132) accused of the crime, and the efforts of Sheriff Campbell to stop them. The plot twists when it is revealed (much to the Sheriff's surprise) that the accused is actually the Sheriff's own long-lost son, Tom, whom he had fathered with a slave he had owned before the war. Present in the story are several of the recurring themes of Chesnutt's fiction: the personal and cultural legacies of slavery, the employment of a mixed-race character, a depiction of a racist Southern society, and the role of law in the perpetuation of racial discrimination. The aspect I want to focus on initially, however, is how the story strives to emphasize its rural setting. Within just the first few paragraphs, the location is specified as the town of Troy—"a hamlet with a population of four or five hundred"– found in the "sequestered district" of Branson County, North Carolina (131). The town has no railroad connection, so that "a traveler, accustomed to the bustling life of cities, could have ridden through Troy on a summer day... [and] fancied himself in a deserted village" (132). Saturday brings "farmer-folk" to trade, but only in the "two or three local stores" (132). Chesnutt carefully establishes the determinedly rural status of Troy (variably a town, a village, and a hamlet) and does so, crucially I argue, in order to establish the setting of the story as at once distant from modern urban life and yet inextricably tied into it. Wiegman's sense that lynching "operat[es] according to a logic of borders" (81) is important because it lends a spatial metaphor to the social psychology of lynching that very often becomes literal in the rural fiction of the period. In exemplary fashion, "The Sheriff's Children" crosses borders of many kinds—color, legal, generic, and, not least, geographical.

Part of the story's concern is the way in which the act of lynching is situated within a spectrum of legal procedures and, in turn, situated in relation to the sympathies of the narrative. When a group of local men gather to discuss the "meanes' murder ever committed in this caounty," they decide that the "wuthless nigger" does not deserve "ordinary justice": "'Hangin' air too good fer the murderer,' said one; 'he oughter be burnt, stidier bein' hung.'" (133–34). The invocation of lynching as a communal response is isolated from the narrative voice at this moment by the careful rendering of local dialect; the men talk in an exaggerated vernacular, transcribed with that familiar typographical zeal, that is in stark contrast to the pointedly correct and sober prose of the narrator. Such differentiation would have held a certain irony for black or mixed-race writers such as Chesnutt, of course, as Gavin Jones notes: although it seems to be employed here in order to "reinscribe a qualitative hierarchy between standard and nonstandard speech" (Jones 46), such hierarchies more usually involved the relegation of black dialects to comic or ignorant stereotypes. Chesnutt's relationship with the mainstream realism of the time—Howells championed him, but also famously condemned *The Marrow of Tradition* (1901) as a "bitter, bitter" book[6]—means that the use of dialect in "The Sheriff's Children" can be read as a signal for the story's general sense of unstable sympathies. "The assumption of Howellsian realism [was] that dialect was a democratic, energetic, and native means of expression" argues Jones, but it could also be the "humorous sign of cultural degeneration" (51). The collective voice of the lynch mob in the story, rendered in a dialect that stands in sharp distinction to the narrative voice, is both a sign of the narrative's realist intent and an ambiguous method of establishing the reader's sympathetic identification.

While such positioning could imply a condemnation of the men from a more enlightened perspective, placing them as vicious rural hicks against the civilized narrator/reader, the way in which the group is subsequently described further unsettles any simple hierarchy of sympathy. They are first called an "informal gathering" (133), but over the course of the next few pages they are variously referred to as a "crowd" (three times), "the lynchers" (three times), "a committee," "the lynching party" (twice), "a mob" (five times), "the group," "a committee of citizens," and "the party." There is, firstly, the deliberate representation of the group as an unindividuated mass; as Wiegman states, lynch mobs frequently "functioned with a panoptic logic" in the sense that they were the "eyes that watched, [but] that rarely had to offer up their own name" (39–40). A notion of panoptic surveillance pervades many of these rural lynching tales, where the pastoral associations of tight-knit communities and local familiarity is shown to have its grotesque underside—the suspicion and occasional violence toward anyone deemed to belong "outside." From Eggleston and Woolson, through Chesnutt and Dunbar, these lynch mobs are rarely depicted as anything but a homogenized collective bringing justice to bear on individuals powerless to resist their collective will and logic.

What is also striking about the way Chesnutt describes the group is not only how often its collective name changes but also how much the connotations of those names change as well. "Mob" and "lynchers" would seem to continue the implicit narrative reproach already established, but "crowd," "group," and "party" posit something more neutral, even innocuous. In those moments in which the third-person narrator uses "committee" and, especially, "committee of citizens," any disapproving moral posture is relaxed altogether; in the midst of a tale that seems to be dramatizing the plight of a racially marked character, a vocabulary of legitimization is suddenly present. Just as readers are encouraged to safely distance themselves from the actions of the group by the politically inflected notion of a "mob," that same political language is turned back on them in the all-too-genteel sounding idea of a "committee." As Ryan Simmons has noted of Chesnutt's novels, he employs "a narrative approach that virtually never privileges one voice or another" (3), and in the first part of "The Sheriff's Children" that deliberate ambiguity underpins even the most apparently polarizing of actions.

Such ambiguities then become important to how the story constructs its central character, Sheriff Campbell. As an official representative of the law who resists the local lynch mob, in some sense he clearly represents a contrast to the insular rural community he inhabits—both in the way he is connected to the cultural and intellectual currents of national geography and the way his economic status is connected to the sectional geography of the recent past:

> The sheriff of Branson was a man far above the average of the community in wealth, education, and social position. His had been one of the few families in the county that before the war had owned large estates and numerous slaves. He had graduated at the State University at Chapel Hill, and had kept up some acquaintance with current literature and advanced thought. He had traveled some in his youth, and was looked up to in the county as an authority on all subjects connected with the outer world. (136–37)

The story establishes its central character, someone who supposedly represents the voice of due process, in the same oddly ambiguous way that the lynch mob has been described—and it is geographical markers that are used to do it. That sense of the Sheriff's modernity—his education, his "acquaintance" with modern culture, his relatively cosmopolitan background—connect him with an "outer" urban world beyond the rural setting, but this is tempered by those ties to the traditions of a Southern plantocracy.

A status vested in both urban and rural locales, as well as antebellum Southern society and postbellum networks of the "outer world," is underlined by the seemingly contradictory attitudes the Sheriff displays toward the attempted lynching at the heart of the story. A member of the lynch mob implores the Sheriff to hand over the accused, arguing that "we've got to do something to teach the niggers their places, or white people won't be able to live in the county" (139). The Sheriff's response condenses the fraught divide between private, communal, and racial senses of self and the more public, codified, and principled roles of official legal culture: "I'm a white man outside, but in this jail I'm sheriff; and if this nigger's to be hung in this county, I propose to do the hanging" (139). Sheriff Campbell is hardly a paragon of heroism, and Chesnutt explicitly characterizes him as someone governed, or at least influenced, by the same racist logic that governs the lynch mob itself. When the mulatto prisoner snatches the Sheriff's gun and threatens to shoot him, the narrator lays out such logic in stark terms: "He [the Sheriff] had relied on the negro's cowardice and subordination in the presence of an armed white man as a matter of course" (141). Furthermore, the conflicted sense of duty that overcomes Sheriff Campbell following the revelation that the prisoner is actually his son is given a geographical quality at the moment the Sheriff is faced with a choice between freeing his son or adhering to his legal duties: "The sheriff was conscientious; his conscience had merely been warped by his environment" (145). The endemic racism of rural Troy is connected, at this moment, to the strict or "positive" adherence to legal procedure. The narrative suggests that letting the prisoner go is the correct moral choice, but the Sheriff hesitates in making that choice because his "environment" has instilled in him a sense of duty geared to the underlying racist values of the community.

In the end, the Sheriff's daughter shoots, wounds, and subdues the prisoner; he spends the night in the cell, during which the Sheriff further wrestles with his conscience: "It occurred to him... that he might permit his prisoner to escape; but his oath of office, his duty as sheriff, stood in the way of such a course" (147). Any narrative force that this moral dilemma might have is soon dissipated, however, when the Sheriff finds the prisoner the next morning—he has torn off his bandages and bled to death in the night. The tension animating the story's plotline—will the lynching take place, or will the prisoner be set free—is deflated by an ending that allows neither moral indignation nor triumphant escape. The sense, instead, is of a story that finally short circuits any melodramatic expectations.

Stephen Knadler, in a discussion of the generic strategies and status of Chesnutt's fiction, points out that in the 1890s "the color line was reproduced and codified within aesthetic boundaries between realism and (black) melodrama" (430). Often excluded from the pantheon of high realism, black authors who dramatized society's racial tensions were usually labeled as peddlers of "infractious melodrama" (Knadler 430); "The Sheriff's Children" skirts this line quite openly, just as it had complicated its identification with realism in the depiction of the lynch mob. The Sheriff is not the lone heroic figure standing up for law and order against a backward mob of rural residents—the morally polarized archetype of melodrama—but an ambivalent agent of an official legal culture that, for African Americans, does not necessarily represent an avenue to justice. It is significant that it is the mulatto himself who voices the story's central irony: "you saved my life," he tells the Sheriff, "but for how long? When you came in, you said Court would sit next week. When the crowd went away they said I had not long to live. It is merely the choice of two ropes" (142). Chesnutt points to how even an official, "modern" legal system did not guarantee anything like justice to black citizens. Setting up a lawless rural mob against a defender of due process is, in a story attentive to race relations at the end of the nineteenth century, no real contest at all—all outcomes lead to the end of a rope. The mulatto figure potently symbolizes the same ambiguity that the story invests in its legal plot: as Hazel Carby states, the mulatto or "octoroon" figure often acted as "a narrative mechanism of mediation frequently used in a period when social convention dictated and increased a more absolute distance between black and white" (313). Chesnutt's attention to the murkiness of the "color line" in Gilded Age society, and attempts by both official and unofficial legal cultures to overwrite that murkiness with simple hierarchies of racial power, find expression in "The Sheriff's Children" in a way that maps the narrative being traced onto a similarly murky, ambiguous, and contested geographical imagination.

Paul Laurence Dunbar's "The Tragedy at Three Forks" brings together a strikingly similar series of narrative concerns, in many ways acting to prefigure his later and better known story "The Lynching of Jube Benson" (1904). Firstly, just like Chesnutt's village of Troy, the story opens with a pointed reference to the "rural settlement of Three Forks" (171), a location frequently reiterated as events unfold. Those events involve another group of incensed local people, this time hunting down two black men who have been falsely accused of burning a local family's house. As in Chesnutt's story, the white residents of the village operate as an undifferentiated collective and are motivated by viciously racist assumptions; when at first the identity of the arsonists is a mystery, the blame is quickly apportioned: "I tell you that's the work o'niggers, I kin see their hand in it" (172). Even the local newspaper joins in the anger and accusations, blaring "NEGROES! UNDOUBTEDLY THE PERPETRATORS OF THE DEED!" (172).

Unlike the ambiguous narrative identification of "The Sheriff's Children," however, the narrator of "The Tragedy at Three Forks" clearly stands a disapproving distance from the actions of the story's characters: "Notwithstanding the utter falsity of these statements,... soon, excited, inflamed and misguided parties of men and boys were scouring the woods and roads in search of the strange 'niggers'" (172). This distance established, the tone becomes increasingly ironic as the supposedly "legal" procedures take place. The district's prosecuting attorney visits the captured men in jail, calling himself a "friend to niggers," and advises them to confess to the crime. "[H]ow kin we 'fess, when we wasn' nowhahs nigh de place?" one of the men protests; "Now there you go with regular nigger stubbornness," the attorney replies, "didn't I tell you that that was the only way out of this? If you persist in saying you didn't do it, they'll hang you; whereas, if you own, you'll only get a couple of years in the 'pen'" (173). Not quite Chesnutt's choice between two ropes, it is nevertheless similar in its depiction of the dilemmas faced by African Americans in parts of the country where extralegal action could wield as much (if not more) authority than any protection official law might offer. The narrator's biting irony seems especially potent in the face of such decisions: "With marvelous and mysterious rapidity, considering the reticence which a prosecuting attorney who was friendly to the negroes should display, the report got abroad that the negroes had confessed their crime" (173). Within a couple of pages, the accused men have been dragged to the village square, hanged, and with "savage glee" the crowd has "emptied their revolvers into the bodies" (175). It is a brutal scene of collective violence, acted out in a sparsely populated district of Kentucky where the law is either powerless against mob justice or, more troublingly, complicit in its operations.

In *To Wake the Nations*, Eric Sundquist discusses the place of law in Chesnutt's work in a way more generally relevant to the current discussion. The sense of irony that pervades Dunbar's story is something present at the deepest levels of social life for African Americans in the period: the law is "a power theoretically capable of justice but also subject to capricious subversions by racism" (445), Sundquist claims, so that "black lawlessness was a cloak behind which white lawlessness might be hidden" (446). The law becomes the technical guarantor of protection against violence, and yet is the system that codifies and legitimizes racist ideologies. The ambiguities of "The Sheriff's Children" and the savage irony of "The Tragedy at Three Forks" dramatize the complex relationship between marginalized and oppressed sections of society and official legal structures. The modernization of law and jurisprudence in the period is both a vitally necessary project—seeking, as it does, a leveling abstraction of the codes of social behavior—and also the very means by which certain people are hierarchized. The relationship between individuals and processes of modernization is, as Chesnutt and Dunbar remind us, always contingent on whatever categories of identity those individuals happen to inhabit. Rural space plays host to these processes in a way that lays their contradictions bare, being the site where the progressive ideology of American modernity and nationhood[7] breaks down in the face of the very real traumas and inconsistencies inherent in its unfolding. These two stories pointedly use the liminality of rural spaces not only as the realistic setting for tales of lynching, but to more symbolically play host to the contested and often tragic meeting of race and law.

* * *

"A Lynching in Mosinee," published in the New York periodical *The Pocket Magazine* in July 1896, never made it into any of Garland's collections of stories, and as such has been virtually lost to contemporary readers and critics. Set in the small Wisconsin town of Mosinee on the day following a presidential election, the story begins when, during a celebratory street parade, band leader and popular local man Captain Frank Willey is shot dead by a stranger in the crowd. The assassin is soon captured, and the story's main dramatic action comes when the town sheriff, Dan Clark, attempts to stop a huge mob of men entering the prison and seizing the murderer. Despite his best efforts, he fails, and the story ends with him returning that night to the now-deserted scene to see "the swinging shape in the tallest elm, moving fitfully in the soft wind" (140). The narrative parameters are kept fairly simple: the question of racial tension is never raised (all concerned are white), and the motive for the murder itself is left curiously unexplained (a point I return to). Instead, the story captures the ongoing evolution of the period's legal culture, the tension between popular expressions of justice and the demands of due-process law, and the altered geographical relations between local rural communities and centers of institutional reform that ultimately underwrote legal structures.

While the narrative centers on local events in a small prairie town, it works hard to broaden the story's implications by explicitly gesturing at national events and concerns. "The Dimblebats were defeated, the Ripupagins were victorious"; so the story opens, pitching us into a postelection celebration that, if we assume the "Dimblebats" and the "Ripupagins" are Garland's thinly veiled fictional equivalent of the Democrats and the Republicans, actually preempts the result of that year's real-life election.[8] This overtly political opening is used, in part, to emphasize the connection between this area of rural Wisconsin and the wider networks of a modernizing America: the news has come through that the state of New York has gone to the "Ripupagins" and therefore sealed victory for the party. Such a moment explicitly situates the town within a nationalized political network, an acknowledgment of modernity's transformations and incursions that is picked up in more material ways elsewhere in the story. The election news is confirmed because a local man declares that the "New York Herald concedes the victory" (113); we learn that electric lights have "lately been put up" (114) in the town; and a larger-than-normal lynching party is able to gather because "they've telephoned the news all over the county" (126). These small but pointed markers of modernity, as well as the more overt situating of the story within national politics, act to extend the geographical parameters of the narrative and locate it within broader social and cultural flows. Such points are not unusual in Garland's fiction, but within the context of this particular story—and within the context of the wider issues around lynching and legal culture that are being traced here—they prove crucial because they signify the narrative's awareness of geographically distant spheres of influence.

But if modernity is indeed present in Mosinee, it is only in these tangible fragments; in other important ways, the town remains locked in a premodern mindset. The prison is one such example: "a cold clammy place" filled with a "sickening odor," and "worst of all" there is "nothing for the convicts to do" (111–12). "Modern civilization is slow in finding its way into a county jail.... If such prisons were once excusable, they are so no longer" (112). The nineteenth century had seen concerted efforts at prison reform, Zebulon Brockway in particular becoming well-known in the 1870s and 80s for his continued work with the pioneering Elmira Reformatory in Upstate New York. The narrator seems to share these general concerns, making clear his disapproval and establishing a moral distance—once again, ground in an urban middle-class sensibility—from the world represented in the story. The framing of rural life through a perspective that implies an urban logic is made visible by the narrative's contrast between prisons located in different times (traditional and modern) and, by association, different spaces (rural and urban).

The motivation behind the lynching also becomes a way of Garland signposting the distance between the residents of rural Wisconsin and contemporary legal thought. Following the murder, an excited crowd gathers around the culprit and Dan the Sheriff as they make their way to the prison:

> [T]here were several voices crying: "Lynch the cowardly son of a dog!"

"Keep your hands off," said Dan, in a significant tone, as he waited for the door to open. "The law'll look out for this feller. Don't worry."
"The law—yes. Some d—d tricky lawyer'll git him off with ten years, just like the—" The speaker's words were lost in the mutter of assent which rose. (118–19)

Two telling metonyms underpin the fundamental conflict in this dialogue. Dan's warning to "keep your hands off" is both a literal address to the pushing crowds and an echo of the metonymical sense of taking the law into your own hands. The idea of communal sovereignty implied by such a statement is exactly what is then denied in Dan's insistence that "the law" will decide what happens to the prisoner, an assertion of a physically intangible and systematic code of social control against the immediate and instinctual action of the corporeal crowd.

While these two distinctly different approaches to law and order vie for authority, one voice from the crowd expresses the suspicion underlying the mob's motivation in the first place: that the law is "tricky," filled with clauses and circumventions that obstruct the impulse for swift justice. Considering the historical moment in which the story was written, it is possible to surmise what sort of "trickiness" the person in the crowd was referring to (and what his tantalizingly unfinished example might have been.) The murderer himself, in the moments after he has shot Captain Willey, offers some clues: he is described as a "wild-eyed...wretch," and we are told that "foam was on his lips, his teeth were clenched," and yet he remains "perfectly silent" (117). He is clearly not in a particularly stable state of mind.

Madness or insanity are never directly mentioned in the story, but two particular sources that Garland might well have been aware of indicate that it is at least partly being inferred. The first was the assassination in 1881 of President James Garfield by Charles Guiteau, who had pleaded insanity at the trial; although his defense failed to convince the jury (Guiteau hanged in June 1882), it sparked a public debate about the status of mental illness in the judicial system. In the same vein, Michael Pfeifer cites another incident that happened just a few years later and that bears a compelling resemblance to the events of Garland's story:

In October 1884, the *La Crosse Morning Chronicle* argued that the hanging by a mass mob of Nathaniel Mitchell, a riverman with a history of unstable personal behavior who had shot to death Frank Burton, a businessman and political leader, as thousands thronged the streets of La Crosse for an election-night parade, resulted from the deleterious effect of the insanity plea upon criminal justice in Wisconsin. (115)

The parallels are striking. As Pfeifer states, "[a]s a result of the Guiteau trial many Americans, particularly rural ones, became convinced of the dangers of the 'insanity dodge'" (115), and the fear that somehow a distant and detached due-process would not deliver a "just" result for local people was an anxiety that motivated many rural lynch mobs in the period. The same fear, although never directly acknowledged, may well lie at the heart of the lynching in Mosinee. The story's apparently anti-modern action, a lynching in a small Wisconsin town, is at least partly motivated by a thoroughly modern concern: the uncertainties and antagonisms—the insanity plea being once such example[9]—attendant in the modernization of law.

The confrontation between Dan the Sheriff and the lynch mob proves to be the moment where these concerns converge. Dan's anger grows as he holds back "that vast flood of men at arm's length alone" (130), unwaveringly holding to a belief in organized law that means he insists "[t]his man has got to be tried" (129). "He represented law and order" (130) the narrator plainly states, a representation that is both literal and figurative: he represents law and order in the town, and he represents the broader modern sense of law and order with which the narrative implicitly sides. Underlining such sympathies is the depiction of the lynch mob itself. Losing any sense of individuality, the crowd of men become a sinister and amorphous mass: they are a "silent swarm" at first (116), but soon become a "wild clamor of voices" (117), a "restless surge" (120), a "pack" (124), a "flood of human faces" at one point (131), "the beasts of a menagerie" at another (125). Similar to the wolf-like mob in Woolson's story, "pack" behavior sometimes renders the crowd animalistic. Dan resists the mob, resorting to shooting men out of the tree as they lift the prisoner up into the branches to be hanged, but their sheer numbers eventually overwhelm him and he is taken away to safety by friends, reduced to "lashing out like a madman" (139). In the story's concluding paragraphs Dan returns to the scene later that night, finding only the hanged body as evidence of the "monstrous outbreak of savagery" (140). The story's sympathies, embodied in Dan, are clearly geared to a disapproval of mob behavior.

Ultimately, however, the plot will not comply to a kind of crude romantic logic and allow the defiant individual to win—the lawless crowd, in the end, gets its man. One understanding of the story's ending might be that Garland's social realism dictates that the lynch mob triumph in order that the story's political message, an anti-lynching one, be given some tragic impetus. Bearing in mind the particularly uncertain place popular justice had in Gilded Age society, however (especially in the rural districts depicted in the story), a more ambiguous reasoning might be detected. Examining newspaper accounts of lynchings from the time, Christopher Waldrep notes that reports of defiant sheriffs could actually confirm a somewhat different understanding of events. "Heroic and determined sheriffs and jailers unable to resist lynch mobs better proved the power of popular sovereignty" Waldrep points out, so that "[i]n the face of enraged citizens, officers seemed so overwhelmed, so often, that stories of their brave but futile resistance seemed further evidence that the people could not be thwarted" (94). The very fact that huge crowds of people were involved, the newspapers seemed to suggest, confirmed that the understanding of lynching displayed by Dimsdale and Cutler was at work within the general populace. Such displays of popular sovereignty transformed the rural villages in which they took place into arenas for the expression of collective will: "In 1872, newspapers reported that three thousand showed up for a lynching in little Celina, Ohio, which had a population of less than nine hundred" (Waldrep 95). The crowd that gathers in Mosinee, likewise, at one point "number[s in the] thousands" (129). As Waldrep goes on to comment, newspaper accounts "incorporated the idea of lynching as [a] spectacular display of popular sovereignty" (95), and such notions were undoubtedly still present in public discourse when Garland came to write his story.

"A Lynching in Mosinee" therefore serves as a record for the antagonistic layers of legal understanding that define the Gilded Age, a narrative that secures its footing in a modern viewpoint of centralized due-process only to represent an incident that itself carries an opposed cultural logic. It attempts to narrate, and in the process give some semblance of coherence to, the simultaneous existence of competing and contradictory ideologies of criminal justice. It is the very fact that the story represents *rural* space—the site where those competing approaches most visibly collide, where residual social practices resist emerging ones most tenaciously—that means it testifies to what Elizabeth Dale called an "alternative history" of nineteenth-century legal change.

This convergence of legal history and literature appears, perhaps most explicitly of all, in a novel that serves as my chronological bookend. Set among the dusty towns and cattle ranches of Wyoming and Idaho in the 1870s and 1880s, Owen Wister's *The Virginian* contains one of the best-known representations of lynching in American literature. Questions of justice and law dominate much of the action, played out in set pieces and vignettes that seem to describe a morally stark world where the status of popular justice is never in doubt. Richard Etulain therefore reads the figure of the Virginian against a polarized conception of law: "although depicted as a law-abiding man who upholds society's institutions, the hero, when necessity arises, can move outside the law" (70). A closer look at the novel's depiction of lynching helps to develop an understanding of the geography of justice in a way that moves beyond fixed ideas of "lawful" and "lawless" and instead grasps the deeply ambivalent notion of law in the period. Through its apparently stereotyped and morally transparent depiction of ranch life and society, *The Virginian* reveals an unsettled generic, thematic, and spatial logic that ultimately speaks of the paradoxes in legal modernization.

A moment where justice appears to be a fairly straightforward concept, for instance, comes after the rancher Balaam has mercilessly worked and then brutally tortured a horse called Pedro. Here the narrative shifts into high sentimentalism, replete with classic generic signatures. There is firstly the maltreatment of a "child"—Pedro is a mere "pony" (196)—whom Balaam "struck...fearfully" until the horse slumped "motionless, his head rolling flat on the earth" (202), while underlining this are suggestions of anthropomorphism: "He played he was tired" Balaam says by way of an excuse, "[h]e played out on me on purpose" (202). Giving the horse these mischievous and childlike qualities induces not just readerly sympathy, but pathos. Establishing this polarized moral universe, if only for a moment, is essential to what the eponymous hero does next: "vengeance like a blast struck Balaam. The Virginian hurled him to the ground, lifted and hurled him again, lifted him and beat his face and struck his jaw....[Balaam] fended his eyes as best he could against these sledgehammer blows of justice" (203). "Justice" here is swift and violent, but justifiable, even commendable, within the generic logic the narrative has set up.[10]

While it appears a simple case of the Virginian's righteous defense of an animal designed to endear him to discerning readers, such a scene in fact reverberates with specific contemporary attitudes to legal reform. The use of a sentimental register when describing Balaam's cruelty toward the horse connects with a growing public sentiment around animals and their treatment in the late nineteenth century, a debate given much impetus by the founding in 1866 of the American Society for the Prevention of Cruelty to Animals. Led by Henry Bergh and initially located in New York City, the Society directed most of its early efforts toward the treatment of horses and found much sympathy among middle-class urbanites; by 1888 other humane societies had appeared in Boston, San Francisco, and Buffalo. In a more generalized sense, as well, the place of animals in society underwent a significant transformation in the nineteenth century. John Berger, in "Why Look at Animals?" points out that the onset of industrialized modernity detaches humans from animals in a way that allows their cultural marginalization (2–3). As animals, and especially horses, are replaced by mechanized tools, our relationship to them can become increasingly sentimental. The Virginian's reaction is therefore understandable according to the sentimental codes that underwrite the action, codes that arise in centers of modern opinion far removed from the setting of the story itself. From this perspective, this scene in *The Virginian* can be read as incorporating a modern, even middle-class and urban-industrial viewpoint, into the enactment of violent justice.

But while sentimentalism does indeed structure the scene leading up to Balaam's beating, something else takes over immediately afterward. Pedro is not quite as badly hurt as we first feared: "[h]e was a young horse, and the exhaustion neither of anguish nor of over-riding was enough to affect him long or seriously"—it is "plain...that he would be a very good horse again" (204). Our sympathy for the horse loosened, the Virginian's mind turns back to the job at hand—walking the horses to a place of work—and finally strips Pedro of any last vestiges of anthropomorphic sentiment: "I'm goin' to trail them hawsses. If you're [Balaam] not comin' with me, your hawss comes with me, and you'll take fifty dollars for him" (204). An economic realism takes over (grounded in a world of premechanized labor) in the reaffirmation of the horse's status as a commodity. It shifts the narrative point of view back to the ranches of Wyoming, where cruelty to animals must be punished not because it offends middle-class tendencies but because an injured horse has less market value. Taken as a whole, the scene constructs through a shift of generic perspectives a sense of justice that is validated both from an urban middle-class viewpoint and a western, rural one.

This incident is important because it outlines the conceptual frame, both in thematic and generic terms, through which the later lynching scene can be understood. The narrative of Gilded Age legal history as a clash of opposed values that also have their geographical correlatives—between what Michael Pfeifer calls "a rural cultural perspective" and the "legal reforms promoted by a rising middle-class in...towns and cities" (29)—is something that the texts examined in this chapter, and especially *The Virginian*, both confirm and unsettle. By representing a site where a "rural cultural perspective" would apparently hold sway, scenes like the one just described are implicated in the affirmation of that perspective even as their strategies of representation sometimes insinuate a different one.

Important to understanding how *The Virginian* mediates between these various positions is the construction of the narrator himself, and more specifically the place of, and his role in, the lynching. Remaining anonymous throughout, when he first arrives in the dusty Wyoming town that serves as the novel's main setting, he immediately announces his Eastern, urban mindset when he warily realizes that he "had stepped into a world new to me indeed" (19)—a world so new and alien, in fact, that he asks himself, "Does this same planet hold Fifth Avenue?" (37). A certain amount of urban naiveté accompanies his early experiences of the ranch lands of Wyoming, and he pines for "the railway, and cities, and affairs" (245).

This overtly modern character is challenged, however, when he is beckoned by an enigmatic letter from the Virginian telling him that he needs to "attend to certain matters in the Wind River country" (246). It is here, far beyond the reaches of civilization—even cartographers: it is in "unmapped spaces" (246)—that the narrator begins to shed his attachment to modern comforts and comply to the different configuration of life the West requires: "to leave behind all noise and mechanisms…made me feel that the ancient earth was indeed my mother and that I had found her again after being lost among houses, customs, and restraints" (246). The mention of "customs and restraints" seems deliberate, placing his awakening feeling of primal freedom not just in the absence of modernity's ubiquitous trappings ("noise" and "houses") but in the structures of social control themselves. Such a feeling speaks not just of the law, but of law's geography: "Jurisdiction marks the domain within which one set of legal authorities can be said to exercize legitimate authority. At the same time, jurisdiction delineates the boundaries beyond which some other law holds sway" (Sarat et al. 2). The narrative places the narrator in a geographically distant space to position him, and the incidents that are about to occur, beyond the jurisdiction of centralized and federalized law.

This suggestion of law's loosening hold proves crucial to what the narrator then experiences. Arriving to find a desolate cluster of stables and tents, the true meaning of the Virginian's business becomes horribly clear:

> Two men sat there together, and a third guarded them. At that sight I knew suddenly what I had stumbled upon; and on the impulse I murmured to the Virginian:—
> "You're hanging them to-morrow."
> He kept his silence.
> "You may have three guesses," said a man behind me.
> But I did not need them. (248)

The captured men are cattle thieves, and in the morning they will be taken out to the cottonwood trees a short ride away and hanged for their crimes. To make matters even more somber, one of the condemned is Steve, a good friend of the Virginian's. Unlike the excited crowds at the lynchings (or near lynchings) in other the texts discussed in this chapter, *The Virginian* depicts lynching as an intimate affair that is less a spontaneous expression of public anger and more a sober, dutiful enactment of law enforcement.

It initially falls to the narrator, in fact, to become the one emotionally affected by the events taking place. As the men wait overnight, he becomes increasingly anxious about what the others are preparing to do: "How could I tell them that I shrunk from any contact with what they were doing, although I knew that only so could justice be dealt in this country?" (250). The absence of "restraints" that he had recognized earlier now becomes a source of his deep uneasiness, his own rejection of lynching a stamp of his difference (his continuing urbanity) from the moral and legal domain he finds himself in. The condemned men clearly inhabit this domain, as over breakfast the next morning "they spoke in a friendly, ordinary way." "They were more at ease now than I was" (252) the narrator states. The lynching's offense to modern moral sensibilities only affects the narrator because he is the only one who shares those sensibilities; he remains an Eastern urbanite at heart, still within the psychological and moral jurisdiction of a social order that utterly condemns lynching as an illegal and immoral act. This embodiment of a modern viewpoint leads to the narrator identifying with the condemned men: a suggestion by one of the lynchers that a prisoner drink some coffee "made it seem like my own execution. My whole body turned cold in company with the prisoner's" (254). Emphasizing his compassionate identification with others, the narrator resembles a classically sentimental figure amid the coldly rational undertaking of the lynching. At work in this particular passage, therefore, is a dual narrative strategy: it represents the Wyoming ranch lands as a world where the jurisdiction of formalized law has yet to take hold and where lynching is the only option, yet it mediates such views through the prism of a first-person narrator who retains a disapproving emotionalism anchored in modern, middle-class moral standards.

This divided stance is reiterated in the representation of the lynching itself—or, rather, in its very lack of representation. The narrator lies in bed as the men ride away to perform the deed, "and next their hoofs grew distant, until all was silence round the stable except the dull, even falling of the rain" (254). The chapter ends at this point, a narrative ellipsis that picks up again at the beginning of the next chapter, post-lynching, with the Virginian returning to the camp. The dramatic crux of this whole section of the novel is elided—just as nearly all of the texts discussed here employ lynching as the absent center of their plots. One explanation for these curious lacunae might be found in Foucault's claim that punishment itself, in the modern era, becomes "the most hidden part of the penal process" (*Discipline and Punish* 9). A chief marker of modern criminal justice is the unspectacular nature of its punishment, the increasing invisibility of justice's outcome: "[T]he publicity has shifted to the trial, and to the sentence; the execution itself is like an additional shame that justice is ashamed to impose on the condemned man; so it keeps its distance from the act, tending always to entrust it to others, under the seal of secrecy." There is a fundamental schism, Foucault argues, between the bureaucratic mechanisms of justice and the punishments those mechanisms dispense: "[J]ustice is relieved of responsibility for it [punishment] by a bureaucratic concealment of the penalty itself" (*Discipline and Punish* 9–10). The "bureaucratic concealment" of punishment was an ongoing process in America during the Gilded Age: New York, New Jersey, and Massachusetts had outlawed public executions in 1835, but it was not until 1888 that New York passed the Electrical Execution Act, "whereby condemned criminals would be electrocuted behind prison walls." Further west, Ohio in 1885 and Indiana, Colorado, and Minnesota in 1889 passed legislation requiring executions to be "enclosed from public view" (Bessler 114).

The difficulty that these works seem to have in describing lynching may be seen as another indication of a modern logic operating behind their representational strategies. In the case of *The Virginian*, Owen Wister's status as a trained lawyer (he graduated from Harvard Law School in 1889) only adds biographical weight to the assertion that traces of contemporary legal thought linger beneath the novel's surface. While the novel implicates lynching as a necessary expression of pseudo-legal enforcement, it "encloses" it from a sensation-seeking public view both by framing it within a sentimental discourse and by denying us the act itself. The bureaucracy that Foucault suggests relieves justice from the "shame" of punishing, and that Wister would have had firsthand experience of, is not something available to the Virginian, or to the ranch lands of Wyoming as a whole. The shame-inducing and onerous task of doing the punishing falls to the actual adjudicators of justice: the Virginian and his friends.

While the lynching is therefore conveyed to the reader in a way that secures the narrative within a modern legal framework, those that carry it out are not simply cast as immoral transgressors operating outside those same moral and social codes. After the event, in a soul-searching conversation with the narrator as they ride away from the scene, the Virginian describes his friend Steve's last moments: "'No play-acting nor last words. He just told good-by to the boys as we led his horse under the limb—you needn't look so dainty,' he broke off. 'You ain't going to get any more shocking particulars'" (258). And we don't. The Virginian refuses to describe the punishment, his account enclosing the execution from public—or from the narrator's, which is also the reader's—view. "Staring ain't courage; it's trashy curiosity" (258) he says, an admonishment to those that turn what he sees as a regrettable but necessary act into a spectacle for public consumption. Furthermore, the Virginian expresses a level of emotional attachment toward his executed friend Steve that, despite the narrator's attempts to assuage his guilt, induces deep regret:

> [L]ogic was useless; he had lost his bearings in a fog of sentiment. He knew, knew passionately, that he had done right; but the silence of his old friend to him through those last hours left a sting....
>
> He gave a sob. It was the first I had ever heard from him, and before I knew what I was doing I had reined my horse up to his and put my arm around his shoulders. I had no sooner touched him than he was utterly overcome. "I knew Steve awful well," he said. (260)

The Virginian's tears are testament to his shame at punishing, but they also testify to the absence of "logic": they are evidence of not only the emergence of progressive attitudes to punishment, of a modern social and moral code that increasingly abhors physical retribution, but also the dangers of the "sentiment" that such attitudes and codes induce. The Virginian, seemingly the embodiment of a form of law that modern sensibilities decry as inexcusable, will not finally adhere to this stereotype and unashamedly perpetrate a lynching. The narrative attempts the problematic task of sympathizing with lynching as a pragmatic expression of popular justice while conveying that sympathy through narrative techniques connoting a disapproving due-process viewpoint. It represents a space where lynching is apparently justified because it is geographically distant from centers of formal law, but it frames that representation within the parameters that formal law promotes.

Through the representation of a specific "legal" practice—and, importantly, a geographical space—*The Virginian* exemplifies the wider point I have been making in this chapter. Lynching, as a distinct and provocative act represented in rural narratives, serves as a synecdoche for the modernizing criminal justice system in Gilded Age America. Its presence may suggest an antimodern approach to law that shuns due process and promotes a kind of lawless popular sovereignty, but through the literary strategies employed to represent it, it becomes a central indicator of the debates and tensions circulating around the period's legal change. Lynching as an occurrence in rural narratives, read in the terms outlined here, encapsulates the ongoing and unresolved mediation between competing and contradictory social positions on law and justice. What is more, lynching forces us to place geography at the center of such considerations by shifting the scene of legal transformation from the legal institutions of urban centers to the rural landscapes of mining, ranching and farming communities. It is an act that suggests not just a diachronic approach to

Gilded Age legal history, but an approach that reinstates rural space into a consideration of modernization.

Toward the end of *The Virginian*, these issues are given voice in a long dialogue between Judge Henry (the Virginian's ranch-owning boss) and Molly (the Virginian's wife to be). Molly is unconvinced by Judge Henry's justifications for lynching at first, but he makes a dubious appeal to Molly to consider the act within its particular context: "We do not torture our criminals when we lynch them. We do not invite spectators to enjoy their death agony. We put no such hideous disgrace upon the United States. We execute our criminals by the swiftest means, and in the quietest way" (283). Judge Henry, appealing to both Molly and the reader, seeks justification for lynching by aligning it with the legal practices of a modernizing, liberal democracy: the amelioration and privacy of the death penalty. Almost in the same breath, however, he appeals to a rather different sentiment—the spirit of popular democratic sovereignty:

> "[The courts] are the hands into which ordinary citizens have put the law.
> ... [W]hen they lynch they only take back what they once gave.... We are in a very bad way, and we are trying to make that way a little better until civilization can reach us. At present we lie beyond its pale.
> ... [F]ar from being a *defiance* of the law, it is an *assertion* of it—the fundamental assertion of self-governing men." (284, emphasis in original)

Here, laid bare in Wister's narrative, are the contradictions that animate the processes of legal modernization through the final decades of the nineteenth century. There is no clear cultural demarcation between due-process and popular justice advocates: as Margaret Vandiver has argued, "proponents of each viewpoint were aware of and sometimes responded to the claims of the other, leading to situations in which the two forms of lethal punishment influenced and imitated each other" (91). In Judge Henry's speech, lynching is first justified on the grounds that it resembles modern forms of punishment, an oddly circuitous argument when it is an initial dissatisfaction with those modern forms of punishment that lead lynchers to bypass them in the first place. Judge Henry seems to regret that lynching must happen, but he champions it as a supreme example of American republican spirit—it is, at once, an interim measure before law can be established and an assertion of law itself. *The Virginian* records, not only in overt moments like Judge Henry's speech but also in traces buried deep in the grain of the narrative, the simultaneous existence of views that were fundamentally opposed and yet drew on the terminology of their opponent.

It is important to think of lynching in regional terms, and it did certainly have its own regional variations, but as historians have claimed—and as the works of fiction examined here have suggested—lynching as a form of popular justice in the late nineteenth century finally transcends regional boundaries and speaks of the ambivalent relationship between localities, regions, and a nation-state still in the process of formation. Through representations of rural life, these fictions attest to what Dale called an "alternative history" of criminal justice: they foreground the relationships of power and authority between centers of legal administration and the scattered, disparate communities of Gilded Age America, and in doing so shift the focal scene of legal history. They do not affirm any clear trajectory of legal modernization and centralization but, through their overt thematic concerns and formal strategies and inconsistencies, illuminate a process of change that is not just socially contested, but culturally traumatic as well.

CHAPTER 5

Landscapes of the Future: Utopias

Across the markedly different topics of the preceding four chapters, the central concern has remained the same: how the attendant cultural and social transformations of urban-industrial modernization in Gilded Age America manifested and embedded themselves in rural fiction. Those four distinct topics have continually coalesced around a concept of modernity that insists on its geographical indiscretion: that modernity can be read in places and spaces that do not immediately present themselves as modern. The intention has been to illustrate how literary representations of rural space—simply, space that is geographically distant and topographically distinct from the urban—can reveal the intricate, contested, and unfolding sense of modernization that marks the era. These chapters have shown that, thematically and generically, rural fiction encodes the social and cultural impact of urbanism, and that the critical neglect of rural fiction as a site of literary-historical investigation has led to an oversimplified conflation of modernity with urban space.

This final chapter, while reinforcing and consolidating the book's overarching argument, takes a somewhat different tack. Rather than identifying a paradigmatic event or figure and then treating it as a synecdoche for a broader theme, it considers in more general terms the conjunction of urban modernity and rural representation in a particular literary genre—namely, utopian fiction.[1] Its aim is to condense and draw together the underlying themes and concerns of the book, and to do this by examining how these depictions of the future reveal the imaginative place of rural life in their own late nineteenth-century context. Through readings of selected utopian novels, all published between 1888 and 1898, I will first show how this hugely popular and prolific genre provides a unique way of grasping the relationship between the spheres of urban and rural life, and how its attempts to imagine the landscapes of the future provides access to the geographical imagination of its own historical moment. Finally, I point to how these works not only reimagine the geographies of the late nineteenth century, but in fact anticipate the efforts to redesign the geographies of the twentieth.

Nineteenth-century utopian fictions were nothing if not abundant. Susan Mizruchi claims that from the late 1880s through the turn of the century, over 150 utopian novels were published, while Jean Pfaelzer lists 183 separate works of fiction published between 1886 and 1896 in her bibliography of utopian writing. As Mizruchi states, it is "a figure unequaled in any other country or historical period" (256). While not all these works enjoyed critical or commercial success, a significant number proved to be highly popular and influential. Edward Bellamy's *Looking Backward* (1888), the novel that sparked the utopian fiction phenomenon in the first place and still the most widely-read example, is frequently mentioned alongside Harriet Beecher Stowe's *Uncle Tom's Cabin* (1852) and Lew Wallace's *Ben-Hur* (1880) as one of the great bestsellers of the nineteenth century. While not all these works are relevant to my argument here, some of the titles of the novels in question give a good initial indication of the kind of geographical and spatial concerns that lie at the heart of my analysis. Joaquin Miller's *The Building of the City Beautiful* (1893), William Bishop's *The Garden of Eden, USA* (1895), and Henry Olerich's *A Cityless and Countryless World* (1893) immediately announce that their visions of the future involve some kind of geographical imaginary that differs from their own contemporary United States.

Here I focus on how these works imagine and represent the planned, architectural landscapes of their utopias, but it should become clear that these landscapes are inevitably indicative of much more abstract concerns. In part, these concerns are what Lefebvre called the "invisible relations" of space: the flows of capital and culture between city and country. In their representations of urban and rural space—categories which, in these utopias, are consciously interrogated and blurred—these works disclose the changing nature of these flows in a more self-conscious way than do the texts examined in previous chapters. The readings of these novels therefore proceed from an assertion that, in representing the future, they unavoidably foreground the context of their own production. Thomas Peyser makes the same point when he says that "any utopian vision is bound to be infected by its unacknowledged affiliations with the culture it pretends to overthrow" (11), while Fredric Jameson refers to the historicity of utopian fictions—their inevitable reliance on topical allusions and recognizable frames of reference—as their "referential subtext" ("Of Islands and Trenches" 85).

Building on this idea, the chapter examines how the referential subtext of these fictions consists of not only the social and cultural reality in which they operate, but also the generic strategies they use as works of narrative fiction in their own right—the relationship between their representations of urban and rural space, and the literary modes they employ to do it. In the end, utopian fiction emerges as an unstable literary genre profoundly concerned with the rapidly changing geography of late nineteenth-century America, one that brings rural space into the center of considerations of modernity.

* * *

One of the key contexts from which utopian fiction emerged is also a key context in terms of the historical conditions surrounding rural life in the fin-de-siècle period: the particularly fraught economic situation of the time that led to agrarian political unrest. The hugely influential land tax theory Henry George proposed in *Progress and Poverty* (1879), the Haymarket Affair of 1886, the passage of acts prohibiting Chinese immigration, and the stock market crash of 1893 influenced the rise of a political movement that placed the conditions of rural life on the national stage. The People's Party (known more commonly as the Populist Party) gained considerable support, especially in the agrarian regions of the South and Midwest, by campaigning against the deflation in agricultural prices—exacerbated, it argued, by the adoption of the gold standard—and the monopolistic practices of railroad companies, as well as by advocating the abolition of national banks.[2] The tumultuous political scene of the time, with its incendiary racial and class antagonisms and its foregrounding of an economically blighted agricultural community, forms one of the essential lenses through which utopian fiction must be read.

This seems especially true when we consider the work of novelist and Populist Party candidate Ignatius Donnelly,[3] who in 1890 published his tale of a dystopian American future, *Caesar's Column*. Set in New York City in 1988, the story is told primarily through a series of letters sent by Gabriel Weltstein to his brother back home in a Swiss sheep-farming colony in Uganda. Brought to the city by economic necessity (it is the home of a wool cartel), Gabriel becomes embroiled in a shadowy proletarian uprising called the Brotherhood of Destruction. Led by Caesar Lomellini, a farmer ruined by the same urban financial monopolies that control the Weltstein's trade, the group plots and eventually succeeds in overthrowing the governing Jewish-Italian plutocracy. Gabriel, witness to the brutality of the revolution when it comes—Caesar's column is in fact a pile of executed corpses set in concrete that rises out of the dust of the city's destruction—eventually flees by airship as America slides into an anarchic civil war and, with his new-found love Estella Washington, heads back to his home in Uganda. Perhaps because of its bizarre mixture of savage social critique, anti-Semitic paranoia, and blood-soaked melodrama, the novel proved a huge popular success, selling over a quarter million copies (Saxton 227).

Most of the action takes place in New York City; it is the utopian community that Gabriel travels from and returns to, however, that proves more critically interesting here. Indeed, the novel opens not with a description of the metropolis, but with a vision of the rural idyll back in Uganda that is clearly inserted to contrast with the urban terrors that are about to unfold. Gabriel's letter is partly a reminiscence of home: "I turn back to the old homestead, amid the high mountain valleys of Africa; to the primitive, simple shepherd-life.... I see the leaning hills, the trickling streams, the deep gorges where our woolly thousands graze" (9). The primitive shepherd-life is quintessential pastoralism, of course, while the "old homestead" has a similarly idyllic ring to it. After Gabriel has excitedly recounted the newfound wonders of New York, the novel embarks on its city-based action, only to return to the Ugandan community, post-revolution, at the conclusion. This circular narrative structure would seem to underline Donnelly's Populism by venerating the farming community, home to the novel's hero and the utopia to which he returns, and bemoaning the economic and social dystopia of the city.

This apparent return to a pastoral haven is something Mizruchi sees in explicitly regressive and conservative terms, the Weltsteins's colony being "safe from 'the dark and terrible throngs' of urban America," a return to a "rural retreat" that "endorses an agrarian democratic ideal against a modern pluralism" (277). Jean Pfaelzer makes a similar argument but states it in terms that emphasize the implicit historical circularity of the novel's geographical arrangement: "the frame of the golden age, the pastoral references at the beginning and the end of the novel, anticipates Donnelly's chiliastic view of time and reinforces the Populist identification of the countryside with the idealized past and future, and the city with the flawed present" (123). It is certainly true that the utopian mountain community is described in isolationist and racially homogenous terms, and that the novel's final chapter provides a model for a future society that explicitly contrasts itself with the corrupt and socially antagonistic metropolis that was the scene of most of its action. In this way, Donnelly (and, as I shall demonstrate, many other writers of utopian fiction) initially appears to use utopian space to reestablish those old urban-rural stereotypes.

Such simple distinctions are troubled, however, when we consider how much this return to a "rural retreat" is actually cyclical; on closer inspection, the description of a utopian future that ends the narrative is a long way from the "primitive shepherd-life" mentioned in the novel's opening pages. The final chapter, titled "The Garden in the Mountains," is an extract from Gabriel's journal, written some time after the events in New York. Initially it was a settlement of "about five thousand" people (230), but when Gabriel comes to describe the colony, its level of social development implies a significant expansion in the population: there are munitions factories (231), universities and colleges (233), and "the state owns all roads, streets, telegraph or telephone lines, railroads and mines" (234). The shepherd-life that Gabriel had left at the beginning of the novel has been transformed into a recognizably modern community—something, in other words, far closer to a city than a pastoral idyll. On the other hand, Gabriel says that the "one town in our colony" is "not much more than a village" (237), and that any future villages will be strictly planned to avoid the dense conglomerations of urban life: "the streets shall be very wide and planted with fruit trees in double and treble rows" (237). Five years later, in another journal entry, the mountain community has constructed further towns but is still described by Gabriel as an "idyl [sic] of the golden age" and "a garden of peace and beauty" (241).

It is, in short, a somewhat confused passage of description. The colony is in some respects a recognizably "urban" settlement, with a municipal government, a presumably large industrial workforce, transportation and communication networks, and even a theater and a concert hall (238). In other ways, however, it seeks an idealized version of rural life, abundant in natural beauty and nothing more than a "village." The narrative attempts to imagine a utopian future that is self-sustaining, progressive, and free of the bonds of labor; yet it has no other referential subtext to call on but the scientific, political, and social developments of its own historical moment. In doing so, it necessarily contradicts the appeals to communal intimacy and the preindustrial technologies of the village life it pines for by constructing a vision of the future that relies on and finally invests its faith in the trappings of modernity.

Such narrative equivocation is clearly an attempt to imbue urban-industrial modernity with the political and geographical values attached to a pastoral or romantic version of the rural. Merging the myth of a rural good life with the bright promises of technological modernity, the narrative therefore needs to invoke two versions of rural life to make its utopia both historically convincing and imaginatively seductive. It abolishes the hard historical conditions of rural life in the late nineteenth century, when concentrations of private capital had held rural communities subservient to urban monopolies, but retains a dehistoricized idealization of rural life that in a cultural sense had served almost as insidiously to distort relations between city and country. It is wrong to claim that Donnelly advocates a return to some kind of prelapsarian social order, but in his alternative to that order—essentially a technological modernity organized around the ideological illusion of "village life"—he tightens the cultural blindfold on the very conditions he seeks to expose. *Caesar's Column* can only imagine a future that silently reinstalls the same relationship between city and country it purports to have dismantled. To put it another way, Donnelly's utopian community testifies to the fundamental disconnection between the historical context of utopian novels (the real economic and political hardships of rural America in the 1880s and 1890s) and the continuing influence of a romanticized representation of rural life. By ultimately failing in their attempts to reimagine the urban-rural relationship, these texts bring the ideological and aesthetic contradictions of that disconnection into focus.

While Donnelly offers a glimpse of how some utopian novels imagined the landscapes of the future, other writers more or less organize their narratives around them. In Olerich's *A Cityless and Countryless World*, the main protagonist is Mr. Midith, a visitor from the planet Mars, who spends much of his time criticizing the problems he sees in the arrangements of urban and rural life on Earth. "It seemed so strange to me when I first arrived on earth," he says, "that about half of your population desire to live in comparatively filthy [and] crowded...cities and towns, while the other half want to live a lonely, toilsome, country life" (32). Preparing us for the "cityless and countryless" utopia that Midith describes, the narrative must adopt two contradictory generic viewpoints: the anti-urban investment in a romantic pastoralism that caricatures cities as filthy and crowded, and the more politically attuned (if still two-dimensional) recognition of "toilsome" rural life that gestures at a kind of social realism. The contradiction that structures this statement between a romantic image of timeless rural life and a historically attuned awareness of agricultural conditions, signals the divided generic stance that becomes fundamental to the whole novel.

It is, firstly, this awareness of the novel's contemporary political context that echoes through much of what Mr. Midith has to say about rural conditions on Earth. He is particularly bewildered by the hard labor that accompanies rural life: "How the agriculturalist, or farmer, fenced his little patch of land, which he worked single-handed so cruelly and toilsomely with a draught animal—ox, horse, etc., which require almost as much food and care as they can earn" (33). Only from the standpoint of the late nineteenth century, when modern technologies offer a viable alternative to these conditions, can such a criticism be raised. In these moments the narrative seems to adopt the stance of realism (or, perhaps more accurately, naturalism) in its sincere efforts to reflect and comment on a politicized and historicized version of rural life. Bearing the traces of its political moment—the novel was published in 1893, a year after the Populist Party had carried four states and won more than a million votes in the presidential election—its realist credentials are further established in its direct challenge to one of the etiological pillars of pastoral idealism: Jefferson's statement in Query 19 of *Notes on the State of Virginia* that "[t]hose who labour in the earth are the chosen people of God" (170). In rejecting the foundational myth of the yeoman farmer, the narrative preconditions its own collectivist vision of utopia later in the novel with a historically updated view of rural life that places it more firmly within the technological-industrial network of urban modernity.

When Mr. Midith begins to describe the utopia they have created on Mars, however, a different descriptive register takes over, one more in line with the romantic construction of a timeless rural idyll. Explaining how they came to be the "cityless and countryless world" of the novel's title, he describes the earlier stage of civilization in strikingly anti-urban terms, claiming that the city was "a noisy, smoky, filthy and unwholesome place to live" that "not only tend[ed] to produce crime, but also shelter[ed] and secrete[d] criminals" (390). Those forced to live in tenements—that is, the working classes—"rarely ever saw and heard a bird, smelled the fragrance of blooming plants, or saw the flowers and green grass grow" (390). The city is "unwholesome" and crime ridden (classic pastoral associations of urban life) because it has lost a connection with rural nature, which is, supposedly, wholesome. Where the idealization of rural life had earlier been implicated as politically distorting, here it necessarily returns to filter our view of urban life. We are primed for the utopia of a cityless and countryless world that Midith goes on to describe, and that I return to in a moment, by the literary double vision the early parts of the novel assumes: the city is viewed through a romantically pastoral lens, and the country is viewed through a more realistic contemporary one. "Just in proportion, then, as the farmer and townsman learned the evils of a crowded, unhealthy and unnecessary city, and also of a lonely and unnecessary country, both the city and country disappeared" (391), Midith concludes.

What should already be clear is that the content of these utopian novels—their representation of a future landscape attempting to be both urban and rural at the same time—leads them into something of a generic dilemma. The point is given more definition when we turn to Fredric Jameson's comments on the form of utopian fiction, and in particular his notion of "critical negativity." The oppositions or antinomies that structure utopian thought—of which the opposition between city and country, he claims, is "one of the most fundamental"—involve the deployment of one pole of that opposition as "a conceptual instrument designed, not to produce some full representation, but rather to discredit and demystify the claims to full representation of its opposite number" (*Archaeologies* 175). The narrative function of "city" or "country" in utopian thought "lies not in itself, but in its capability radically to negate its alternative" (*Archaeologies* 175). Jameson provides, by way of an illustration, an example that resonates with the current discussion: "[The City] rebukes everything that is complacent and specious, celebratory and deluded, about ideologies of nature; while the serenity of the village casts the silence of an equally final judgment on a febrile urban agitation" (*Archaeologies* 176). The invocation of urban or rural space serves to negate and discredit its opposite number's ability to provide a truly utopian future. The result is a literary mode that simultaneously neutralizes and yet authorizes the romantic *and* the realist claims for narrative ascendancy.

This disjunction between the geography of utopia and the literary genres employed to describe it comes to the fore again in Olerich's novel when Midith describes the architectural layout and social advancements back on utopian Mars. In place of dense cities and sparse countryside people now live in highly ordered "communities" of about 120,000 people (59), all housed in self-sustaining apartment blocks: "grand, magnificent structures about eight stories high" that "accommodate about a thousand men, women and children" (53). These are "built about a half a mile apart all around rectangular fields" (56) that resemble parkland, which in turn are bordered by orchards and gardens a thousand feet wide. Gone is Jefferson's yeoman farmer, replaced by huge farms ploughed by "a powerful land locomotive" driven by electricity—"not a human hand [touches] straw or grain" Midith proudly proclaims (61–62). Ordered, geometrical landscapes are emptied of the old geographical diversities, and even of labor itself. Later in the novel, Midith offers a succinct summation of the living conditions back home: "Thus we did away with the solitude of the country and the evil effects of the city. We are all living in splendid parks" (392). The cityless and countryless utopia is less an amalgam of the two and more a negation of either. Urban life is rejected as evil, echoing the ideology of romantic pastoralism, whereas the country is considered solitary and toilsome, an attitude born out of an urban middle-class desire for modern conveniences and an antipathy for physical labor.

This discussion can be developed by turning to one of the more prominent utopian novels of the period, William Dean Howells's *A Traveler from Altruria* (1894). Although different in tone and style to the other two novels discussed so far, Howells's utopian vision of the future bears a close similarity to those of Donnelly and Olerich. Narrated by Mr. Twelvemough, a successful society novelist of genteel romances, it tells the story of Aristedes Homos, a visitor from the utopian country of Altruria. Spending his time at a New England rural resort for wealthy cosmopolitan tourists, a somewhat bewildered Homos encounters the political and cultural contradictions of late nineteenth-century society, innocently asking the kind of probing questions that expose the inconsistencies of upper- and middle-class ideology. Although Homos's reaction is fired in part by the same Populist anger that motivated Donnelly's novel, Howells offers a more transparent and cogent critique of society by placing the scene of the action squarely in contemporary America. In the descriptions of this society, Howells's satirical impulse finds particularly fertile ground and forms a damning vision of modern American life that prepares the way for the utopian society described at the end of the novel. It is this vision, however, that partly unsettles Howells's satire, registering in intriguing ways the complexities of establishing a utopian space.

Especially pertinent here is the substantial amount of time the novel spends over describing urban-rural relations, a discussion given the most room when the wealthy urbanites Twelvemough and Mrs. Makely, along with Homos, take a day trip away from the resort to a nearby village. The episode provides Howells with an opportunity to launch a satiric swipe at the urban idealization of rural life when, for Homos's benefit, the party actually gets down from its carriage and visits a farmer in his humble cottage. Mrs. Makely, the snobbish elderly woman who represents everything about bourgeois urbanity that Howells finds reprehensible, addresses the farmer:

> "[H]ow I envy you all this dear old, home-like place! I never come here without thinking of my grandfather's farm in Massachusetts.... If I had a place like this, I should never leave it."
>
> "Well, Mrs. Makely...you can have this place cheap... [or] almost any other place in the neighborhood." (101)

Mrs. Makely admonishes the farmer, telling him that to suggest farm life is "cheap" is like "going back on the Declaration." His response carries all the political and cultural baggage that weighs so heavily on the idealization of rural life: "The Declaration is all right, as far as it goes, but it don't help us to compete with the western farm operations" (101–02). Howells points out that a nostalgia for rural life—either in personal childhood memories or in the continuing cultural veneration of a mythical Jeffersonian republic—willfully obscures the contemporary economic conditions for Eastern farmers being priced out of the market by the advent of industrialized agribusiness in the Midwest.

Howells is writing in his firmly realist mode here, exposing the distortions of literary romanticism and grounding the drama of the action in the social and political context of the 1890s. His critique of rural idealization, a vision consolidated in the urban middle classes the novel centers on, is even more overtly established when the usually unapologetic narrator comments on the distorted relationship between the tourists and the local farming community:

> [W]e city people see so little of the farming life, when we come into the country. I have been here now for several seasons, and this is the first time I have been inside a farmer's house.... [M]ost city people come and go, year after year, in the country, and never make any sort of acquaintance with the people who live there the year round. (108)

Twelvemough's recognition of how city people treat the countryside comments not so much on the disconnection between the two, but on the middle-class treatment of rural life as a picturesque backdrop to touristic excursions. The metaphor he conjures up to explain this social relationship to Homos emphasizes the idea of the leisurely exploitation of the countryside: "It has sometimes seemed to me as if our big hotel there were a ship, anchored off some strange coast. The inhabitants come out with supplies...but we never speak to them.... We sail away at the close of the season" (109).

The narrative establishes this point of view—that of an exploitative, monied, condescending urban class—in order that it might place its utopian representative in direct contrast to it. Homos refuses to play the tourist: "The Altrurian was greatly interested, not so much in the landscape—though he owned its beauty, when we cried out over it from point to point—but in the human incidents and features" (88). Resisting the reduction of rural space to a pastoral "landscape," Homos brings no nostalgic or aesthetic preconditions to his relationship with it and so recovers the human input hidden within that landscape. When Twelvemough is showing Homos around the resort at the beginning of the novel, for instance, Twelvemough proudly shows off the "tender gloom of the forest," which he romanticizes to almost comic proportions: "the music of the hermit-thrushes rang all round us, like crystal bells, like silver flutes...like the choiring of still-eyed cherubim" (17). Coming into a clearing in the forest, however, Homos notices something rather less picturesque: "I saw the Altrurian staring about him...in a kind of horror. It was squalid ruin, a graceless desolation, which not even the pitying twilight could soften" (18). A farmer has burned his forest because it is worth more to him as building plots than it is as timber. The charred and smoking remains of the forest stand as a stark symbol of the economic pressures on rural life in the 1890s, establishing a contrast with Twelvemough's romantic reverie that underlines its absurd detachment from real life. The distance between the two visions is, therefore, a conjunction of realist and romantic viewpoints that becomes a microcosm of the wider point Howells labors throughout many similar episodes in the novel. One aspect of modern society that differentiates America from Altruria, the thing that keeps the former from achieving its own kind of utopia, is the continuation of an economically and culturally exploitative relationship between city and country.

In these sections of the novel, the narrative is partly invested in the type of realism that Howells personally did so much to propagate. It is worth dwelling on these points, especially in the light of Peyser's claim that "realism and utopia seem remarkable for their apparent incompatibility" because "utopia seeks to place the widest possible distance between its own procedures and those associated with the realist novel, which prides itself on being deeply suffused by the ethos of the times" (7, 8). This apparent distance leads Tom Moylan to suggest that "utopia can be understood to be a development within the paradigm of romance" as it falls "under the category of the fantastic rather than the realistic" (31). Utopian fiction becomes an exaggerated version of romanticism because, as Moylan states, "the romantic mode is centered around a process of wish-fulfilment...that aims at a *displacement or transfiguration* of the given historical world" (31, emphasis in original). The utopian worlds or nations appearing in these novels are romantic constructions in that they actively seek to remove themselves from their contemporary reality—to imagine, in fact, an alternative to that reality.

This categorization does not, however, fully explain their narrative mode. The ideological and aesthetic context from which all these novels emerge, especially in the case of *A Traveler from Altruria*, fixes their representations in the "ethos of the time" and the "given historical world" they define themselves against. Pfaelzer suggests that utopian visions are necessarily an extrapolation of current realities, and that their credibility as fictions therefore relies on a "realistic or plausible representation of the new world" (15): "the utopian future... is seemingly predicated on logical principles that give it the aura of possibility. The utopian society... must be credible and, consequently, not fantastic" (16). Peyser makes a similar point when he insists that "without realist attention to fact, utopia floats away into the realm of mere escapist fantasy" (12).

This mixed critical account of utopian fiction, situating it in an uncertain and vacillating position between romance and realism, underlines a point that has been developing in this chapter. The utopian novel diagnoses the conditions of its own time, directly discussing the social and political problems it perceives in its extratextual reality in order to propose a future that is also a cure. Training a realist's eye on the sickness in the American countryside at the end of the century, these works finally seek to heal that sickness by creating worlds that are romantic and seemingly evasive projections of the future, all the while maintaining roots in historical realities. The point about utopian fiction both neutralizing and authorizing realist and romantic modes comes about partly because its object of representation requires both of those modes to be in operation at the same time.

These issues converge in Howells's novel (as they had done in Donnelly's and Olerich's) when the narrative turns to its descriptions of the utopian society and, in particular, the utopian landscape. When at the end of the novel Homos delivers his lecture on the conditions in Altruria, one of the most notable aspects of his society is the absence of the urban-rural antagonisms that had marked the descriptions of contemporary America. "We had, of course, a great many large cities under the old egoistic conditions," he tells the audience, a mixture of resort residents and local people, but "[a]lmost from the moment of the Evolution the competitive and monopolistic centers of population began to decline" (187).

The conditions that replaced them, however, ring with a certain note of familiarity—not only in terms of the other fictional utopias of the period, but also to some extent in terms of America's already existing geography:

> "There are now no cities in Altruria, in your meaning, but there are capitals, one for each of the Regions of our country.... These capitals are for the transaction of public affairs... and they are the residences of the administrative officials.... In the capitals are the universities, theaters, galleries, museums, cathedrals, laboratories and conservatories, and the appliance of every art and science, as well as the administration buildings." (188–89)

The "capitals" Homos describes, despite his suggestion to the contrary, sound uncannily like cities already in existence in America: seats of cultural arbiters, scientific progress, political power, and religious hierarchies.

It is, however, the actual environment of these cities that marks them as utopian: "[o]ur capitals are as clean and quiet and healthful as the country" (189) he points out. The economic relationship of city to country may have changed, but the spatial relationship remains largely the same. The major difference is that now the cities are imbued with the "timeless virtues" associated with rural life—cleanliness, quietness, and healthfulness—that the narrative's earlier realist mode had seen as a romantic distortion.

This problematic return to a vision of the rural idyll is underlined when Homos moves on to describe conditions in the countryside (unlike on Olerich's Mars, such differentiations are still possible). Romantic visions of rural life take further hold, only now it is the more specifically American notion of Jeffersonian agrarian virtue that returns, forgiven and redeemed despite its mocking dismissal earlier in the novel. "If it can be said that one occupation is honored above another with us, it is that which we all share, and that is the cultivation of the earth," he says. "We believe that this ... brings man into the closest relations to the deity ... and that it not only awakens a natural piety in him, but that it endears to the worker that piece of soil which he tills, and so strengthens his love of home" (190). The combination of nature's regenerative powers and Christian ethics that underlies Altruria's veneration of farming—linking man not just to God, but to his community—owes as much to Jeffersonian politics as it does to a more specifically literary romanticism. If Altruria's cities are to be as "healthful as the country," then the country itself must be restored to something innately healthful; the realism of the tired-out and physically demanding farmlands described earlier in the novel is neutralized to make way for a vision of social perfection. The description of Altruria becomes the moment where the coexistence of romantic and realist generic stances finally short-circuits, a space where city and country—and romantic and realist narrative perspectives—cancel each other out.

I am not suggesting that Howells merely replicates the problems of contemporary America in his imagined geography of Altruria, just that what Jameson called the "referential subtext" comes to constrain and ultimately limit his conception of how urban and rural space could be transformed. Howells is stuck in a historical and generic quandary, wishing to abolish the unjust spatial relationships of the present but finding only a discredited romantic mode available for the representation of the utopian alternative. Mizruchi's claim that "Howells's utopia betrayed nostalgia for a preindustrial, agrarian social order" (285) too simplistically reduces the novel to the description of the utopia itself, missing the rejection of agrarian nostalgia in the novel's earlier sections. Pfaelzer's reading suggests a more nuanced historicity to Altruria's landscape; it is "a literary border country that lies between the nineteenth-century city and the eighteenth-century country" (63). The idea of a "border country" is useful, but it suggests some synthetic third term that somehow encompasses both. Instead, the generic oscillations of the novel, its paradoxical need to keep both realist and romantic visions in play at the same time, are mirrored and manifested in Altruria's own oddly divided geography. Seeking to level the urban-rural divide that lies at the heart of economic exploitation in the period of urban-industrial modernity, Altruria, in the end, only restores those conditions in its spatial arrangement: the concentrations of social, cultural, and political power in the "capitals," and an agricultural landscape of seemingly blissful yeoman farmers.

What this all amounts to is a reading of utopian fiction that finds critical purchase in the very failure of the texts its analyses. Again, it is Jameson who clarifies this point most eruditely: "on the social level," he says, "our imaginations are hostages to our own mode of production (and perhaps to whatever remnants of past ones it has preserved)" (*Archaeologies* xiii). The implications of this for the utopian novel are significant, as it suggests that "at best Utopia can serve the negative purpose of making us more aware of our mental and ideological imprisonment…the best Utopias are those that fail the most comprehensively" (*Archaeologies* xiii). It is the inability of these texts to project a future truly emancipated from the present and the past (in terms of both form and content) that make them such valuable windows into the same critical issues that the rest of this book has been tracing. In trying to imagine a landscape that is neither urban nor rural and yet somehow both, late nineteenth-century utopian novels reveal the extent to which the conditions of modernity govern the representation of rural space—and the extent to which we can recover the historical conditions of urban modernity by approaching it indirectly, through that rural representation.

Here, I want to turn to two works by the figure who almost single-handedly generated the phenomenon of utopian writing in Gilded Age America. Edward Bellamy's *Looking Backward* (1888) and its sequel *Equality* (1897) in fact mark the chronological span of the texts I consider in this chapter, and the landscapes they describe help to clarify and nuance many of the points already discussed. *Looking Backward*, although easily the most critically discussed American utopian novel, is actually of less interest here; the novel is set almost entirely in the city of Boston, either in 1887 or 2000, and any discussion of rural life outside the city environs is largely absent.[4] Julian West's first account of Boston in 2000 is worth dwelling on for a moment, however, because in its subtle evocation of the natural world it sets up some of the themes integral to the more developed descriptions of the utopian landscape found in *Equality*. The Boston that West finds when he awakes from his century-long sleep seems to be, like the cities of the future found in other utopian novels, an attempt to import the presumed benefits of rural nature into a transformed urban landscape: "At my feet lay a great city. Miles of broad streets, shaded by trees and lined with fine buildings ... set in larger or smaller inclosures [sic], stretched in every direction. Every quarter contained large open squares filled with trees, among which statues glistened" (22). The leafiness of Boston is immediately apparent to West, but what is also clear is what Matthew Beaumont calls the city's "impeccable abstraction": "The absence of people signals the absence of social contradiction. In this respect it is in dramatic contrast to the nineteenth-century city in which he had lived at the beginning of the novel" (xxi). The urban scene of *Looking Backward* attempts to remove all traces of "social contradiction," not just by emptying it of its people, but also by blurring the distinction between urban and rural space: the insistent visibility of nature and the diffused density of buildings hint at an absent but determining rural landscape. The pseudo-rurality of Boston in 2000 "literally contains the cityscape and offers continuity for West" (Auerbach 28), a lingering presence of a recognizable past that provides a psychic buffer against the shock of the new.

These initial suggestions come to fruition in Bellamy's longer, less successful sequel, *Equality*. The structure of the book is largely the same as that of its predecessor: West is shown around a variety of locations by Dr. Leete, who explains in exhaustive detail (few characters in American literature can ever have done so much talking) the principles behind the transformed society of the twenty-first century. It is in this book that Bellamy, partly as a response to the questions raised by *Looking Backward*, gives a fuller account of how America's landscape has developed. Behind those changes is the same socialist vision that was outlined in the previous book: "There are few respects, I suppose ... in which the effect of the nationalization of production and distribution on the basis of economic equality has worked a greater transformation than in the relations of city and country" (290). The spatial densities that characterize a society based on "private capitalism" have disappeared, replaced by a decentralization of capital that renders cities unnecessary: "now there had ceased to be any economic advantages in city life, [people] were attracted by the natural charms of the country" (294). The "natural" state of man, it is suggested, is to live a rural life.

Even those cities that remain have dissolved into large, leafy towns: "I fancy your first impression [of Manhattan] would be that the Central Park of your day had been extended all the way from the Battery to Harlem

River ... some two hundred and fifty thousand people living there among the groves and fountains" (294). With the population much more thinly spread, and surrounded by "[p]arks, gardens, and roomy spaces" (295)—in other words, imbued with the supposed qualities of pastoral nature—cities were "as pleasant places to live in as was the country itself" (295). In abolishing a certain economic form, America has seemingly reverted to an idea of itself as an agrarian republic, a "tendency countryward" (294). The final confirmation comes when West gazes down from an "air car" at the landscape below him: "mile after mile, league after league," the world below "presented the same parklike aspect that marked the immediate environs of the city" (296). When West asks Dr. Leete how big the park is, he replies simply, "It extends to the Pacific Ocean" (296).

There is a contradiction in Bellamy's vision, however, and it is one signals a deeper issue with his imagined landscapes of the future. The "parklike" landscape of America automatically suggests a carefully managed version of nature, a use of the land that is economically distinct from agriculture; a landscape that is, in fact, designed to create a perfected and laborless version of the natural world.[5] This distance between the necessary use of nature (farming, food, employment) and its use as an idealized background for human pleasure becomes clearer when we discover that farming itself, that overtly economic and decidedly human use of the land, is now a pleasurable pursuit devoid of the hardships of late nineteenth-century agriculture. Ploughs are huge electric machines manned by "a young man or woman with quite the air of persons on a pleasure excursion" (298), while even spades and forks are now driven by electricity. As Dr. Leete explains to West, "an intelligent boy can excavate a trench or dig a mile of potatoes quicker than a gang of men in your day" (299). The imaginative construction of a perfected America involves abolishing the economic injustices and physical difficulties that mark Gilded Age rural life, but in the process a version of rurality is created that seems both romanticized and, in the end, not much like rural life at all: a pleasurable, easy leisure time in a parklike environment.

Dr. Leete's summation of how rural life has changed since West's 1880s condenses many of the points I have raised so far:

> The poets from Virgil up and down have recognized in rural pursuits and the cultivation of the earth the conditions most favorable to a serene and happy life. Their fancies in this respect have, however, until the present time, been mocked by the actual conditions of agriculture.... [B]efore the nineteenth century had reached its last third, ... by the inevitable operation of private capitalism, the farmer began to go down hill toward the condition of serfdom. (303–4)

Attuned to its own historical circumstances, the utopian impulse in *Equality* strives to alter the conditions of urban-industrial modernity to make them more favorable for rural people; yet the ultimate aim of this alteration is a realization of the pastoral myth that had provided an ideological prop to those unfavorable conditions in the first place. The political energy generated by the novel's naturalistic attention to the social inequalities of late nineteenth-century rural life finds its utopian realization in a romanticized countryside that, ultimately, confirms the ideological vision of an urban-capitalist order.

There is a logic at work in Bellamy's writing that replicates the same paradox I have identified in other utopian novels: a realist literary mode that enlists a romantic conception of rural space. This vision of the future is tacitly reinforced by the utopian landscapes these writers imagine: dreams of decentralization that dissolve the volatile conglomerations of the nineteenth-century city, or rural landscapes emptied of the farmers who threatened political upheaval in the 1880s and 1890s. Progressive technologies and benevolent governments have done away with the laboring classes altogether. The divided generic approach of these novels is, ultimately, only the inevitable result of the landscapes they seek to represent; governed by the referential subtext of the urban-industrial society they emerge from, these texts reflect and help to reinforce the ideology of an urban ruling class.

This use of rural space in utopian fiction—enlisted for its timeless idyllic qualities even as its historically specific conditions motivate that enlistment—occurs again and again throughout the genre. In the future, they seem to proclaim, the promises of modernity will finally free rural space from its current hardships, so that it can become what the romantic "structure of feeling" always insisted it was: idyllic, restorative, and an antidote to the evils of the city. It is perhaps no surprise that King Camp Gillette, one of the great capitalists of the age, confirms such a vision in his own contribution to the genre, *The Human Drift* (1894). Here he suggests that the whole population of America should be re-housed into a vast city of 40,000 skyscrapers, each one set within beautiful gardens and surrounded by wide belts of rural space. Those rural areas provide a buffer against the overcrowded misery of the nineteenth-century city, but they are themselves to be "restructured to facilitate large-scale production and give rural inhabitants access to thoroughly equipped and modernized facilities (libraries, theaters, restaurants, schools)" (Mizruchi 266). Like the others discussed here, Gillette's vision is potentially contradictory. Keen to transform the economic conditions, physical hardships, and social isolation of rural life (issues that had a particular cultural resonance at the end of the nineteenth century), his prescription for the future involves an ideologically confused landscape. The 40,000 towers take the faith in Progressive-era reasoning to its logical conclusion: a true reflection, in its orderly, rectilinear, geometrical uniformity, of urban-industrial rationalism. Yet underpinning this is a vestige of something far less reasoned, a romantic belief in the psychologically and socially regenerative power of rural life.

Conceived in a historical moment bristling with political unrest, these utopias project a future that quells that unrest by bringing together both a faith in technological modernity and an idealization of rural life. Their imagined future landscapes therefore provide an explicit expression of the deeper argument of this book: in their generically unstable representation of rural space, they reflect the unsettled and vacillating nature of their own cultural moment. The representational uncertainties of the landscapes of utopian fiction are an imaginative access point to the competing series of associations surrounding urban and rural life in the Gilded Age.

* * *

In the sense that utopian fictions project rural space into the center of modernity, it is worth finally mentioning the striking relationship between these literary landscapes and those conceived (and sometimes realized) by twentieth-century modernist architects and planners. Peter Hall, pointing out what he acknowledges is now a commonplace assertion in architectural history, says that "twentieth-century city planning, as an intellectual and professional movement, essentially represents a reaction to the evils of the nineteenth-century city" (7). Such a motivation lies behind Mr. Midith's condemnation of nineteenth-century cities in *A Cityless and Countryless World*—and, in one way another, virtually all of the utopian visions considered in this chapter. One strand of this book has traced the uncertain line between romantic and realist generic modes as framed by Gilded Age rural fiction, but these utopian texts allow that discussion, if only tentatively and briefly, to broaden out in an alternative direction. The utopian fiction of the late nineteenth century, read against the plans drawn up by the most prominent modernist planners of the twentieth, emerges as a significant anticipation of the intellectual life of rural space within the ideological and aesthetic imagination of modernism.

Echoes of these literary landscapes can be found, for instance, in the ideas put forward by one of the earliest and most influential modernist planners, Ebenezer Howard. His only book, *Garden Cities of To-morrow* (1902) (originally published in 1898 as *To-morrow: A Peaceful Path to Real Reform*), outlines a plan for the built environment that sounds not unlike

Midith's Mars: "32,000 people, living in 1,000 acres of land...surrounded by a much larger area of permanent green belt" (Hall 93). The deployment of rural space as an antidote to all that is perceived to be wrong with urban living underpins nineteenth-century literary utopias just as it underpins the grander ambitions of twentieth-century modernist planning. In a markedly different way, Le Corbusier's strictly regimented city plans—first unveiled in Paris in 1922, and then prescribed in detail in his book *Urbanisme* (1924) (published in English under the title *The City of To-morrow and Its Planning*)—were perhaps the ultimate statement of rationalized modernity.[6] Outlining a plan for "eighteen uniform 700-foot-high towers" (Hall 207), Le Corbusier's fanatical pursuit of orderliness would consist of a city grid of "geometrically arrayed skyscrapers...[rising] out of parks, gardens, and superhighways" (Fishman 10). To make way for Le Corbusier's grand dreams of the future, most of historic Paris north of the Seine would be demolished. Such drastic measures had been proposed, however, in Bellamy's Boston some forty years before, while the sterile uniformity of such a landscape mirrors almost exactly the utopias of Olerich and Gillette. "The whole city is a park," Le Corbusier wrote in the 1920s (177), just as Julian West and Mr. Midith had exclaimed in novels written back in the 1890s.

It was the American architect Frank Lloyd Wright, however, who would exemplify the combination of beliefs now familiar from my reading of utopian fiction: a faith in technological modernity coupled with a romantic view of rural life.[7] In his only attempt at a comprehensive city plan, called Broadacre City and first exhibited in New York in April 1935, Wright presented a vision where "all cities larger than a county seat have disappeared. The center of society has moved to the thousands of homesteads which cover the countryside" (Fishman 9). A plan for the profound decentralization of urban life, Broadacre City, low rise and spread out between acres of parks and wide boulevards, is "not a city at all" but "the point at which the urban/rural distinction no longer exists" (Fishman 92). In this way, Wright's vision of an American future seems precisely what the writers of the 1880s and 1890s were dreaming of, a place where "the new technological forces could recreate...a nation of free independent farmers" (Hall 287). Well into the twentieth century, Wright was expressing the same ideological and philosophical underpinnings to his landscapes of the future that all the writers discussed here had done: acknowledging the social and economic problems of their own time, they sought to escape them by bringing timeless rural qualities into the heart of a thoroughly modern landscape.

Drawing these brief parallels shows just how integral utopian fictions are to understanding the relationship between rural representation and urban modernity in Gilded Age America. In a way that epitomizes and condenses the argument that has unfolded in the preceding chapters, the worlds imagined by the utopian writers of the late nineteenth century require us to read their generic and thematic strategies diachronically—that is, to see how the mixed literary modes of their representation are both a constituent and a symptom of the mixed geographical arrangement of their future landscapes. The movement back and forth between romantic, realist, and naturalist literary registers signposts the same movement between a resolutely historicized attention to the conditions of social life and the belief in an illusory, idyllic past. That such uncertainties become a keynote in modernism's own visions of a future landscape testifies to the way rural fictions cannot be fitted into any neat historical templates, and that, in the end, it is their instability and uncertainty that makes them such a critical site in understanding the tangled mesh of influences at work within the unfurling experience of urban modernity.

Conclusion

For much of this book, my method of reading rural fiction has required a kind of archaeological scrutiny. I have attempted to unearth the traces of modernity buried within rural fiction in a way that reveals the intimate and inextricable connection between the two, and such a method has necessarily required a certain degree of "reading against the grain"—suggesting that even the representations of rural life that seem to evade the implications of an increasingly urbanized society do, in fact, bear witness to its unavoidable impact. This is not to say, however, that rural fiction was a wholly disengaged or unconscious discourse in the late nineteenth century; often enough, as I have also shown, writers tackled such concerns head on, seeking to represent and understand the rapidly changing nature of everyday life through its connection to geographical experience.

Turning to such an example now, one that acts as an illustrative companion to the more oblique quote I opened this book with, I end with a moment from William Dean Howells's *Suburban Sketches* (1871). In the sketch "Mrs. Johnson," the narrator offers this assessment of the Boston suburb of Charlesbridge:

> The neighborhood was in all things a frontier between city and country. The horse-cars, the type of such civilization—full of imposture, discomfort, and sublime possibility—as we yet possess, went by the head of our street, and might, perhaps, be available to one skilled in calculating the movements of comets; while two minutes' walk would take us into a wood so wild and thick that no roof was visible through the trees. We learned, like innocent pastoral people of the golden age, to know the several voices of the cows pastured in the vacant lots, and, like engine-drivers of the iron age, to distinguish the different whistles of the locomotives passing on the neighboring railroad. The trains shook the house as they thundered along, and at night were a kind of company, while by day we had the society of innumerable birds. (13)

From material signifiers of modernity, through the close proximity of a natural landscape, to the different forms of knowledge necessary to inhabit this environment, this description of a New England suburb speaks to many of the governing concerns of my argument. "Civilization" is in the process of arriving in Charlesbridge, but the town is within minutes of a thickly wooded forest—a place the narrative implies is antithetical to that civilization. On the "frontier" between the urban and the rural, forms of knowledge associated with both become part of everyday life: the "pastoral" ability to distinguish cows from one another, and the "iron age" ability (a historically ambiguous label in itself) to distinguish different trains. Finally, these same trains become "a kind of company" at night, as do the personified birds during the day—a time when, presumably, no trains pass by.

On one level, this passage helps to reiterate the point that literary narratives are a particularly fruitful way of understanding the changing nineteenth-century landscape. What is interesting in this passage is not only that it succinctly distills so many of the complexities of the urban-rural relationship I have been tracing, but that it does so as a literary discourse partly by employing different generic registers. The attention the passage pays to those material signifiers of modernity adopt the realist's stance of locating the action within a specific and recognizably contemporary historical moment, while within the same paragraph the self-conscious evocation of a pastoral "golden age" and the personified animals gesture at a sentimentalized and romanticized viewpoint. One of the recurring themes in this book has been the generic instability of the texts in question, and I have argued that such instabilities are not only further testament to the complexities of nineteenth-century literary genres, but are also a symptom of the deeply divided and unstable nature of the geographical space being described. This passage from *Suburban Sketches* helps to bring these issues to a focal point, exposing in a quite straightforward way the relationship between historical context, literary representation, and geographical space that runs as a current through the subjects of the preceding chapters.

The passage also proves to be a fitting place to end because it takes us directly to the overarching subject that explicitly and implicitly lies at the heart of my discussion, one that has received much attention in previous scholarly work: the relationship between modernity and literature. What marks this book out from much of the work that has come before, however, is my attention to an aspect of modernity—rural space and rural life—that, often cast as anti- or premodern, has frequently been marginalized in such discussions. In this way, I have argued against the dismissive notion that rural fiction is somehow only capable of expressing the issues and day-to-day experiences of a circumscribed agricultural life, and instead placed it front and center in the understanding of literary modernity. There was a gradual expansion of the scale of the argument as the book progressed, from opening with the suggestive fragment of James Lane Allen's *Summer in Arcady* to the grand reimaginings of the American landscape in the prolific genre of utopian fiction. Regardless of the breadth of the frame of reference, what underlies my readings is an attempt to secure rural fiction as a vital entry point to the themes, concerns, currents, and transformations of urban modernity.

Pushing these ideas a little further, however, my argument suggests an approach to the urban and the rural that finally destabilizes the very terms of its engagement. While this book is organized around the connections between urban and rural life, it has become clear that the vocabulary we employ to trace that relationship undergoes a significant realignment during the nineteenth century. Fixed notions of "the city" and "the country" become increasingly obsolete under the conditions of modernization because those processes I outlined in my introduction—the spread of an "urban fabric," the disembedding and distanciation of social relations, and the rise of a mature, rationalized capitalism—necessarily bring city and country into an ever-tighter orbit, initiating flows of commerce and knowledge between the two in a way that is only partly reflected in the built environment. Howells's suburbia points to the fuzziness of spatial categories because as a "suburb" it has no inherent identity of its own; it is only representable as a frontier between the two preexisting cultural and geographical categories of city and country. While I have therefore taken rural fiction as a way to read the presence of the urban in Gilded Age life, what the texts analyzed in this book ultimately testify to is the need to read beyond prescriptive categories like city and country (and even suburb) and understand the inextricable connections that bring them together.

By rejecting conventional regionalist frameworks, as well as author-centered chapters, I have reframed a number of works of fiction and the expectations we have of them in a way that draws specific attention to the broad themes being discussed in each chapter. This is why the method of employing synecdochal counterparts has proved integral to the argument I have staked out—the train, the circus, the country doctor, and the lynching, by their frequency and conspicuousness in the large body of rural fiction produced during this period, become distinct ways to read the modernization of different areas of American life. Each has its own particular history and set of implications, and each stands alone as a way of thinking about the more abstract processes—transportation technologies, the business of popular entertainment, developments in medical knowledge, and finally, the shifting cultural attitudes to law and justice—that they have been used to represent. What unites these different strands are the kind of issues that literary utopias more directly addressed: the changing nature of the period's geographical imagination, and the way in which urban modernity was irrevocably altering, not just the physical and epistemological landscape, but the human relationship to that landscape as well.

While other periods might prove valuable in developing an idea of rural fiction in American literary historiography, the Gilded Age seems an especially conducive one. There is no doubt that the American landscape, and the relationship between urban and rural life (indeed, what was even recognized as urban and rural life), witnessed rapid, profound, and often quite traumatic changes in the period. The fact that a full-fledged modernity was yet to take hold meant that the vestiges of an older order often still governed thought and action, especially in the rural locales I have described. The positioning of this period means that the broad identification of urban modernity—as a coming into being of a rationalized, industrialized, mature capitalism—was always tempered, always somehow infected, by the older orders that it was both a product of and a reaction against. The very indeterminacy of those big social and cultural currents in this period is what makes it such a fascinating window on the processes of modernization and what makes rural fiction, with all its conflicting impulses and strategies, such a valuable perspective on those processes.

By grasping them through literary representation, however, the concern becomes less for the grand explanatory powers of those metanarrational concepts, and more for the intricate relationship between people and their culture. Rural fiction, at first glance, can sometimes seem to operate in a place that evades or resists the deeper structural changes affecting Gilded Age life—continue to perpetuate, in other words, an imaginative version of rural life that even today is often called upon to symbolize an idealized and politically regressive version of American national identity. The value of recovering it in the way this book has attempted is that a more intricate picture of modernization can be established, one that gives full recognition to the way that rural space formed a central component of a culture arriving headlong into an inchoate modernity it was yet to fully absorb. In the novels and short stories of Gilded Age rural fiction we find a society alive to the rush of modernity's demands—and the responses, in all their varieties, of the people caught up in it.

NOTES

INTRODUCTION

1. The exact chronological boundaries of what historians understand to be 'the Gilded Age' are open to debate, but throughout this book I take it to mean the period from the late 1860s to the turn of the century.
2. The influential criticism on American realism that emerged in the 1980s certainly attached a critical relationship between the geography of nineteenth-century America and its prevailing literary forms. Daniel Borus argues quite straightforwardly in *Writing Realism* (1989) that "American realism...became predominantly an urban literature. Not only did the city allow realists to trace the new social relations, but it also opened the way for the depiction of the flood of artefacts and commodities that inundated men and women" (22). Similarly, Amy Kaplan in *The Social Construction of American Realism* (1988) sees "urban spaces" as both the social source and "unproblematic setting of the realistic novel" (12). More abstractly, although explaining this equation of spatial form with aesthetic practice, realism has frequently been seen as the literary mode expressive of "bourgeois class-interests and...capitalist habits of thought" (Glazener 11), traits that have traditionally been characterized as both symptoms and constituents of urban space. This affinity between setting and literary mode is most directly taken up by Philip Fisher in *Hard Facts: Setting and Form in the American Novel* (1985). Here Fisher argues that the city is one of the "privileged settings" of late nineteenth-century American literature, explicitly aligning particular geographical types with historically periodized literary modes: "[T]he modest homestead or family farm with its corrosive fact of slavery and its appropriate form, the sentimental novel...[and] the city with its core reality of the object world and exchange patterns and its popular form in the naturalist novel" (10). Fisher sees the antebellum sentimental novel, haunted as it is by the travesty that slavery had made of Jefferson's agrarian idealism, as belonging essentially to a rural setting. In distinction, the social turmoil of Gilded Age America shifts its chosen arena of expression to the city. This kind of critical characterization effectively erases rural fiction from considerations of modal transition by conflating a type of space (the urban) with a particular historical period (the final third of the nineteenth century). Henderson is one critic who has briefly alluded to, and sought to disturb, this same tendency (n219).
3. There are, for instance, some interesting parallels between *The Hoosier School-Master* and Irving's "The Legend of Sleepy Hollow" (1820). Irving's Ichabod Crane is also a newly arrived provincial schoolmaster who excites the attention of at least one female admirer, a similarity that Eggleston seems to allude to at

a crucial moment of his novel. Ralph, besotted with Hannah Thomson, takes a late-night walk across pastures "white with moonlight" (42), but his contemplation is disturbed when he hears "the thud of horses' hoofs coming down the road" (43) and he ducks behind a fence as the men rush pass: "[t]hey galloped on, and he stood shivering with a nervous fear" (43). The sound of those galloping hooves are surely Eggleston's own affectionate echo of the Headless Horseman chasing down a lovelorn Ichabod on his own secluded moonlit road.

4. A full roll call of urban literature studies would be a project in itself, but it is worth highlighting a few prominent titles to emphasize the relatively unproblematic way in which the category of the urban has been deployed in recent literary criticism. To pick some examples almost at random, they range from quite specific studies about particular social categories in the city, such as Dana Brand's *The Spectator and the City in Nineteenth-Century American Literature* (Cambridge: Cambridge University Press, 1991) and Betsy Klimasmith's *At Home in the City: Urban Domesticity in American Literature and Culture, 1850–1930* (Lebanon: University of New Hampshire Press, 2005), to generalized uses of "the city" or "the urban" as a critical category: Hana Wirth-Nesher's *City Codes: Reading the Modern Urban Novel* (Cambridge: Cambridge University Press, 1996); Carlo Rotella's *October Cities: The Redevelopment of Urban Literature* (Berkeley and Los Angeles: University of California Press, 1998); Richard Lehan's *The City in Literature: An Intellectual and Cultural History* (Berkeley and Los Angeles: University of California Press, 1998); Robert Alter's *Imagined Cities: Urban Experience and the Language of the Novel* (New Haven: Yale University Press, 2005); Christoph Lindner's edited collection *Urban Space and Cityscapes* (London and New York: Routledge, 2006); and Thomas Heise's *Urban Underworlds: A Geography of Twentieth-Century American Literature and Culture* (Piscataway, NJ.: Rutgers University Press, 2011).

5. For the record, the three novels Sherman cites as the "forerunners" of twentieth-century rural fiction are Hamlin Garland's *Main-Travelled Roads* (wrongly identified as a novel, in fact), Eggleston's *The Hoosier School-Master*, and E.W. Howe's *The Story of a Country Town* (1884; New York: Holt, Rinehart and Winston, 1964).

6. See Florian Freitag, "Naturalism in its Natural Environment? American Naturalism and the Farm Novel," *Studies in American Naturalism* 4.2 (Winter 2009): 97–118, and Stacey Denton, "Nostalgia, Class and Rurality in *Empire Falls*," *Journal of American Studies* 45.3 (August 2011): 503–18.

7. Two prominent recent examples are indicative of a wider tendency. In Greil Marcus's and Werner Sollors's *A New Literary History of America* (Cambridge, MA: Harvard University Press, 2009), the rural only gets a serious mention in Sarah Vowell's entry on Grant Wood's 1930 painting *American Gothic*. The more conventional *Cambridge History of the American Novel* (Cambridge and New York: Cambridge University Press, 2011) devotes its second section to the late nineteenth and early twentieth centuries, where an entry on "Dreiser and the City" by Jude Davies (who talks about the "American city novel") and a contribution from Tom Lutz called "Cather and the Regional Imagination" can be found. Any notion of a transregional rural identity is missing.

8. Farland goes on to suggest that, as an alternative to the regionalist rubric that I am questioning, "considerations of rural space are almost wholly subsumed into questions of environmentalism, ecology, and nature writing. In this rarefied domain, rural nature assumes significance as an 'other' with which human

beings attempt to forge an ethical relationship, and the social problems of rural people are elided or ignored" (913). The very same might be said of that other, rather more deeply rooted geo-cultural idea, 'the wilderness.' Whether we see rural space as subsumed to regionalism, the wilderness, or to eco-criticism (and all are true to some extent), the same fundamental elision of "the rural" lies at the heart of mine and Farland's concerns. This apparent absence of the rural as an analytic category in American literary criticism is particularly strange when we consider that city-and-literature studies have been open to the fields of urban geography and sociology, embracing the interdisciplinary potential of such collaborations, while there is no equivalent association of literature with rural geography. The geographers, it seems, have less of a problem with the rural as a field of study: just the last few years have seen the publication of the *Handbook of Rural Studies* edited by Paul Cloke, Terry Marsden and Patrick H. Mooney (London: Sage, 2006), *Rural Geography* by Michael Wood (London: Sage, 2005), and *Geographies of Rural Cultures and Societies* edited by Lewis Holloway and Moya Kneafsey (Aldershot: Ashgate, 2004). The *Journal of Rural Studies*, meanwhile, has been published four times a year since 1985.

9. Glazener offers a somewhat more imprecise definition, stating that rural writing is that which is concerned "not only with life on farms, but also life in villages and towns" (191). Rural geographers have long wrangled over the difficulty of defining the rural; Paul Cloke and Nigel Thrift suggest that such anxieties have moved from purely sociological or demographic demarcations—defining the rural as "dominated by extensive land use,... small settlements which are strongly related to the surrounding landscape and which are recognized as different from the urban by their residents"—to viewing the rural as a social and cultural construct rooted in a host of textual determinants and ideological prejudices (2–3).

10. Marx would offer a modification and development of these ideas in his essay "Pastoralism in America," included in the now-classic collection edited by Sacvan Bercovitch and Myra Jehlen, *Ideology and Classic American Literature* (Cambridge: Cambridge University Press, 1986). Here his interest is more is in the continuing ideological currency of pastoralism, and as such the term becomes even less of a relevant tool when trying, as I am here, to think about literature and rural life in a specific historical period.

11. It is important to state here that "regionalism" is not straightforwardly synonymous with the "rural," even if in the hands of some critics it often is. For a nonrural approach to the idea of literary regionalism, see especially Stephanie Foote's chapters on Jacob Riis and Tammany Hall in *Regional Fictions*. Equally important to point out is that although the notion of "regionalism" as a body of texts is often identified with the "local color" writing of the late nineteenth century, it has become a broader theoretical approach to literature in general, often used in discussions of twentieth- and twenty first-century fiction.

12. There is a large and diverse body of scholarship on nineteenth-century literary regionalism, and my point is not to do away with the category of the regional. For illuminating approaches toward and theorizations of regionalism, see Howard, Hsu, Lutz, and Zagarell. More recently, a special edition of the journal *Modern Fiction Studies* was dedicated to regionalism in a twentieth-century context, specifically in relation to aesthetic modernism (55.1, spring 2009), and Sarah Gleeson-White has suggested a transregional and diachronic approach to reading Southern regionalism in "William Faulkner's *Go Down, Moses*: An

American Frontier Narrative," *Journal of American Studies* 43.3 (December 2009): 389–405.

13. Nancy Glazener argues that the various outlets for regional fiction in the period created different expectations and implied different types of reader, in particular seeing a difference between the middle-class urbanity of the *Atlantic*-group magazines and the less New England–centric *Overland* and *Arena*. See Glazener, especially the chapter "Regional Accents" (189–228).

14. Two quite different mythologies were attached to the idea of rural life in the late nineteenth century, and implicitly inform Kaplan's and Brodhead's views here: the conventional romanticization inherited from both pastoralism and Jeffersonian idealism, and what Maria Farland calls an "anti-rural" strain that viewed rural life and rural people as degenerate, backward, and idiotic. This latter view was reinforced, in part, by negative sociological and anthropological studies of rural life, most notoriously Richard Dugdale's *The Jukes: A Study in Crime, Pauperism, Disease and Heredity* (1877).

15. For a wide-ranging discussion of the idea of "minor" canonical works centered on the work of Sarah Orne Jewett, see Louis A. Renza, *"A White Heron" and the Question of Minor Literature* (Madison: University of Wisconsin Press, 1984).

16. Lutz forcefully argues that the "antihegemonic reading seems to maintain the...arrogant (and ahistorical) assumption that the regionalist authors' politics mirrors critics' own" (27). I am in total agreement, and in general Lutz's assessment of regionalist criticism and its problems is spot on (24–28).

17. Like Marshall Berman, I use the terms modernity and modernization in quite pointed distinction to modernism. Modernity is a broad label for a particular set of historical processes, whereas modernism evokes a more narrowly defined aesthetic reaction to these conditions that existed within a relatively specific period. For a way to wade through the often entangled debates surrounding this point, see Susan Stanford Friedman, "Definitional Excursions: The Meanings of Modern/Modernity/Modernism." *Modernism/Modernity* 8.3 (2001): 493–513.

18. A glance at Adna Weber's classic statistical study *The Growth of Cities in the Nineteenth Century* (1899) gives some indication of the demographic changes taking place in the period. Taking the census reports' measure of urbanity as a settlement of 8,000 or more persons, the number of cities in America leapt from 141 in 1860 to 448 in 1890. This is, of course, partly accounted for simply by the growth in population overall, yet as Weber notes, "in the great cereal regions of the West, the cities have grown entirely out of proportion to the rural parts, resulting there...in an increasing concentration of the population" (20). More pertinent, then, is the percentage of the population accounted for by urban dwellers: 16% in 1860, and 29% by 1890. It is not the case that the population of the United States lived predominantly in cities by the end of this period; in fact, it is under a third. It would be misleading here to suggest that the rural population suffered a decline inversely proportional to the urban population's growth. However, beneath these statistics there are more complex flows taking place. The rate of increase in urban population was 59% between 1860 and 1870, and 61% between 1880 and 1890; yet in comparison, the rate of increase of rural population was just 15% in both periods.

19. See especially David B. Danbom, *Born in the Country: A History of Rural America* (Baltimore: The Johns Hopkins University Press, 1995) and Hal S. Barron, *Mixed Harvest: The Second Great Transformation in the Rural North, 1870–1930* (Chapel Hill: The University of North Carolina Press, 1997).

20. On this last point, see especially the famous report "The Influence of Railway Travelling on Public Health" published in the British medical journal *The Lancet*, January 4, 1862.

CHAPTER 1

1. *The Huge Hunter* went through several reprints, proved the inspiration for many subsequent dime novels, and spawned a whole subgenre of "steam men" fiction—itself the forerunner for several sub-genres of science fiction. The author, Edward Sylvester Ellis, must count as one of the most remarkably prolific writers in American literary history. Between the 1860s and the early 1890s, writing under his own name as well as at least a dozen pseudonyms, he managed to produce over 200 dime novels for various publishing houses (mainly boys' fiction about frontier life) not to mention over 50 volumes of history—including the 1,500-page "Youth's History of the United States" and the 6,000-page "History of the German People." See Albert Johannsen's notes on Ellis at Northern Illinois University's dime novel digitization project: http://www.ulib.niu.edu/badndp/ellis_edward.html
2. Thompson's small place in American literary history tends to be centered on his critical writings (and his quarrel with Howells over the nature of realism) rather than his fiction. See Link (43–44) and Gary Scharnhorst, "Maurice Thompson's Regional Critique of William Dean Howells," *American Literary Realism* 9 (1976): 57–63.
3. This slippage between realist and romantic registers, and the way it is explicitly connected to gender, echo Michael Davitt Bell's argument in *The Problem of American Realism* that realism came to be understood as a masculine answer to the effeminacy of sentimental and romantic fiction. The complex matrix of genre and gender in this passage are underpinned, I argue, by the equally complex connotations of the railroad.
4. There are several excellent accounts of the adoption of standard time in America. See especially O'Malley, and the first chapter of Jack Beatty's *The Age of Betrayal: The Triumph of Money in America, 1865–1900* (New York: Alfred A. Knopf, 2007).
5. Both the *Old Farmers' Almanac* (published since 1792) and *Farmers' Almanac* (published since 1818) are journals dedicated to rural matters, including, most famously, long-range weather forecasting, and astronomical data. They were ubiquitous and invaluable handbooks for farmers throughout the nineteenth century.
6. These stories are now hard to track down, but appeared in various collections of Jewett's stories published in her lifetime. "A Late Supper" was first collected in *Old Friends and New* (1879); "A Little Traveler" first appeared in *Good Company* (1880); and "The Dulham Ladies" first appeared in *A White Heron and Other Stories* (1886). However, this is complicated by the fact that Jewett is known to have published alternative versions of "A Little Traveler" and "The Dulham Ladies." These can all be found online at the Sarah Orne Jewett Text Project: http://www.public.coe.edu/~theller/soj/contents.htm. For an exemplary reading of "A Late Supper," see Howard, "Unraveling Regions, Unsettling Periods."
7. The standardization of British local time began in the 1840s, and by 1855 the majority of public timekeeping adhered to London time.
8. John Stilgoe goes as far as to provide a summary of the level of detail visible from a train window at particular speeds: "At five miles an hour, an intent

observer can discern flowers and other elements of the scene immediately adjacent to the rails, but at ten miles an hour he must look at objects fifteen feet from the side of the car. At thirty miles an hour, everything within the thirty- to forty-foot mark appears blurred.... At ninety miles an hour, the railroad passenger intrigued by the passing scene must fix his attention only on very distant objects; doing otherwise creates eyestrain and headache" (250).
9. It is worth quoting Simmel himself here as his analysis of the sensory experiences of the metropolis compared with that of rural life are pertinent to my own discussion of the experience of train travel: "Lasting impressions, impressions which differ only slightly from one another, impressions which take a regular and habitual course...—all these use up, so to speak, less consciousness than does the rapid crowding of changing images, the sharp discontinuity in the grasp of a single glance.... These are the psychological conditions which the metropolis creates.... [T]he city sets up a deep contrast with small town and rural life with reference to the sensory foundations of psychic life. The metropolis exacts from man...a different amount of consciousness than does rural life" (175).
10. The description of the "swaying caparisons" in the Pullman carriage is interesting in itself. "Caparison" can mean, in its general sense, anything richly adorned, but also more specifically refers to the embroidered cloth covering of a horse. With the metaphor of the "iron horse" part of the common lexicon, such a pointed use of the word may have been an ironic gesture on Tarkington's part, but might also be read as a specific moment where the vocabularies of the pre-modern and modern worlds slip suggestively between each other.
11. For more on Dickson and early westerns in general, see Scott Simmon, *The Invention of the Western Film* (Cambridge: Cambridge University Press, 2003) and Nanna Verhoeff, *The West in Early Cinema: After the Beginning* (Amsterdam: Amsterdam University Press, 2006)
12. Stilgoe, for instance, states that in a "speeding passenger car, coach or Pullman...the gazing passenger entered a theatrelike, cinemalike...state" (252). For an extended and thorough analysis of the relationship between the train and early cinema, see Kirby.
13. A possible source for the novel's use of the train in this respect is Richard Harding Davis's popular travel narrative *The West from a Car-Window* (New York: Harper and Brothers, 1892). Describing his journey through Texas, Oklahoma, and Colorado, mainly by train, Davis's account records both the scenic landscapes and traditional life of the West as well as the first signs of the industrial and commercial growth that would transform the region. The idea of viewing the rapidly transforming West from the comforts of a train carriage seems to chime with Wister's opening scene.

CHAPTER 2

1. Gender and sexuality studies have, of course, been the predominant critical lenses through which Jewett's work has been read—which is partly the reason for my pursuit of an alternative approach here. For an influential reading of *Deephaven* along these lines, however, see Judith Fetterley, "Reading *Deephaven* as a Lesbian Text" in *Sexual Practice/Textual Theory: Lesbian Cultural Criticism*. Oxford: Blackwell, 1993: 164–83.
2. "Caravan" was a common colloquialism for circuses at the time.

3. Once again, Helen and Kate are the detached observers/listeners for the majority of the scene. They are on the other side of the tent looking at some monkeys when Mrs. Kew begins speaking to the giantess, at which point, "with great interest...we went nearer" (78). Nearly two pages of dialogue between Mrs. Kew and the giantess follow, all reported in Helen's first-person narrative, but it is only when Mrs. Kew mentions Helen's and Kate's names that they turn around (79). The whole passage Helen has just recounted was an eavesdropped conversation.
4. Hamlin Hill has noted the presence of the circus in *A Connecticut Yankee*, but to suggest that Hank Morgan may be modeled on P. T. Barnum himself. Hill points out that when Hank first sees Camelot at the start of the novel and assumes, somewhat oddly, that he is in Bridgeport, Connecticut, that it may be Twain making a playful reference to Barnum's own house. Inspired by a trip to the Brighton Pavilion when Barnum was in England, the house—named "Iranistan"—was built in 1848 and instantly became a famous local landmark. Constance Rourke's description goes some way to doing it justice when she lists the "balconies, wide wings, shining domes, spires [and] minarets," and grounds including a "huge fountain... bronze deer... and the fair semblance of an English park" (qtd. in Hill 615). Sadly, the house would only stand for eight years before it burned to the ground in 1857, but a woodcut of it appeared in Barnum's autobiography, *Struggles and Triumphs*, published in 1869, a book that became one of Twain's favorites. Both Hill and David Sloane have suggested that when Twain came to write *A Connecticut Yankee* "P. T. Barnum was... very much in [his] consciousness" (Sloane 147). After all, Hank Morgan is an entrepreneurial, straight-talking Connecticut man in the Barnum mold, a character who spends the novel creating ever-more elaborate displays of showmanship and illusion.
5. William Dean Howells, in *A Boy's Town* (1890), recalls that children in his hometown would often try to pull the same trick Huck does. Not only that, but getting into the circus without paying was considered an admirable achievement: "The boys held it to be a high and creditable thing to hook into a show of any kind, but hooking into a circus was something that a fellow ought to be held in special honor for doing" (778). In fact, Howells's description of his boyhood visit to the circus bears a remarkable similarity to the passage in *Huckleberry Finn*: apart from sneaking into the circus without paying, both the young Howells and Huck are particularly captivated by an act where a supposedly drunken man from the audience volunteers to ride a misbehaving horse, much to the ridicule of the watching crowd, only to effortlessly gallop around the ring—taking off layers of clothes as he does so to reveal a series of colorful costumes underneath. Whereas Huck is convinced the whole thing is a prank at the expense of the ringmaster—"he *was* the sickest ring-master you ever see, I reckon. Why, it was one of his own men! He had got up that joke all out of his own head, and never let on to nobody" (194, emphasis in original)—Howells is wise with hindsight: "The big boys have known all along that he was not a real country-jake" (780).
6. For a more developed discussion of the role that Barnum's circuses play in Twain's writing, see Mark Storey, "Huck and Hank Go to the Circus: Mark Twain under Barnum's Big Top," *European Journal of American Culture* 29.3 (2011):217–28.

7. Garland seems to be misquoting the opening of a poem (perhaps from memory) by Hannah F. Gould, written in 1839, called "The Wheat Field." The correct version reads:

> Fields of wheat, so full and fair,
> Showing thus thy silvery hair,
> Lightly waving either way,
> Where the gentle breezes play...

8. A proto-feminist movement on both sides of the Atlantic in the last decades of the nineteenth century, the "New Woman" ideal was partly a reaction to the stereotyped gender roles that the Cult of Domesticity had established. *Rose of Dutcher's Coolly* has been read in this light; see Newlin.
9. Archaic plural of "cow."
10. In the immediate context of when this story was written, the 1892 Geary Exclusion Act had served to extend and solidify several earlier Chinese Exclusion Acts.
11. This brings to mind the notion of the "uncanny"; *das Unheimliche* literally translates as "the unhomely," and there are few more "homely" symbols in nineteenth-century usage than the peaceful rural village. The circus clearly stands as a stark contrast to such homeliness. Anthony Vidler, however, in *The Architectural Uncanny* (1992), sees the uncanny as something that was "born out of the rise of the great cities," a consequence of "their disturbingly heterogeneous crowds" (4). He goes on to argue that "generalized as a condition of modern anxiety, an alienation linked to its individual and poetic origins in romanticism, the uncanny finally became public in metropolis" (6). According to Vidler, the uncanny becomes the defining psychopathology of urban modernity: "As a concept...the uncanny has, not unnaturally, found its metaphorical home...in the city, where what was once walled and intimate, the confirmation of community,...has been rendered strange by the spatial incursions of modernity" (11). The modern city, in its ceaseless manifestation of the unfamiliar, is seen as the prime and originating location of an uncanny condition. While I do not wish to pursue a notion of the "rural uncanny" here, it is worthy of note that the circus operates precisely as one of the "spatial incursions of modernity" that Vidler discusses—and illustrates, once again, how rural space is often removed from theoretical considerations of modernity.
12. Game used for gambling and, more often than not, as a confidence trick. The operator places a pea under one of three shells and rapidly shuffles them on a flat surface. The participant then bets on which shell the pea is under, not realizing that the operator has in fact palmed the pea anyway. Common at fairs and circuses throughout the nineteenth century, the shell game became a favorite trick in the repertoire of famed confidence trickster Jefferson "Soapy" Smith (1860–1898).
13. This rapid assault of visual stimuli returns us to a point made in chapter 1 about the links between urban experience and visual perception; see the quote from Georg Simmel in note 9.

CHAPTER 3

1. While these two men do indeed represent the dominant trend in the medical profession of their time, the notion that antebellum medicine was devoid

of scientific thinking is inaccurate. See especially John Harley Warner, "The History of Science and the Sciences of Medicine," *Osiris* 2.10 (1995): 164–93.
2. Foucault uses the term "library" metonymically to mean, "not only the books and treatises traditionally recognized as valid, but also all the observations and case-histories published and transmitted, and the mass of statistical information...that can be supplied to the doctor by public bodies" (*Archaeology of Knowledge*, 57). Anywhere, in other words, where medical knowledge is officially deposited in written form.
3. The book's full title is worth recounting if only because it typifies the age in its inclusive circuitousness and taxonomic anxiety: *New Guide to Health; or, Botanic Family Physician, containing a Complete System of Practice, on a Plan Entirely New; with a Description of the Vegetables made use of, and Directions for Preparing and Administering Them to Cure Disease, to Which is Prefixed, a Narrative of the Life and Medical Discoveries of the Author* (2nd edition. Boston: J.Q. Adams, 1835).
4. The slippery elm (*Ulmus rubra*) is native to the northeastern quarter of North America within which the novel is set. Its bark was traditionally used either as a tea or a nutrient-rich gruel to sooth digestive irritations, but it was also used as an abortifacient.
5. In its broadest application to the history of science, the notion of incommensurability is something Thomas Kuhn elaborates on in his classic study *The Structure of Scientific Revolutions* (1962). At its simplest level, Kuhn's influential thesis is that when a field of science undergoes a paradigm shift—or, as Kuhn puts it in terms that echo Weberian terminology, a "change of world view"—the new fields of theory that open up cannot be straightforwardly compared to the ones they have replaced because the very standards of evaluation have also changed. "[W]hen paradigms change," Kuhn states, "the world itself changes with them" (111)—or, more accurately, "the scientist afterward works in a different world" (121). It would be overreaching to suggest that a metanarrational theory like Kuhn's is wholly applicable here, not least because medicine and science are not simply synonymous; but the expansion of critical terminology that Kuhn introduces is useful to this discussion.
6. For Foucault's own exploration of medicalization, see *The Birth of the Clinic: An Archaeology of Medical Perception* (New York: Pantheon Books, 1973).
7. Folk remedies, often passed down through families and communities, ranged from the simple application of herbs to elaborate, exhausting concoctions of botanicals and animal products. Ann Anderson cites this midwestern recipe for a rheumatism-relieving massage oil from the mid-nineteenth century: "Take a young fat dog and kill him, scald and clean him as you would a pig, then extract his guts through a hole previously made in his side, and substitute in the place thereof, two handfuls of nettles, two ounces of brimstone, one dozen hen eggs, four ounces of turpentine, a handful of tanzy, a pint of red fishing worms, and about three-fourths of a pound of tobacco, cut up fine; mix all those ingredients well together before deposited [sic] in the dog's belly, and then sew up the whole [sic], then roast him well before a hot fire, save the oil, anoint the joints and weak parts before the fire as hot as you can bear it" (27). Whether anyone decided to just live with the rheumatism is not recorded.
8. Eric Carl Link discusses the way in which various authors who have been associated most directly with American naturalism—Frank Norris especially—practiced a form of writing that included both realistic and romantic elements. The naturalism I am suggesting in Murfree's story is more along the lines of

philosophical naturalism, what Link describes as "a worldview that precludes the operation of *super*natural forces and stresses the notion that all phenomena...can be explained in terms of material causation" (11, emphasis in original). Murfree's story introduces a supernatural element but refuses to confirm whether or not it is "really" a ghost or merely a hallucination.

9. The other novel frequently mentioned in connection with these two is William Dean Howells' *Doctor Breen's Practice* (1881). Indeed, Phelps was yet another Gilded Age writer in correspondence with Howells, and the two discussed the subject of women doctors in literature at some length (see Davis 103–21).
10. See especially Browner, Glazener, and Baym.
11. Homeopaths—believing in the treatment of disease by application of hugely diluted medicines that would induce the same symptoms as the disease itself—had a long-running and often acrimonious struggle with regular doctors (or "allopaths"), who sought to treat disease by administering treatments that would have an opposed effect. This iconoclastic approach to orthodox medicine's fundamental assumptions meant homeopaths were excluded when the American Medical Association was formed in 1847, a decision that would effectively discredit homeopathy and condemn it to professional marginalization by the end of the century.
12. A key context here, of course, is the changing place of women within the medical profession. In 1860 there were just 200 practicing female physicians in the United States, a number that had risen to over 7000 by the turn of the century (Baym 176). As prominent representations of professional women, both Phelps's and Jewett's novels have been widely discussed in relation to feminist history and literary scholarship; see especially Baym, Davis, and Browner. For a broader historical account of women physicians in late nineteenth-century America, see Regina Morantz-Sanchez, *Sympathy and Science: Women Physicians in American Medicine* (Chapel Hill: University North Carolina Press, 2000).
13. Dr. Benjamin Rush (1746–1813), hugely influential physician and co-signer of the Declaration of Independence, advocated the aggressive and drastic treatments that typified the "heroic" medicine of the eighteenth and early nineteenth centuries.
14. Jewett returned to this idea in an uncollected story published ten years later, "In a Country Practice" (1894). Dr. John Ashurst decides to commit to a rural life rather than follow his mentor to New York, and in the final part of the story, while his daughters sift through the contents of his study following his death, they encounter a series of objects that suggest their father's medical knowledge was based more on instinct and experience than on a sustained immersion in modern science: among an old wasp's nest and a bust of Dante there is a picture of Thomas Sydenham, celebrated seventeenth-century English physician, and a copy of *Religio Medici* by Sir Thomas Browne, published in 1643.
15. There is a poignant biographical note worth mentioning here. The model for Dr. Leslie seems to have been Sarah's own father, Theodore Jewett, a respected physician and surgeon who served the town of Berwick, Maine, and, later, the state medical school. Sarah herself would write his obituary in 1879 (it was published anonymously), and there is a touching sense throughout that her father's career never achieved the recognition it deserved because his own delicate health required that he live a provincial life: "It could not help being, at times, somewhat a lonely life, for he was shut out from the larger circle of professional friends, with its pleasures and advantages, to which he would have belonged in a

city" (*Country Doctor* 267). Such personal sentiments seem to have been part of Jewett's narrative concerns in *A Country Doctor*.
16. Myers offers a brief summary of the various readings of the novel, from Larzer Ziff's through to his own, pointing out that what they share is a notion of the central characters—Father Forbes, Celia Madden, and Sister Soulsby, as well as Ledsmar—as "representations of the social forces that were transforming America" (61n).

CHAPTER 4

1. Such a situation was not uncommon in scenes of popular justice. Margaret Vandiver, discussing Southern lynching in particular but commenting on this aspect of popular justice in general, points out that "mob members held trials in an attempt to give an aura of legality to the murder they intended to commit" (93)
2. There are several excellent histories of lynching concerning the late-nineteenth and early-twentieth-century periods. Philip Dray's *At the Hands of Parties Unknown: The Lynching of Black America* (New York: Modern Library, 2002) is a rich source of statistics and analysis, and Amy Wood's *Lynching and Spectacle: Witnessing Racial Violence in America, 1890–1940* (Chapel Hill: University of North Carolina Press, 2009) continues the cultural-historical approach similar to Goldsby's. What is interesting about these two studies is that they indicate the way in which "lynching" only became generally synonymous with racially aggravated violence at the very end of the nineteenth century, an equation that has tended to be applied retroactively through the whole of the postbellum period.
3. Gonzales-Day succinctly summarizes this problem of usage when he writes that "even the most ambitious researchers are challenged to distinguish substantial differences between the practices referred to as vigilance committees, lynch mobs, kangaroo courts, hanging parties, and sheriff's posses" (11). For a concise overview of lynching's changing and troublesome definition see Waldrep's introduction; indeed, he sees his entire book as an attempt "to trace the history of the word lynching" (4).
4. One figure who typified this approach was Christopher Columbus Langdell, dean of Harvard Law School between 1870 and 1895 and famous in legal circles as the man who introduced the casebook method to legal education. Langdell believed in the essentially scientific study of law, insisting that it was a "highly specialized discipline" that must be "largely purified of external considerations" (Feldman 92). In Langdell's conception of law, legal principles were not derived from social opinion or preexisting moral absolutes outside the legal system, but were "immanent in and exist only through cases" (97). Langdellian logic, as Feldman points out, appears circular: "the legal scientist studied a series of cases and then reasoned inductively upward to discover the principles. But once discovered, these high-level principles served as the fountainhead for chains of deductive logic, reasoning downward to generate precisely classified and arranged formal systems" (97). For a more detailed account of Langdellian thought, see Feldman (91–101).
5. A broadly defined but usefully pithy account of the terms comes in Walter Benjamin's essay on law and justice, "Critique of Violence": "Natural law attempts, by the justness of the ends, to 'justify' the means, positive law to 'guarantee' the justness of the ends through the justification of the means" (278)—in other

words, the first argues for how law "ought" to be, the second for how law "is" (McLeod 19). With these categories in mind, the text that critics concerned with law and literature during the Gilded Age have most frequently seized upon is Herman Melville's *Billy Budd, Sailor* (left unfinished on Melville's death in 1891 and eventually published in 1924). The story of a court-martial and execution aboard a British ship, Dolin notes that the story "has been read as an allegory of the clash between the two systems of jurisprudence": "the execution of Billy represents the tragic outcome of a strict application of the Code [of law] and the exclusion of any consideration of personal justice" (27). See also Brook Thomas, and Robert A. Ferguson, *Law and Letters in American Culture* (Cambridge, MA: Harvard University Press, 1984).

6. For a full discussion of the Chesnutt-Howells relationship, and of Chesnutt's realism more generally, see Simmons.
7. Lloyd Pratt discusses a similar notion in relation specifically to the heterogeneous modes of temporality in the antebellum period, arguing that they disrupted progressive narratives of national destiny (5).
8. The story appeared in July 1896, during the election campaign that in November of that year would result in Republican William McKinley defeating the Democratic candidate William Jennings Bryan. "A Lynching in Mosinee" seems to anticipate this result, even down to the fact that New York went to the Republicans. Garland's connection with the Populist Party is well-known (the Populists were particularly strong in the rural Midwest, where the story is set) and the election of 1896 is seen as a watershed moment for the party: they nominated Bryan as their candidate, but still insisted on their independence from the Democratic Party. The convergence of the two parties was inevitable, however, and by the early twentieth century the Populist Party had disappeared. For an introduction to and selection of Garland's political writings, see Donald Pizer, editor, *Hamlin Garland, Prairie Radical: Writings from the 1890s* (Urbana: University of Illinois Press, 2010).
9. The insanity plea was not solely a Gilded Age phenomenon, and it caused much controversy on both sides of the Atlantic throughout the nineteenth century. See Allen D. Spiegel and Marc B. Spiegel, "The Insanity Plea in Early Nineteenth Century America," *Journal of Community Health* 23.3 (June 1998): 227–247, and Richard Moran, "The Modern Foundation for the Insanity Defense: The Cases of James Hadfield (1800) and Daniel McNaughtan (1843)," *Annals of the American Academy of Political and Social Science* 477 (Jan. 1985): 31–42.
10. Robert Shulman points out that the beating of Pedro is taken from a real incident in Wister's life that happened while he was out West. Out riding, Wister's host turned on his own horse and beat it so brutally that the animal's eye was gouged out. Wister took no action at the time and later expressed his guilt for not doing so; the scene in *The Virginian* might well be read as his attempt at some kind of atonement. See Shulman (348n in Wister).

CHAPTER 5

1. "Utopian fiction" here refers to the body of texts published in America during the last fifteen or so years of the nineteenth century, a category that encompasses the whole range of writing in this genre including fiction that represents a dystopian vision.

2. There are many studies of the rise of the Populist Party in the late nineteenth century; see especially Robert C. McMath's *American Populism: A Social History 1877–1898* (New York: Hill and Wang, 1993) and the chapter "The Politics of the Future" in Jack Beatty's *The Age of Betrayal* (New York: Alfred A. Knopf, 2007: 303–45).
3. Ignatius Donnelly (1831–1901) had been a Republican congressman and senator for Minnesota in the 1860s and 1870s, but was also well-known as the author of two grandly ambitious pseudohistories: *Atlantis: The Antediluvian World* (1882) claimed that Atlantis—a real place—had been destroyed in an apocalyptic natural disaster, and *Ragnarok, the Age of Fire and Gravel* (1883) proposed that a comet had struck earth in prehistoric times. He also gained a certain degree of notoriety for his theory, proposed in *The Great Cryptogram* (1888), that Francis Bacon was in fact the writer of Shakespeare's plays. For more on the life of this extraordinary man, see Martin Ridge, *Ignatius Donnelly: The Portrait of a Politician* (St. Paul: Borealis Books, 1991).
4. For a basic discussion of the differences between the geographical descriptions in *Looking Backward* and those in *Equality*, see John R. Mullin, "Edward Bellamy's Ambivalence: Can Utopia be Urban?", *Utopian Studies*, 11 (2000): 51–65.
5. Such visions of the reformed urban landscape had their parallels in the City Beautiful movement of the 1890s and 1900s, an attempt by progressive urban planners and architects to ameliorate inner-city problems through beautification of the built environment. The insistence on the parklike landscapes of the future also owes much to the work and legacy of Frederick Law Olmsted (1822–1903), celebrated landscape architect and designer of (among many urban parks in the United States) Central Park in New York City and, with Daniel Burnham, the 1893 World's Fair in Chicago. Many of the fictional utopian landscapes examined in this chapter clearly echo these well-known plans and designs. On the City Beautiful movement, see William H. Wilson, *The City Beautiful Movement* (Baltimore: Johns Hopkins University Press,1989) and on Olmsted, see Witold Rybczynski, *A Clearing in the Distance: Frederick Law Olmsted and America in the Nineteenth Century* (New York: Scribner, 1999).
6. In the chapter "The Contemporary City," Le Corbusier states his ambitious plan: a radical centralization of city living coupled with a massive increase in open spaces. "We must *increase the open spaces and diminish the distances to be covered*. Therefore the centre of the city must be constructed *vertically*" (163, emphasis in original). The belief in the strength of rational, reasoned city planning achieves a kind of apotheosis in Le Corbusier's Paris of the future: "The city of to-day is a dying thing because it is not geometrical" (171) he states. See pp. 159–78.
7. For an extended analysis of Frank Lloyd Wright and Le Corbusier along these same lines, see Richard A. Etlin, *Frank Lloyd Wright and Le Corbusier: The Romantic Legacy* (Manchester: Manchester University Press, 1994). It is also worth pointing out that this often paradoxical connection between romantic and modernist philosophies would lie at the heart of fascist visions of the city in the 1930s; see George L. Mosse, *The Crisis of German Ideology: The Intellectual Origins of the Third Reich* (New York: Grosset and Dunlap, 1964).

WORKS CITED

PRIMARY SOURCES

Allen, James Lane. *Summer in Arcady: A Tale of Nature*. New York: Macmillan & Co., 1896.
Bellamy, Edward. *Looking Backward, 2000–1887*. 1888. Edited by Matthew Beaumont. Oxford: Oxford University Press, 2007.
Bellamy, Edward. *Equality*. 1897. New York: AMS Press, 1970.
Brown, Alice. "Strollers in Tiverton." *Meadow-Grass: Tales of New England Life*. Boston and New York: Houghton, Mifflin and Company, 1895. 278–315.
Brown, Alice. "Horn o' the Moon." *Tiverton Tales*. Boston and New York: Houghton, Mifflin and Company, 1899. 98–128.
Chesnutt, Charles. "The Sheriff's Children." 1889. *Charles W. Chesnutt: Stories, Novels and Essays*. Edited by Werner Sollors. New York: The Library of America, 2002. 131–48.
Crane, Stephen. "The Bride Comes to Yellow Sky." 1898. *The Open Boat and Other Stories*. New York: Dover Publications, 1993. 79–88.
Donnelly, Ignatius. *Caesar's Column: A Story of the Twentieth Century*. 1890. Edited by Nicholas Ruddick. Middletown, CT.: Wesleyan University Press, 2003.
Dunbar, Paul Laurence. "The Ordeal at Mt. Hope." 1898. *The Complete Stories of Paul Laurence Dunbar*. Edited by Gene Andrew Jarrett and Thomas Lewis Morgan. Athens: Ohio University Press, 2005. 11–24.
Dunbar, Paul Laurence. "The Tragedy at Three Forks." 1900. *The Complete Stories of Paul Laurence Dunbar*. Edited by Gene Andrew Jarrett and Thomas Lewis Morgan. Athens: Ohio University Press, 2005. 171–76.
Eggleston, Edward. *The Hoosier School-Master*. 1871. Bloomington: Indiana University Press, 1984.
Eggleston, Edward. *The Mystery of Metropolisville*. 1873. Charleston, SC: Bibliobazaar, 2006.
Ellis, Edward Sylvester. *The Huge Hunter, or The Steam Man of the Prairies*. 1868. *Eight Dime Novels*. Edited by E.F. Bleiler. New York: Dover Publications, 1974. 107–21.
Frederic, Harold. *The Damnation of Theron Ware or Illumination*. 1896. New York: The Modern Library, 2002.
Garland, Hamlin. "God's Ravens." *Main-Travelled Roads*. 1891. New York: Perennial Classics, 1956. 191–206.
Garland, Hamlin. "The Return of a Private." *Main-Travelled Roads*. 1891. New York: Perennial Classics, 1956. 108–26.

Garland, Hamlin. "Uncle Ethan Ripley." *Main-Travelled Roads*. 1891. New York: Perennial Classics, 1956. 179–91.

Garland, Hamlin. "Up the Coolly." *Main-Travelled Roads*. 1891. New York: Perennial Classics, 1956. 42–85.

Garland, Hamlin. *Rose of Dutcher's Coolly*. 1895. Edited by Keith Newlin. Lincoln and London: University of Nebraska Press, 2005.

Garland, Hamlin. "A Lynching in Mosinee." *The Pocket Magazine*. 2.3 (July 1896): 108–40.

Harte, Bret. "Tennessee's Partner." 1869. *The Luck of Roaring Camp and Other Writings*. Edited by Gary Scharnhorst. New York: Penguin, 2001. 49–57.

Howells, William Dean. *Suburban Sketches*. 1871. Stroud, UK: Nonsuch Publishing, 2005.

Howells, William Dean. *Their Wedding Journey*. 1871. Boston and New York: Houghton, Mifflin and Company, 1899.

Howells, William Dean. *A Boy's Town*. 1890. *Selected Writings of William Dean Howells*. Edited by Henry Steele Commager. New York: Random House, 1950. 711–880.

Howells, William Dean. *A Traveler from Altruria*. 1894. New York: Hill and Wang, 1957.

Jewett, Sarah Orne. *Deephaven*. 1877. *Sarah Orne Jewett: Novels and Stories*. Edited by Michael Davitt Bell. New York: Library of America, 1994. 1–141.

Jewett, Sarah Orne. *A Country Doctor*. 1884. Edited by Frederick Wegener. New York: Penguin Books, 2005.

Jewett, Sarah Orne. "Going to Shrewsbury." 1889. *Sarah Orne Jewett: Novels and Stories*. Edited by Michael Davitt Bell. New York: Library of America, 1994. 700–09.

Jewett, Sarah Orne. *The Country of the Pointed Firs*. 1896. *The Country of the Pointed Firs and Other Stories*. Edited by Alison Easton. London: Penguin Books, 1995.

Kirkland, Joseph. *Zury: The Meanest Man in Spring County*. 1887. Urbana: University of Illinois Press, 1956.

Murfree, Mary Noailles [Charles Egbert Craddock]. "The Romance of Sunrise Rock." *In the Tennessee Mountains*. Boston: Houghton, Mifflin and Company, 1884. 182–214.

Olerich, Henry. *A Cityless and Countryless World*. 1893. New York: Arno Press and the New York Times, 1971.

Phelps, Elizabeth Stuart. *Doctor Zay*. 1882. New York: The Feminist Press, 1987.

Tarkington, Booth. *The Gentleman from Indiana*. London: T. Nelson and Sons, 1899.

Thompson, Maurice. "Hoiden." *Hoosier Mosaics*. New York: E. J. Hale and Son, 1875. 127–61.

Twain, Mark. *Adventures of Huckleberry Finn*. 1884. Edited by Victor Fischer and Lin Salamo. Berkeley and Los Angeles: University of California Press, 2001.

Twain, Mark. *A Connecticut Yankee at King Arthur's Court*. 1889. Edited by Justin Kaplan. London: Penguin Classics, 1986.

Wister, Owen. *The Virginian: A Horseman of the Plains*. 1902. Edited by Robert Shulman. Oxford: Oxford University Press, 1998.

Woolson, Constance Fenimore. "Peter the Parson." *Castle Nowhere: Lake Country Sketches*. 1875. Ann Arbor: University of Michigan Press, 2004. 65–90.

SECONDARY SOURCES

Adams, Bluford. *E Pluribus Barnum: The Great Showman and the Making of U.S. Popular Culture*. Minneapolis: University of Minnesota Press, 1997.

Allen, Thomas M. *A Republic in Time: Temporality and Social Imagination in Nineteenth-Century America*. Chapel Hill: The University of North Carolina Press, 2008.
Anderson, Ann. *Snake Oil, Hustlers and Hambones: The American Medicine Show*. Jefferson, NC, and London: McFarland and Company, 2000.
Atherton, Lewis. *Main Street on the Middle Border*. 1954. Bloomington: Indiana University Press, 1984.
Auerbach, Jonathan. "'The Nation Organized': Utopian Impotence in Edward Bellamy's *Looking Backward*." *American Literary History*. 6.1 (Spring 1994): 24–47.
Bakhtin, Mikhail. *Rabelais and His World*. Translated by Helene Iswolsky. Cambridge, MA: The M.I.T. Press, 1968.
Barthes, Roland. "The Reality Effect." 1968. *French Literary Theory Today*. Edited by Tzvetan Todorov. Translated by R. Carter. Cambridge: Cambridge University Press, 1982.
Baym, Nina. *American Women of Letters and the Nineteenth-Century Sciences: Styles of Affiliation*. New Brunswick: Rutgers University Press, 2002.
Beaumont, Matthew. Introduction. *Looking Backward: 2000–1887*. By Edward Bellamy. Oxford: Oxford University Press, 2007. vii–xxx.
Beaumont, Matthew and Michael Freeman. "Introduction: Tracks to Modernity." *The Railway and Modernity: Time, Space, and the Machine Ensemble*. Edited by Matthew Beaumont and Michael Freeman. Oxford: Peter Lang, 2007. 13–43.
Beck, E.M. and Stewart E. Tolnay. "When Race Didn't Matter: Black and White Mob Violence against Their Own Color." *Under Sentence of Death: Lynching in the South*. Edited by W. Fitzhugh Brundage. Chapel Hill and London: The University of North Carolina Press, 1997. 132–154.
Bell, Michael Davitt. *The Problem of American Realism: Studies in the Cultural History of a Literary Idea*. Chicago: Chicago University Press, 1993.
Benjamin, Walter. "Critique of Violence." 1921. *Reflections: Essays, Aphorisms, Autobiographical Writings*. Translated by Edmund Jephcott. New York: Harcourt Brace Jovanovich, 1978.
Bentley, Nancy. *Frantic Panoramas: American Literature and Mass Culture, 1870–1920*. Philadelphia: University of Pennsylvania Press, 2009.
Berger, John. "Why Look at Animals?" 1977. *About Looking*. New York: Vintage International, 1991.
Berman, Marshall. *All That Is Solid Melts into Air: The Experience of Modernity*. 1982. London and New York: Verso, 1997.
Bernard, Claude. *An Introduction to the Study of Experimental Medicine*. 1865. Translated by H. C. Greene. New York: Dover Publications, 1957.
Bessler, John D. *Legacy of Violence: Lynch Mobs and Executions in Minnesota*. Minneapolis: University of Minnesota Press, 2003.
Blomley, Nicholas K. *Law, Space, and the Geographies of Power*. New York and London: The Guildford Press, 1994.
Borus, Daniel H. *Writing Realism: Howells, James, and Norris in the Mass Market*. Chapel Hill: University of North Carolina Press, 1989.
Brodhead, Richard. *Cultures of Letters: Scenes of Reading and Writing in Nineteenth Century America*. Chicago and London: University of Chicago Press, 1993.
Brodhead, Richard. "The American Literary Field, 1860–1890." *The Cambridge History of American Literature, Vol. 3: Prose Writing, 1860–1920*. Edited by Sacvan Bercovitch. Cambridge: Cambridge University Press, 2005.

Brown, Bill. *The Material Unconscious: American Amusement, Stephen Crane, and the Economies of Play*. London: Harvard University Press, 1996.
Brown, Richard Maxwell. *Strain of Violence: Historical Studies of American Violence and Vigilantism*. New York: Oxford University Press, 1975.
Browner, Stephanie P. *Profound Science and Elegant Literature: Imagining Doctors in Nineteenth-Century America*. Philadelphia: University of Pennsylvania Press, 2005.
Brundage, W. Fitzhugh. *Lynching in the New South: Georgia and Virginia, 1880–1930*. Urbana: University of Illinois Press, 1993.
Burns, Sarah. *Pastoral Inventions: Rural Life in Nineteenth-Century American Art and Culture*. Philadelphia: Temple University Press, 1989.
Campbell, Donna. "Realism and Regionalism." *A Companion to the Regional Literatures of America*. Edited by Charles L. Crow. Oxford: Blackwell Publishing, 2003. 92–110.
Carby, Hazel V., "'On the Threshold of Woman's Era': Lynching, Empire, and Sexuality in Black Feminist Theory." *"Race," Writing, and Difference*. Edited by Henry Louis Gates, Jr. Chicago: University of Chicago Press, 1986: 301–16.
Certeau, Michel de. *The Practice of Everyday Life*. Translated by Steven Rendall. Berkeley: University of California Press, 1984.
Clark, T.J. *The Painting of Modern Life: Paris in the Art of Manet and His Followers*. London: Thames and Hudson, 1984.
Cloke, Paul and Nigel Thrift. "Refiguring the 'Rural.'" *Writing the Rural: Five Cultural Geographies*. Edited by Paul Cloke et al. London: Paul Chapman Publishing, 1994.
Crary, Jonathan. *Suspensions of Perception: Attention, Spectacle, and Modern Culture*. Cambridge, MA: The M.I.T. Press, 1999.
Cohn, Dorrit. *Transparent Minds: Narrative Modes Presenting Consciousness in Fiction*. Princeton: Princeton University Press, 1978.
Condit, Carl W. *The Railroad and the City: A Technological and Urbanistic History of Cincinnati*. Columbus: Ohio State University Press, 1977.
Conlogue, William. *Working the Garden: American Writers and the Industrialization of Agriculture*. Chapel Hill: The University of North Carolina Press, 2001.
Cronon, William. *Nature's Metropolis: Chicago and the Great West*. New York: W. W. Norton & Company, 1991.
Cutler, James Elbert. *Lynch-Law: An Investigation into the History of Lynching in the United States*. New York: Longman, Greens, and Co., 1905.
Dale, Elizabeth. "Criminal Justice in the United States, 1790–1920: A Government of Laws or Men?" *The Cambridge History of Law in America: Volume 2, The Long Nineteenth Century (1789–1920)*. Edited by Michael Grossberg and Christopher Tomlins. Cambridge: Cambridge University Press, 2008.
Daly, Nicholas. "Railway Novels: Sensation Fiction and the Modernization of the Senses." *ELH: English Literary History*. 66 (Summer 1999): 461–87.
Danbom, David B. *Born in the Country: A History of Rural America*. Baltimore: The Johns Hopkins University Press, 1995.
Davis, Cynthia J. *Bodily and Narrative Forms: The Influence of Medicine on American Literature, 1845–1918*. Palo Alto, CA: Stanford University Press, 2000.
Davis, Janet M. *The Circus Age: Culture and Society under the American Big Top*. Chapel Hill and London: The University of North Carolina Press, 2002.
Debord, Guy. *The Society of the Spectacle*. 1967. Translated by Donald Nicholson-Smith. New York: Zone Books, 1994.

Dickens, Charles. *Hard Times.* 1854. Edited by Kate Flint. London: Penguin, 1995.
Dierig, Sven, Jens Lachmund and J. Andrew Mendelsohn. "Toward an Urban History of Science." *Osiris.* 18 (2003): 1–19.
Dimsdale, Thomas J. *The Vigilantes of Montana, or Popular Justice in the Rocky Mountains.* 1865. Butte, MT: McKee Publishing Co., 1950.
Dolin, Kieran. *Fiction and the Law: Legal Discourse in Victorian and Modernist Literature.* Cambridge: Cambridge University Press, 1999.
Dreiser, Theodore. *Sister Carrie.* 1900. Oxford: Oxford University Press, 1998.
Duffy, John. *The Healers: A History of American Medicine.* Urbana: University of Illinois Press, 1979.
Eagleton, Terry. *Walter Benjamin, or Towards a Revolutionary Criticism.* 1981. London: Verso, 1992.
Entrikin, J. Nicholas. *Towards a Geography of Modernity.* London: Macmillan, 1991.
Esteve, Mary. *The Aesthetics and Politics of the Crowd in American Literature.* Cambridge: Cambridge University Press, 2003.
Etulain, Richard W. *Telling Western Stories: From Buffalo Bill to Larry McMurtry.* Albuquerque: The University of New Mexico Press, 1999.
Farland, Maria. "Modernist Versions of Pastoral: Poetic Inspiration, Scientific Expertise, and the 'Degenerate' Farmer." *American Literary History.* 19.4 (Winter 2007), 905–36.
Feldman, Stephen M. *American Legal Thought from Premodernism to Postmodernism: An Intellectual Voyage.* New York and Oxford: Oxford University Press, 2000.
Fetterley, Judith and Marjorie Pryse. *Writing Out of Place: Regionalism, Women, and American Literary Culture.* Urbana and Chicago: University of Illinois Press, 2003.
Fishman, Robert. *Urban Utopias in the Twentieth Century: Ebenezer Howard, Frank Lloyd Wright, and Le Corbusier.* New York: Basic Books, 1977.
Foote, Stephanie. *Regional Fictions: Culture and Identity in Nineteenth-Century American Literature.* Madison: University of Wisconsin Press, 2001.
Foote, Stephanie. "The Cultural Work of American Regionalism." *A Companion to the Regional Literatures of America.* Edited by Charles L. Crow. Oxford: Blackwell Publishing, 2003.
Foucault, Michel. *The Archaeology of Knowledge.* 1969. Translated by A. M. Sheridan Smith. London: Routledge Classics, 2002.
Foucault, Michel. *Discipline and Punish: The Birth of the Prison.* 1975. Translated by Alan Sheridan. London: Penguin, 1991.
Friedman, Lawrence M. *A History of American Law.* New York: Simon and Schuster, 1973.
Friedman, Lawrence M. *Crime and Punishment in American History.* Baltimore and London: John Hopkins University Press, 1995.
Giddens, Anthony. *The Consequences of Modernity.* Cambridge: Polity Press, 1990.
Gillette, King Camp. *The Human Drift.* Boston: New Era Publishing, 1894.
Glazener, Nancy. *Reading for Realism: The History of a U.S. Literary Institution, 1850–1910.* Durham and London: Duke University Press, 1997.
Goist, Park Dixon. *From Main Street to State Street: Town, City and Community in America.* Port Washington, NY: Kennikat Press, 1977.
Goldsby, Jacqueline. *A Spectacular Secret: Lynchings in American Life and Literature.* Chicago and London: University of Chicago Press, 2006.
Gonzales-Day, Ken. *Lynching in the West: 1850–1935.* Durham and London: Duke University Press, 2006.

Gordon, Sarah H. *Passage to Union: How the Railroads Transformed American Life, 1829–1929*. Chicago: Elephant Paperbacks, 1997.

Graulich, Melody. "Monopolizing 'The Virginian' (Or, Railroading Wister)." *Montana: The Magazine of Western History*. 56.1 (Spring 2006): 30–41.

Habermas, Jürgen. *The Philosophical Discourse of Modernity*. Translated by Frederick Lawrence. Cambridge: Polity Press, 1987.

Hall, Peter. *Cities of Tomorrow: An Intellectual History of Urban Planning and Design in the Twentieth Century*. Updated edition. Oxford: Blackwell Publishers, 1996.

Halliburton, David. *The Color of the Sky: A Study of Stephen Crane*. Cambridge: Cambridge University Press, 1989.

Harris, Neil. *Humbug: The Art of P. T. Barnum*. Chicago: University of Chicago Press, 1973.

Henderson, George L. *California and the Fictions of Capital*. New York: Oxford University Press, 1999.

Higham, John. "The Matrix of Specialization." *The Organization of Knowledge in Modern America, 1860–1920*. Edited by Alexandra Oleson and John Voss. Baltimore: The Johns Hopkins University Press, 1979.

Hill, Hamlin. "Barnum, Bridgeport, and 'The Connecticut Yankee.'" *American Quarterly* 16.4 (Winter 1964): 615–16.

Hofstadter, Richard. *Anti-Intellectualism in American Life*. London: Jonathan Cape, 1964.

Hogue, Bev. "Forgotten Frontier: Literature of the Old Northwest." *A Companion to the Regional Literatures of America*. Edited by Charles Crow. London: Blackwell, 2003.

Horwitz, Morton J. *The Transformation of American Law, 1870–1960: The Crisis of Legal Orthodoxy*. Oxford: Oxford University Press, 1992.

Howard, June. *Form and History in American Naturalism*. Chapel Hill and London: The University of North Carolina Press, 1985.

Howard, June. "Unraveling Regions, Unsettling Periods: Sarah Orne Jewett and American Literary History." *American Literature*. 68.2 (June 1996): 365–84.

Hsu, Hsuan L. *Geography and the Production of Space in Nineteenth-Century American Literature*. Cambridge: Cambridge University Press, 2010.

James, Henry. *The American Scene*. 1907. Edited by John F. Sears. Harmondsworth: Penguin, 1994.

Jameson, Fredric. "The Vanishing Mediator; or, Max Weber as Storyteller." *The Ideologies of Theory: Essays 1971–1986. Vol. 2: The Syntax of History*. Minneapolis: University of Minnesota Press, 1988. 3–34.

Jameson, Fredric. "Of Islands and Trenches: Neutralization and the Production of Utopian Discourse." *The Ideologies of Theory: Essays 1971–1986. Vol. 2: The Syntax of History*. Minneapolis: University of Minnesota Press, 1988. 75–101.

Jameson, Fredric. *Archaeologies of the Future: The Desire Called Utopia and Other Science Fictions*. London and New York: Verso, 2005.

Jefferson, Thomas. *Notes on the State of Virginia*. 1785. Edited by Frank Shuffelton. New York: Penguin, 1999.

Jones, Gavin. *Strange Talk: The Politics of Dialect Literature in Gilded Age America*. Berkeley and Los Angeles: University of California Press, 1999.

Joseph, Philip. *American Literary Regionalism in a Global Age*. Baton Rouge: Louisiana State University Press, 2007.

Kaplan, Amy. "Nation, Region, and Empire." *The Columbia History of the American Novel*. Edited by Emory Elliot. New York: Columbia University Press, 1991: 240–66.

Kasson, John F. *Houdini, Tarzan, and the Perfect Man.* New York: Hill and Wang, 2001.
Kirby, Lynne. *Parallel Tracks: The Railroad and Silent Cinema.* Exeter: University of Exeter Press, 1997.
Knadler, Stephen P. "Untragic Mulatto: Charles Chesnutt and the Discourse of Whiteness." *American Literary History.* 8.3 (Autumn 1996): 426–48.
Kuhn, Thomas S. *The Structure of Scientific Revolutions.* Chicago: University of Chicago Press, 1962.
Lears, Jackson. *Fables of Abundance: A Cultural History of Advertising in America.* New York: Perseus, 1994.
Le Corbusier. *The City of To-morrow and Its Planning.* 1929. Translated by Frederick Etchells. London: The Architectural Press, 1971.
Lee, Julia H. "Estrangement on a Train: Race and Narratives of American Identity." *ELH.* 75.2 (Summer 2008): 345–65.
Lefebvre, Henri. *The Urban Revolution.* 1970. Translated by Robert Bononno. Minneapolis: University of Minnesota Press, 2003.
Link, Eric Carl. *The Vast and Terrible Drama: American Literary Naturalism in the Late Nineteenth Century.* Tuscaloosa: The University of Alabama Press, 2004.
Lupton, Deborah. "Foucault and the Medicalisation Critique." *Foucault, Health and Medicine.* Edited by Alan Petersen and Robin Bunton. London and New York: Routledge, 1997. 94–110.
Lutes, Jean M. "Lynching Coverage and the American Reporter-Novelist." *American Literary History.* 19.2 (Summer 2007): 456–81.
Lutz, Tom. *Cosmopolitan Vistas: American Regionalism and Literary Value.* Ithaca and London: Cornell University Press, 2004.
Machor, James L. *Pastoral Cities: Urban Ideals and the Symbolic Landscape of America.* Madison: University of Wisconsin Press, 1987.
Marx, Leo. *The Machine in the Garden: Technology and the Pastoral Ideal in America.* Oxford: Oxford University Press, 1964.
McLeod, Ian. *Legal Theory.* 3rd edition. Basingstoke: Palgrave Macmillan, 2005.
Meyer, Roy W. *The Middle Western Farm Novel in the Twentieth Century.* Lincoln: University of Nebraska Press, 1965.
Mizruchi, Susan L. *The Rise of Multicultural America: Economy and Print Culture, 1865–1915.* Chapel Hill: The University of North Carolina Press, 2008.
Moylan, Tom. *Demand the Impossible: Science Fiction and the Utopian Imagination.* New York and London: Methuen, 1986.
Myers, Robert M. "Antimodern Protest in *The Damnation of Theron Ware.*" *American Literary Realism.* 26.3 (1994): 52–64.
Newlin, Keith. Introduction. *Rose of Dutcher's Coolly.* By Hamlin Garland. Lincoln: University of Nebraska Press, 2005. vii–xxvi.
Nietzsche, Friedrich. *Human, All Too Human.* 1878. Translated by Helen Zimmern and Paul V. Cohn. Mineola, NY: Dover Publications, 2006.
Ober, K. Patrick. *Mark Twain and Medicine: "Any Mummery Will Cure."* Columbia: University of Missouri Press, 2003.
Ohmann, Richard. *Selling Culture: Magazines, Markets, and Class at the Turn of the Century.* London and New York: Verso, 1996.
O'Malley, Michael. *Keeping Watch: A History of American Time.* Washington and London: Smithsonian Institution Press, 1990.
Osler, William. "Medicine in the Nineteenth Century." 1901. *Aequanimitas.* London: H.K. Lewis, 1948.

Penry, Tara. "'Tennessee's Partner' as Sentimental Western Metanarrative." *American Literary Realism*. 36.2 (2004): 148–65.
Peyser, Thomas. *Utopia and Cosmopolis: Globalization in the Era of American Literary Naturalism*. Durham and London: Duke University Press, 1998.
Pfaelzer, Jean. *The Utopian Novel in America, 1886–1896: The Politics of Form*. Pittsburgh: The University of Pittsburgh Press, 1984.
Pfeifer, Michael J. *Rough Justice: Lynching and American Society, 1874–1947*. Urbana and Chicago: University of Illinois Press, 2004.
Pratt, Lloyd. *Archives of American Time: Literature and Modernity in the Nineteenth Century*. Philadelphia: University of Pennsylvania Press, 2010.
Pryse, Marjorie. "'I Was Country When Country Wasn't Cool': Regionalizing the Modern in Jewett's *A Country Doctor*." *American Literary Realism*. 34.3 (Spring 2002): 217–32.
Renoff, Gregory J. *The Big Tent: The Traveling Circus in Georgia, 1820–1930*. Athens and London: University of Georgia Press, 2008.
Richter, Amy G. *Home on the Rails: Women, the Railroad, and the Rise of Public Domesticity*. Chapel Hill and London: The University of North Carolina Press, 2005.
Rothfield, Lawrence. *Vital Signs: Medical Realism in Nineteenth-Century Fiction*. Princeton: Princeton University Press, 1992.
Rothstein, William G. *American Physicians in the Nineteenth Century: From Sects to Science*. Baltimore: The Johns Hopkins University Press, 1972.
Sarat, Austin, Lawrence Douglas and Martha Merrill Umphrey. "Where (or What) Is the Place of Law? An Introduction." *The Place of Law*. Edited by Austin Sarat, Lawrence Douglas and Martha Merrill Umphrey. Ann Arbor: The University of Michigan Press, 2003. 1–20.
Sartisky, Michael. Afterword. *Doctor Zay* by Elizabeth Stuart Phelps. 1882. New York: The Feminist Press, 1987. 259–21.
Saxton, Alexander. "*Caesar's Column*: The Dialogue of Utopia and Catastrophe." *American Quarterly*. 19.2 (Summer 1967): 224–38.
Schivelbusch, Wolfgang. *The Railway Journey: The Industrialization of Time and Space in the Nineteenth Century*. 1977. Berkeley: University of California Press, 1986.
Schlereth, Thomas J. *Victorian America: Transformations in Everyday Life, 1876–1915*. New York: HarperPerennial, 1991.
Seltzer, Mark. *Bodies and Machines*. New York and London: Routledge, 1992.
Sherman, Caroline B. "The Development of American Rural Fiction." *Agricultural History*. 12.1 (Jan. 1938): 67–76.
Shulman, Robert. Introduction and Notes. *The Virginian* by Owen Wister. Oxford: Oxford University Press, 1998.
Simmel, Georg. "The Metropolis and Mental Life." 1903. *Simmel on Culture: Selected Writings*. Edited by David Frisby and Mike Featherstone. London: Sage Publications, 1997. 174–85.
Simmons, Ryan. *Chesnutt and Realism: A Study of the Novels*. Tuscaloosa: The University of Alabama Press, 2006.
Singer, Ben. *Melodrama and Modernity: Early Sensational Cinema and Its Contexts*. New York: Columbia University Press, 2001.
Sloane, David E. E. *Mark Twain as Literary Comedian*. Baton Rouge: Louisiana State University Press, 1979.
Starr, Paul. *The Social Transformation of American Medicine*. New York: Basic Books, 1982.
Stilgoe, John R. *Metropolitan Corridor: Railroads and the American Scene*. New Haven and London: Yale University Press, 1983.

Stoddart, Helen. *Rings of Desire: Circus History and Representation*. Manchester: Manchester University Press, 2000.

Stradling, David. *Making Mountains: New York City and the Catskills*. Seattle: University of Washington Press, 2007.

Sundquist, Eric. "The Country of the Blue." *American Literary Realism: New Essays*. Edited by Eric Sundquist. Baltimore and London: The Johns Hopkins University Press, 1982. 3–24.

Sundquist, Eric. *To Wake the Nations: Race in the Making of American Literature*. Cambridge, MA: The Belknap Press, 1993.

Szczygiel, Bonj and Robert Hewitt. "Nineteenth-Century Medical Landscapes: John H. Rauch, Frederick Law Olmsted, and the Search for Salubrity." *Bulletin of the History of Medicine*. 74.4 (Winter 2000): 708–34.

Thomas, Brook. *Cross-Examinations of Law and Literature: Cooper, Hawthorne, Stowe, and Melville*. Cambridge: Cambridge University Press, 1987.

Trachtenberg, Alan. *The Incorporation of America: Culture and Society in the Gilded Age*. New York: Hill and Wang, 1982.

Vadillo, Ana Parejo and John Plunkett. "The Railway Passenger; or, The Training of the Eye." *The Railway and Modernity: Time, Space, and the Machine Ensemble*. Edited by Matthew Beaumont and Michael Freeman. Oxford: Peter Lang, 2007. 45–67.

Vandiver, Margaret. *Lethal Punishment: Lynchings and Legal Executions in the South*. New Brunswick: Rutgers University Press, 2006.

Vidler, Anthony. *The Architectural Uncanny: Essays in the Modern Unhomely*. Cambridge, MA: The M.I.T. Press, 1992.

Vorpahl, Ben Merchant. "Murder by the Minute: Old and New in 'The Bride Comes to Yellow Sky.'" *Nineteenth-Century Fiction*. 26.2 (Sept. 1971): 196–218.

Vowell, Sarah. "Going Home for Good." *A New Literary History of America*. Edited by Greil Marcus and Werner Sollors. Cambridge, MA: Harvard University Press, 2009. 640–44

Waldrep, Christopher. *The Many Faces of Judge Lynch: Extralegal Violence and Punishment in America*. New York: Palgrave Macmillan, 2002.

Weber, Adna Ferrin. *The Growth of Cities in the Nineteenth Century: A Study in Statistics*. 1899. Ithaca: Cornell University Press, 1965.

Weber, Max. "Prefatory Remarks to *Collected Essays in the Sociology of Religion*." *The Protestant Ethic and the "Spirit" of Capitalism and Other Writings*. Edited and translated by Peter Baehr and Gordon C. Wells. London: Penguin, 2002.

Wegener, Frederick. Introduction. *A Country Doctor*. By Sarah Orne Jewett. New York: Penguin Books, 2005.

Whitman, Walt. "To a Locomotive in Winter." *Leaves of Grass*. Edited by Jerome Loving. Oxford: Oxford University Press, 1990.

Wiegman, Robyn. *American Anatomies: Theorizing Race and Gender*. Durham and London: Duke University Press, 1995.

Williams, Raymond. *The Country and the City*. St. Albans: Paladin, 1973.

Williams, Raymond. *Marxism and Literature*. Oxford: Oxford University Press, 1977.

Williams, Raymond. *Culture and Society, 1780–1950*. New York: Columbia University Press, 1983.

Wirth, Louis. "Urbanism as a Way of Life." *The American Journal of Sociology*. 44.1 (July 1938). 1–24.

Zagarell, Sandra A. "Troubling Regionalism: Rural Life and the Cosmopolitan Eye in Jewett's *Deephaven*." *American Literary History*. 10.4 (Winter 1998). 639–663.

INDEX

Adam Forepaugh Circus, 57
Adams, Bluford, 57–58
Allen, James Lane, 1, 3, 4, 170
Allen, Thomas, 34
American Medical Association, 87
American Society for the Prevention of Cruelty to Animals, 140
animal cruelty, 140–41, 184n.10
Atherton, Lewis, 57, 73

Bailey, James A., 55
Bakhtin, Mikhail, 58, 70
Barnum, P.T., 55–56, 59, 61, 66, 179n.4
Barillas, William, 10
Barthes, Roland, 20, 73
Baym, Nina, 100, 109
Bell, Michael Davitt, 63, 177n.3
Bellamy, Edward, 23
   Equality, 161, 162–64
   Looking Backward, 149, 161–62
Benjamin, Walter, 183–84n.5
Bentley, Nancy, 59
Berger, John, 140
Bergh, Henry, 140
Berman, Marshall, 14, 19, 176n.17
Bernard, Claude, 85, 89
Billings, John Shaw, 86
Borus, Daniel, 5–6, 173n.2
Brockway, Zebulon, 136
Brodhead, Richard, 12, 176n.14
Brown, Alice, 23, 60
   "Horn o' the Moon," 85, 111, 114–15
   "Strollers in Tiverton," 75–77
Brown, Bill, 2, 20, 65, 69, 70
Brown, Joshua Purdy, 55
Browner, Stephanie, 104

Campbell, Donna, 13
Carby, Hazel, 133
Carnival. *See* circuses
Castello, Dan, 55
Certeau, Michel de, 40, 41, 42, 46
Chesnutt, Charles, 23, 118
   "The Sheriff's Children," 129–33, 134–35
   The Marrow of Tradition, 130
circuses, 21, 22, 54–82
   advertising of, 54, 61–62, 63, 68–69, 76
   carnival and, 58
   spectacle and, 58, 66, 69, 81–82
   See also realism
City Beautiful movement, the, 185n.5
Cohn, Dorrit, 75
Condit, Carl, 28
Conlogue, William, 8
country doctors. *See* medicine
Coup, W.C., 55
Crane, Stephen, "The Bride Comes to Yellow Sky," 23, 28, 45–48, 53
Crary, Jonathan, 59
Cronon, William, 3, 31
crowds, 56, 77–79, 80, 81, 130–31, 137, 138
Cutler, James, 123, 139

Darwin, Charles, 98, 102, 113
Davis, Janet, 56, 77, 80
Davis, Richard Harding, 178n.13
Debord, Guy, 58, 59, 63, 82
dialect in fiction, 5, 24, 75, 88, 93, 100, 130
Dickens, Charles, 59, 64–65
Dickson, William K. L., 51–52
Dimock, Wai Chee, 6

Dimsdale, Thomas, 122–23, 139
Donnelly, Ignatius, *Caesar's Column*, 150–53, 156, 159, 185n.3
Dugdale, Richard, 176n.14
Dunbar, Paul Laurence, 23, 118, 130
  "The Lynching of Jube Benson," 133
  "The Ordeal at Mt. Hope," 26–27
  "The Tragedy at Three Forks," 129, 133–35
Dreiser, Theodore, 25, 119–20

Eagleton, Terry, 70
Eakins, Thomas, 86
eco-criticism, 174–75n.8
Eggleston, Edward, 7, 23, 92, 118, 127, 130
  The Hoosier School-Master, 5–6, 32, 88–90, 124–26, 173–74n.3, 174n.5
  The Mystery of Metropolisville, 32–33
Electrical Execution Act, 144
Ellis, Edward Sylvester, 29, 177n.1
Entertainment. *See* circuses
Esteve, Mary, 77

Farland, Maria, 7, 8, 174–75n.8, 176n.14
Farmers' Almanac, 177n.5
Fetterley, Judith and Marjorie Pryse, 11, 13, 23
Fisher, Philip, 173n.2
Foote, Stephanie, 12–13, 111
Foucault, Michel, 85–86, 89, 105, 125, 143–44, 181n.2
Frederic, Harold, *The Damnation of Theron Ware*, 85, 110–14
Friedman, Lawrence, 117

Garfield, James, 137
Garland, Hamlin, 23, 28, 60, 118, 184n.8
  "God's Ravens," 38
  "A Lynching in Mosinee," 129, 135–139
  Main-Travelled Roads, 25, 36, 95, 174n.5
  "The Return of a Private," 36–38
  Rose of Dutcher's Coolly, 38–39, 41–42, 54, 68–74, 75, 79, 82, 180n.7
  "Uncle Ethan Ripley," 94–96
  "Up the Coolly," 25, 26, 27, 33, 39–40, 41, 42, 49, 50

George, Henry, 150
Giddens, Anthony, 14, 19, 34
Gilette, King Camp, 164–65
Glazener, Nancy, 7, 175n.9, 176n.13
Goldsby, Jacqueline, 120, 123
Gonzales-Day, Ken, 120, 183n.3
gothic, 6, 42, 99, 100
Gould, Hannah F., 180n.7
Guiteau, Charles, 137

Habermas, Jürgen, 17–18
Halliburton, David, 46, 48
Harris, Neil, 56, 59, 82
Harte, Bret, "Tennessee's Partner," 23, 116–119, 127
Harvard Law School, 144
Hawthorne, Nathaniel, 10
Haymarket Affair, 150
Henderson, George, 8, 173n.2
Hofstadter, Richard, 113
Homeopathy. *See* medicine
Howard, Ebenezer, 165–66
Howard, June, 13, 119–20
Howe, E.W., 174n.5
Howells, William Dean, 23, 71, 109, 130, 177n.2, 182n.9
  A Boy's Town, 54, 179n.5
  Suburban Sketches, 168–69, 170
  Their Wedding Journey, 28, 43–44, 45, 50
  A Traveler From Altruria, 156–61
Hsu, Hsuan, 3

Inness, George, 26
insanity defense, 137–38, 184n.9
Irving, Washington, 6, 43, 44, 173–74n.3

James, Henry, 7, 12, 79
James, William, 77
Jameson, Fredric, 4, 5, 6, 149, 155, 160, 161
Jefferson, Thomas, 9, 30, 154, 157, 160, 173n.2, 176n.14
Jewett, Sarah Orne, 12, 23, 28, 35, 177n.6
  A Country Doctor, 35, 85, 100, 104–107, 109–10, 178n.1, 182n.12, 182–83n.15
  The Country of the Pointed Firs, 91–92

Deephaven, 54, 55, 60–64, 65, 68, 69, 73
"Going to Shrewsbury," 33, 34–35, 36, 44–45
"In a Country Practice," 182n.14
Jones, Gavin, 6, 130
Joseph, Philip, 23

Kaplan, Amy, 12, 173n.2, 176n.14
Kasson, John, 71–72
Kirby, Lynne, 32, 34, 40
Kirkland, Joseph, *Zury: The Meanest Man in Spring County*, 23, 28, 35–36, 83–84, 88, 92–94
Kuhn, Thomas, 181n.5

landscape, 21, 71, 101, 109, 119, 169, 171, 178n.13, 185n.5
  as expression of economic conditions, 16, 28, 32, 40–41, 155, 162–63
  and medicine, 83–84 (*see also* medicine)
  trains and the, 26, 28, 30, 31, 32, 39–53 (*see also* trains)
Langdell, Christopher Columbus, 183n.4
law. *See* lynching
Lawrence, D. H., 10
Lears, Jackson, 18–19, 68, 69
Le Corbusier, 166, 185n.6
Lefebvre, Henri, 16–17, 32, 86, 149
Lutz, Tom, 13, 174n.7, 176n.16
lynching, 22, 116–147, 183nn.1–3
  legal theory and, 117, 121–24, 183–84n.5
  race and, 118, 120–21, 123, 128–35
  as spectacle, 143–44

Machor, James, 11
Marx, Leo, 10–11, 26, 31, 175n.10
medicine, 21, 22, 83–115. *See also* realism
  herbalism as a form of, 87–92, 98, 114
  homeopathy and, 101–2, 182n.11
  patent, 92–96
  professionalization of, 87, 97
Melville, Herman, 184n.5
Meyer, Roy W., 8
Mizruchi, Susan, 149, 151, 160

modernism, 60, 82, 165–67, 175n.12, 176n.17
modernization, theories of, 17–18
Moffett, Cleveland, 56
Morrison, Toni, 10
Moylan, Tom, 158
Murfree, Mary Noailles, "The Romance of Sunrise Rock," 23, 85, 97–100

naturalism, 6, 11, 22, 24, 74, 82, 98–99, 100, 119–20, 154, 181–82n.8
Nietzsche, Friedrich, 41, 77
Norris, Frank, 181n.8

Ohmann, Richard, 17, 19
Old Farmers' Almanac, 177n.5
Olerich, Henry, *A Cityless and Countryless World*, 149, 153–55, 156, 159, 160, 165, 166
Olmsted, Frederick Law, 185n.5
O'Malley, Michael, 33
orientalism, 76
Osler, William, 85, 89

panoramas, 40
pastoralism, 30, 41–42, 43, 45, 49, 50, 75, 77, 103, 104, 109, 111, 118, 130, 168–69, 175n.10, 176n.14
  American literary history and, 8–11, 13, 15
patent medicine. *See* medicine
People's Party, the. *See* populism
Peyser, Thomas, 149, 158, 159
Pfaelzer, Jean, 149, 151, 158 59, 160–61
Pfeifer, Michael, 117, 121, 122, 126, 137–38, 141
Phelps, Elizabeth Stuart, *Doctor Zay*, 23, 85, 100–03, 107–09, 182n.9
Plessy v. Ferguson, 26
populism, 80–81, 150, 151, 154, 156, 184n.8
Pratt, Lloyd, 6, 33, 35, 184n.7
prison reform, 136
Pullman carriages, 26, 45, 46–47, 49, 50, 51, 52, 178n.10. *See also* trains

Radam, William, 93
railroad, *see* trains
rationalization, 18, 32, 33, 34, 55, 56

realism, 5–6, 11, 20, 24, 36, 43, 120, 130, 132–33, 138, 141, 173n.2, 177nn.2–3
    circuses and, 22, 59–60, 64, 65, 70–71, 73, 74, 82 (see also circuses)
    medicine and, 91, 92, 100, 108, 109, 110 (see also medicine)
    in painting, 86
    utopia and, 153, 154, 158–59, 160 (see also utopian fiction)
regionalism, 9, 11–15, 23, 24, 175n.8, 175–76nn.11–13, 176n.16
Richter, Amy, 30, 34
Ringling Brothers, 55
Rothfield, Lawrence, 91
rural fiction, definitions of, 7–9, 175n.9
Rush, Benjamin, 182n.13

Sandow, Eugen, 72
Schivelbusch, Wolfgang, 21, 32
Schlesinger, Arthur M, 2
Seltzer, Mark, 40, 41, 42, 43
sensation fiction, 35
Seurat, Georges, 59
Simmel, Georg, 42, 45, 178n.9
Singer, Ben, 42, 45
Smith, Henry Nash, 10
Starr, Paul, 93, 97, 108
Stilgoe, John, 49, 177–78n.8, 178n.12
Stoddart, Helen, 59
Stowe, Harriet Beecher, 149
suburbia, 170
Sundquist, Eric, 6, 134

Tarkington, Booth, *The Gentleman from Indiana*, 23, 28, 45, 48–50, 54, 57, 60, 77–82, 178n.10
Thompson, Maurice, "Hoiden," 23, 28, 29–32, 177n.2
Thomsonianism, 87–88. See also medicine
time, standardization of. See trains
Trachtenberg, Alan, 17, 64, 69, 79
trains, 10, 20, 21–22, 25–53, 169, 177–78n.8
    early cinema and, 40, 51–52
    gender and, 30, 43
    race and, 26–27
    temporality and, 28, 33–39, 47–48, 177n.7
    visual experience and, 28, 39–46, 48–52
    See also landscape
transcontinental railroad, 29. See also trains
transport. See trains
traveling circuses. See circuses
Twain, Mark, 6, 23, 60
    Adventures of Huckleberry Finn, 66–67, 179n.5
    A Connecticut Yankee at King Arthur's Court, 65–66, 179n.4

urbanization, 2–3, 15–17, 18
urbanism, 16–17, 28, 148
utopian fiction, 22, 148–67
    landscapes in, 149, 154, 155, 157, 161–67 (see also landscape)
    pastoralism in, 151–55, 157, 163, 164 (see also pastoralism)
    See also realism

Vidler, Anthony, 180n.11
Vigilantism. See lynching

Waldrep, Christopher, 120, 138–39, 183n.3
Wallace, Lew, 149
Weber, Adna, 176n.18
Weber, Max, 18, 65, 69, 181n.5. See also rationalization
western (genre), 24, 119
White, Morton and Lucia, 10
Whitman, Walt, 28, 68
wilderness, the, 175n.8
Wiegman, Robyn, 121, 129, 130
Williams, Raymond, 4, 41, 64–65
    The Country and the City, 9, 15, 17, 40, 103
Wirth, Louis, 16
Wister, Owen, *The Virginian*, 23, 28, 45, 51–53, 118, 129, 139–46, 178n.13, 184n.10
Woolson, Constance Fenimore, "Peter the Parson," 23, 118, 126–28, 130, 138
Wright, Frank Lloyd, 166

Zagarell, Sandra, 61, 64

www.ingramcontent.com/pod-product-compliance
Ingram Content Group UK Ltd.
Pitfield, Milton Keynes, MK11 3LW, UK
UKHW042006230426
12048UKWH00009B/587